POCKET BIRDS
OF NORTH AMERICA
EASTERN REGION

CONSULTANT EDITORS
STEPHEN KRESS, ELISSA WOLFSON

THE ULTIMATE PHOTOGRAPHIC GUIDE

AMERICAN MUSEUM OF NATURAL HISTORY

Consultant
Jill Hamilton
Global Business Development
Jennifer Chow

REVISED EDITION

Senior Art Editor Pooja Pipil
Art Editor Aarushi Dhawan
Managing Art Editors Sudakshina Basu, Michael Duffy
Jacket Designer Gayatri Menon
DTP Designer Mrinmoy Mazumdar
Production Editor Anita Yadav
Production Controller Laura Andrews
Design Head Malavika Talukder
Art Director Karen Self
Design Director Phil Ormerod

Senior Editor Dharini Ganesh
Editor Saumya Agarwal
US Editor Jill Hamilton
Managing Editors Rohan Sinha, Angeles Gavira Guerrero
Jacket Design Development Manager Sophia MTT
Pre-Production Manager Balwant Singh
Production Manager Pankaj Sharma
Editorial Head Glenda Fernandes
Associate Publishing Director Liz Wheeler
Publishing Director Jonathan Metcalf

FIRST EDITION

Consultant Editors
Stephen Kress, Elissa Wolfson

Design team Michael Duffy, Anjana Nair, Ina Stradins, Mahua Sharma, Simar Dhamija, Jomin Johny, Vaishali Kalra, Shanker Prasad
Production team David Almond, Mary Slater, Anita Yadav, Harish Aggarwal, Sachin Singh
Production Managers Pankaj Sharma, Balwant Singh
Art Director Karen Self
Associate Publishing Director Liz Wheeler

Editorial team Angeles Gavira Guerrero, Rohan Sinha, Miezan van Zyl, Dharini Ganesh, Tina Jindal, Nisha Shaw
US Editors Jill Hamilton, Shannon Beatty
Jacket team Mark Cavanagh, Claire Gell, Suhita Dharamjit, Juhi Sheth, Ira Sharma
Managing Jackets Editor Saloni Singh
Jacket Design Development Manager Sophia MTT
Publishing Director Jonathan Metcalf

For the curious
www.dk.com

CONTENTS

GREEN HERON   KING EIDER   ROUGH-LEGGED HAWK

150 YEARS | AMERICAN MUSEUM
of NATURAL HISTORY

The **American Museum of Natural History**, founded in 1869, is one of the world's preeminent scientific, educational, and cultural institutions. The Museum encompasses more than 40 permanent exhibition halls, including the Rose Center for Earth and Space and the Hayden Planetarium, as well as galleries for temporary exhibitions. The Museum's Department of Ornithology maintains one of the largest collections of bird specimens in the world, representing all continents and oceans and more than 99 percent of all species.

How this book works

This guide covers 374 North American bird species found in the Eastern half of the continent. It is organized into chapters of related birds, with a group introduction preceding the species profiles. Within each chapter, the birds are arranged broadly by family and genus, so that related species appear together for ease of comparison. The main index lists the common and scientific names of each featured bird.

▽ **INTRODUCTION**
Each chapter opens with an introductory page, briefly describing each family's shared characteristics.

COMMON NAME

SCIENTIFIC NAME

DESCRIPTION
Conveys the main features and essential characteristics of the species; may include interesting facts or notable behaviors.

PHOTOGRAPHS
Illustrate the bird in different views, sexes, or plumage variations. Unless otherwise stated, the bird shown is an adult.

Ducks, Geese, and Swans

▷ **SINGLE-PAGE ENTRIES**
More commonly seen species are given a full-page entry, often showing more photos with varieties of age, sex, and plumage.

236 WOOD W

Cape M

Setophaga tigrina

The Cape May Warl increases during ou chase away other bi they use their thin, the nectar from blo plucking them from

Cerulea

Setophaga cerule

This unusually colo it spends the major deciduous forests. I the Ohio River Vall and development. the Andean foothi

OTHER KEY INFORMATION
VOICE: *a description of the bird's calls and songs.*
NESTING: *type of nest and its usual location; number of eggs in a clutch; number of broods in a year; breeding season.*
FEEDING: *how, where, and what the bird feeds upon.*
HABITAT: *a description of the bird's preferred habitats in North America.*
LENGTH AND WINGSPAN: *length is tip of tail to tip of bill; measurements are averages or ranges.*

▽ **SPECIES ENTRIES**
The typical page describes two bird species. Each profile follows the same easy-to-access structure and features photographs taken in the bird's natural setting.

STATUS
The conservation status of the species, based loosely on the US Fish and Wildlife Services Endangered Species list. Some species are given two statuses, referring to different populations.

S Stable   **T** Threatened

D Declining   **E** Endangered

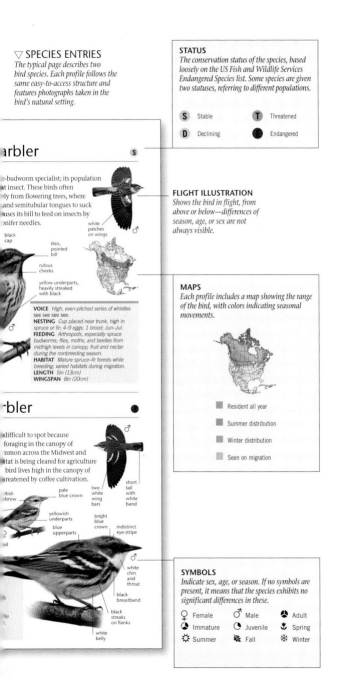

arbler ⓢ

e-budworm specialist; its population
t insect. These birds often
·ly from flowering trees, where
and semitubular tongues to suck
onifer needles.

black
cap

thin,
pointed
bill

rufous
cheeks

white
patches
on wings ♂

yellow underparts,
heavily streaked
with black

FLIGHT ILLUSTRATION
Shows the bird in flight, from above or below—differences of season, age, or sex are not always visible.

VOICE *High, even-pitched series of whistles see see see see.*
NESTING *Cup placed near trunk, high in spruce or fir; 4–9 eggs; 1 brood; Jun–Jul.*
FEEDING *Arthropods, especially spruce budworms; flies, moths, and beetles from midhigh levels in canopy; fruit and nectar during the nonbreeding season.*
HABITAT *Mature spruce–fir forests while breeding; varied habitats during migration.*
LENGTH *5in (13cm)*
WINGSPAN *8in (20cm)*

MAPS
Each profile includes a map showing the range of the bird, with colors indicating seasonal movements.

■ Resident all year

■ Summer distribution

■ Winter distribution

▩ Seen on migration

·bler ⬤

difficult to spot because
foraging in the canopy of
nmon across the Midwest and
itat is being cleared for agriculture
bird lives high in the canopy of
reatened by coffee cultivation.

itish
·brow

pale
blue crown

two
white
wing
bars

short
tail
with
white
band ♂

yellowish
underparts

blue
upperparts

bright
blue
crown

indistinct
eye-stripe

white
chin
and
throat ♂

black
breastband

black
streaks
on flanks

white
belly

SYMBOLS
Indicate sex, age, or season. If no symbols are present, it means that the species exhibits no significant differences in these.

♀ Female   ♂ Male   ● Adult

◗ Immature   ◔ Juvenile   ✿ Spring

☀ Summer   🍂 Fall   ❄ Winter

Anatomy

In spite of their external diversity, birds are remarkably similar internally. For birds to be able to fly, they need light and rigid bones, a lightweight skull, and hollow wing and leg bones. In addition, pouchlike air sacs are connected to hollow bones, which reduce a bird's weight. The breast muscles, crucial for flight, are attached to the keeled sternum (breastbone).

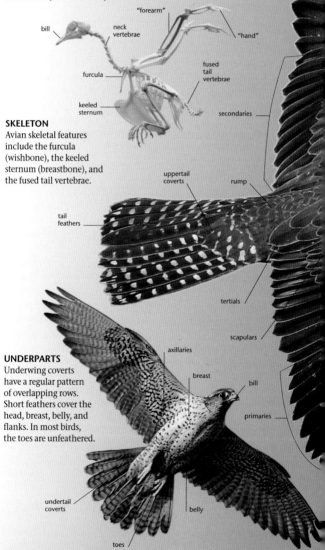

"forearm"

bill

neck vertebrae

"hand"

fused tail vertebrae

furcula

keeled sternum

secondaries

SKELETON
Avian skeletal features include the furcula (wishbone), the keeled sternum (breastbone), and the fused tail vertebrae.

uppertail coverts

rump

tail feathers

tertials

scapulars

UNDERPARTS
Underwing coverts have a regular pattern of overlapping rows. Short feathers cover the head, breast, belly, and flanks. In most birds, the toes are unfeathered.

axillaries

breast

bill

primaries

undertail coverts

belly

toes

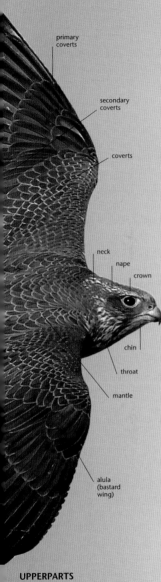

primary
coverts

secondary
coverts

coverts

neck
nape
crown

chin

throat

mantle

alula
(bastard
wing)

Feathers

Feathers serve two main functions: insulation and flight. Small down feathers form an insulating underlayer, and are also the first feathers that nestlings have after hatching. Contour feathers cover the head and body. The rigidity of the flight feathers helps create a supporting surface that birds use to generate thrust and lift.

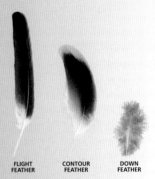

FLIGHT FEATHER

CONTOUR FEATHER

DOWN FEATHER

Feet and toes

When we talk about a bird's feet, we really mean its toes. The structure of the foot can give clues to a bird's characteristics and habits.

WALKING
Ground-foraging birds usually have a long hind claw.

CLIMBING
Most climbers have two toes forward and two backward.

SWIMMING
Water-loving birds have webbing between their toes.

HUNTING
Birds of prey have powerful toes and strong, sharp claws.

UPPERPARTS

The wing feathers from the "hand" of the bird are the primaries and those on the "forearm" are the secondaries. Each set has its accompanying row of coverts—contour feathers that overlap the flight feathers. The tertials are adjacent to the secondaries.

Identification

Some species are easy to identify, but in many cases, identification is tricky. In North America, a notoriously difficult group to identify is the wood warblers, especially in the fall, when most species have similar greenish or yellowish plumage. Gulls and shorebirds are also challenging.

Geographic range

Each bird species in North America lives in a particular area that is called its geographic range. Some species have a restricted range; others range from coast to coast and from northern Canada to Mexico. Species with a broad range usually breed in a variety of vegetation types, while species with narrow ranges often have a specialized habitat.

BROAD RANGE
Red-tailed Hawks range from coast to coast in North America and south down to Mexico, and are found in a wide variety of habitats.

RESTRICTED RANGE
Whooping Cranes breed only in Wood Buffalo National Park in Alberta and the Northwest Territories.

Size

The weight and size of North American birds range from hummingbirds, which weigh a fraction of an ounce and are only 4in (10cm) long, to Tundra Swans, which average more than 15lb (6.8kg) and are up to 5ft (1.5m) long. Size can be measured in several ways, including the length of a bird from bill-tip to tail-tip, its wingspan, or even its weight. Comparing the sizes of two birds can also be helpful: for example, the less familiar Bicknell's Thrush can be compared with the well-known American Robin.

SIZE MATTERS
Smaller shorebirds, with short legs and bills, forage in shallow water, and larger ones with longer legs and bills can feed in deeper water.

SEMIPALMATED PLOVER

LONG-BILLED CURLEW

General shape

Bird body shapes vary widely and can give clues to the habitat in which they live. The American Bittern's long, thin body blends in with the reed beds that it favors. The round-bodied Sedge Wren hops in shrubby vegetation or near the ground, where slimness is not an advantage.

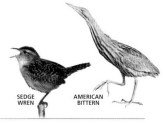

SEDGE WREN

AMERICAN BITTERN

Bill shape

In general, bill form, including length or thickness, corresponds to the kind of food a bird consumes. With its pointed bill, the Mountain Chickadee picks tiny insects from crevices in tree barks. At another extreme, dowitchers probe mud with their long thin bills, feeling for worms.

AMERICAN ROBIN — worms and fruit

MOUNTAIN CHICKADEE — tiny insects, seeds

HOUSE FINCH — seeds and caterpillars

LONG-BILLED DOWITCHER — worms from deep mud

AMERICAN AVOCET — small shrimp in water

GREAT BLUE HERON — fish

GOLDEN EAGLE — mammals and birds

SURF SCOTER — marine mollusks

Wing shape

Birds' wing shapes are correlated with their flight style. The long, round-tipped wings of the Red-tailed Hawk are perfect for soaring, while the tiny wings of hummingbirds allow them to hover in front of flowers for a meal of nectar.

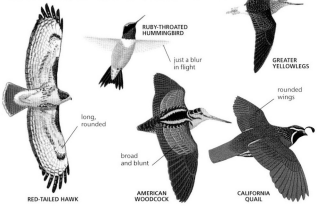

RUBY-THROATED HUMMINGBIRD — just a blur in flight

GREATER YELLOWLEGS — angled, pointed

RED-TAILED HAWK — long, rounded

AMERICAN WOODCOCK — broad and blunt

CALIFORNIA QUAIL — rounded wings

Tail shape

Tail shapes vary as much as wing shapes, but are not as clearly linked to a function. Irrespective of shape, tails are needed for balance. In some birds, tail shape, color, and pattern are used in courtship displays or in defensive displays when threatened.

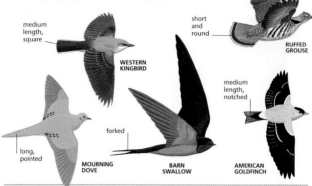

medium length, square

WESTERN KINGBIRD

short and round

RUFFED GROUSE

medium length, notched

AMERICAN GOLDFINCH

long, pointed

MOURNING DOVE

forked

BARN SWALLOW

Colors and markings

Colors and markings, including stripes, bars, patches, and spots, can be helpful in identifying a species. Look for wing and tail patterns, which may be noticeable only when the bird opens its wings or spreads its tail, or distinctive patterns on the head.

BLACK-AND-WHITE WARBLER

black-and-white streaks

black spots

LAZULI BUNTING

white wing bars

black-and-white head pattern

WHITE-CROWNED SPARROW

WOOD THRUSH

streaking on belly

BARRED OWL

white eye-ring

BLUE-HEADED VIREO

Seasonality

Some bird species in North America are year-round residents, although a few of them move away from where they hatched at some time in the year. However, a large number of North American species are migratory. For example, many songbirds fly from their breeding grounds in North America's boreal forests to Mexico and northern South America. Some species, like the American Robin, are partial migrants, meaning that some populations are resident year-round and others migrate out of their breeding range.

NEOTROPICAL MIGRANT
The Blackpoll Warbler breeds in boreal forests, then migrates south to its wintering grounds in the Caribbean, or Central or South America.

Nests and eggs

Most bird species build their own nests while some use old ones; exceptions include the parasitic cowbirds, which lay their eggs in other species' nests. Nest-building is often done by the female alone, but in some species the male may help or even build it himself. Nests range from a simple scrape in the ground with a few added pebbles to an elaborate woven basketlike structure. Plant matter forms basic nest material.

EGG CUP
Robins lay their eggs in a cup lined with grass stems, built either in shrubs or trees.

NATURAL CAVITY
This Northern Saw-whet Owl is nesting in a tree cavity, likely excavated by a woodpecker.

NEST BOX
Cavity-nesting bluebirds will nest in human-made structures.

COMPLEX WEAVE
Orioles weave intricate nests from dried plant material, high in trees.

Egg shapes

There are six basic egg shapes among birds. The most common egg shapes are longitudinal and elliptical. Many cliff-nesting birds lay pear-shaped eggs. Formerly believed to prevent eggs from rolling off ledges, recent studies suggest that the pointed shape facilitates more efficient incubation. Spherical eggs with irregular red blotches are characteristic of birds of prey. Pigeons and doves lay white oval eggs, and the eggs of many songbirds are conical and have a variety of dark markings on a pale background. Owls lay the roundest eggs.

PEAR-SHAPED

LONGITUDINAL

ELLIPTICAL

OVAL

CONICAL

SPHERICAL

COLOR AND SHAPE
Birds' eggs vary widely in terms of shape, colors, and markings. The American Robin's egg shown above is a beautiful blue.

Ducks, Geese, and Swans

Ornithologists group most geese and swans together into the subfamily Anserinae. Geese are generally intermediate between swans and ducks in body size and neck length. They are more terrestrial than either swans or ducks, often being seen grazing on dry land. Like swans, geese pair for life. They are also highly social, and most species are migratory, flying south for the winter in large flocks.

Swans are essentially large, long-necked geese. Ungainly on land, they are extremely graceful on water. When feeding, a swan stretches its long neck to reach water plants at the bottom, submerging up to half its body as it does so.

Classified into several subfamilies, ducks are more varied than swans or geese, and are loosely grouped by their feeding habits. Dabblers, or puddle ducks, eat plants and invertebrates by upending on the surface of shallow water. Diving ducks, by contrast, dive deep underwater for their food.

GAGGLING GEESE
Gregarious Snow Geese form large, noisy flocks during migration and on winter feeding grounds.

Snow Goose

S

Anser caerulescens

The abundant Snow Goose has two subspecies. The "Greater" (*A. c. atlantica*) is slightly larger and breeds farther east; the smaller "Lesser" (*A. c. caerulescens*) breeds west. Snow Geese have two color forms—white and "blue" (actually dark grayish-brown with a white head)—and there are also intermediate forms. Their heads are often stained rusty-brown from minerals in the soil. Snow Geese fly with direct, strong wingbeats, in either V-shaped or bunched flocks.

gray wing patch

WHITE

black patch on long bill

blackish-brown back

elongated white head

long neck

dark belly

pale wing feathers

BLUE FORM

white upperparts

WHITE FORM

pink legs

VOICE *Nasal whouk, kowk, or kow-luk, higher-pitched heenk; feeding call hu-hu-hur.*
NESTING *Scrapes on hummock, lined with plant material and down; 2–6 eggs; 1 brood; May–Jul.*
FEEDING *Aquatic and terrestrial vegetation, including stems, seeds, leaves, tubers, and roots; grain.*
HABITAT *Tundra while breeding, and interior valleys and coastal marshes in winter.*
LENGTH *27–33in (69–83cm)*
WINGSPAN *4¼–5½ft (1.3–1.7m)*

Cackling Goose

S

Branta hutchinsii

The Cackling Goose is distinguished from the Canada Goose by its smaller size, short, stubby bill, steep forehead, and short neck. There are at least four subspecies of Cackling Goose, which vary in breast color—ranging from quite dark in *B. h. minima* and medium dark in *B. h. leucopareia* to pale in *B. h. hutchinsii*. Cackling Geese fly in bunched V-formations.

plain, grayish-brown wings

small, black head

white, U-shaped patch on rump

dark brown breast

B. h. minima

white chin strap

small, stubby bill

B. h. hutchinsii

black tail

no black under chin

pale breast

VOICE Males: honk or bark; females: higher pitched hrink; also high-pitched yelps.
NESTING Scrape lined with available plant matter and down; 2–8 eggs; 1 brood; May–Aug.
FEEDING Plants in summer; in winter, grass in livestock and dairy pastures, and agricultural fields.
HABITAT Rocky tundra slopes while breeding; pastures and agricultural fields in winter.
LENGTH 21½–30in (55–75cm)
WINGSPAN 4¼–5ft (1.3–1.5m)

Canada Goose

S

Branta canadensis

The Canada Goose is the most common, widespread, and familiar goose in North America. Given its colossal range, it is not surprising that the Canada Goose has much geographic variation, and 12 subspecies have been recognized. With the exception of the Cackling Goose, from which it has recently been separated, it is difficult to confuse this species—with its distinctive white chin strap, black head and neck, and grayish-brown body—with any other species of goose. It is a monogamous species, and once pairs are formed, they usually stay together for life.

plain, grayish-brown wings with darker flight feathers

white, U-shaped patch on rump

smaller white chin strap

dark brown overall

black head

very long neck

broad white chin strap

grayish-brown upperparts and sides

paler upper breast

white undertail feathers

VOICE *Males: honk or bark; females: higher pitched* hrink.
NESTING *Scrape lined with plant matter and down, near water; 2–12 eggs; 1–2 broods; May–Aug.*
FEEDING *Grasses, sedges, leaves, seeds, agricultural crops, and berries; insects.*
HABITAT *Inland near water, including grassy urban areas, marshes, prairies, parkland, forests, and tundra; agricultural fields, saltwater marshes, lakes, and rivers in winter.*
LENGTH *2¼–3½ft (0.7–1.1m)*
WINGSPAN *4¼–5½ft (1.3–1.7m)*

Brant

(S)

Branta bernicla

A small-billed, dark, stocky sea goose, the Brant winters on the East and West Coasts of North America: the pale-bellied "Atlantic" Brant (*B. b. hrota*) in the East, and the darker "Black" Brant (*B. b. nigricans*) in the West. In addition, there is an intermediate gray-bellied form that winters in the Puget Sound region of the Washington State coast.

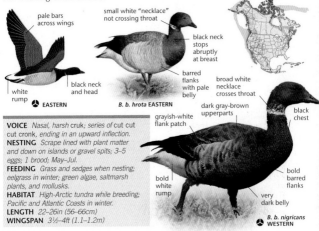

pale bars across wings

white rump

black neck and head

🦆 **EASTERN**

small white "necklace" not crossing throat

black neck stops abruptly at breast

barred flanks with pale belly

B. b. hrota **EASTERN**

grayish-white flank patch

broad white necklace crosses throat

dark gray-brown upperparts

black chest

bold barred flanks

bold white rump

very dark belly

B. b. nigricans 🦆 **WESTERN**

VOICE *Nasal, harsh cruk; series of cut cut cut cronk, ending in an upward inflection.*
NESTING *Scrape lined with plant matter and down on islands or gravel spits; 3–5 eggs; 1 brood; May–Jul.*
FEEDING *Grass and sedges when nesting; eelgrass in winter; green algae, saltmarsh plants, and mollusks.*
HABITAT *High-Arctic tundra while breeding; Pacific and Atlantic Coasts in winter.*
LENGTH *22–26in (56–66cm)*
WINGSPAN *3½–4ft (1.1–1.2m)*

Mute Swan

(S)

Cygnus olor

The Mute Swan was introduced from Europe due to its graceful appearance on water, if not on land, and easy domestication. However, this is an extremely territorial and aggressive bird. When threatened, it points its bill downward, arches its wings, hisses, and then attacks. Displacement of native waterfowl species and overgrazing have led to efforts to reduce its numbers in North America.

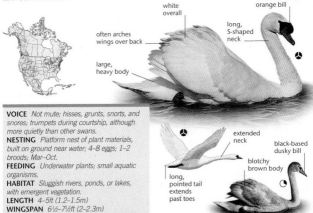

conspicuous black knob at base of orange bill

white overall

often arches wings over back

long, S-shaped neck

large, heavy body

extended neck

black-based dusky bill

blotchy brown body

long, pointed tail extends past toes

VOICE *Not mute; hisses, grunts, snorts, and snores; trumpets during courtship, although more quietly than other swans.*
NESTING *Platform nest of plant materials, built on ground near water; 4–8 eggs; 1–2 broods; Mar–Oct.*
FEEDING *Underwater plants; small aquatic organisms.*
HABITAT *Sluggish rivers, ponds, or lakes, with emergent vegetation.*
LENGTH *4–5ft (1.2–1.5m)*
WINGSPAN *6½–7½ft (2–2.3m)*

Trumpeter Swan

(S)

Cygnus buccinator

North America's quintessential swan and heaviest waterfowl, the Trumpeter has made a remarkable comeback after numbers were severely reduced by hunting; by the mid-1930s, fewer than a hundred were known to exist. Reintroduction efforts were made in Ontario and the upper Midwest in the US to reestablish the species. The Trumpeter Swan's characteristic call is usually the best way to identify it.

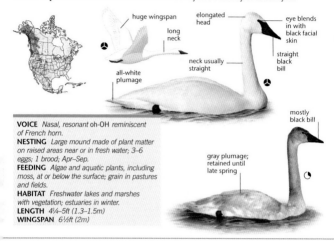

huge wingspan

long neck

elongated head

eye blends in with black facial skin

straight black bill

neck usually straight

all-white plumage

mostly black bill

gray plumage; retained until late spring

VOICE *Nasal, resonant oh-OH reminiscent of French horn.*
NESTING *Large mound made of plant matter on raised areas near or in fresh water; 3–6 eggs; 1 brood; Apr–Sep.*
FEEDING *Algae and aquatic plants, including moss, at or below the surface; grain in pastures and fields.*
HABITAT *Freshwater lakes and marshes with vegetation; estuaries in winter.*
LENGTH *4¼–5ft (1.3–1.5m)*
WINGSPAN *6½ft (2m)*

Tundra Swan

(S)

Cygnus columbianus

Nesting in the Arctic tundra, this well-named species is North America's most widespread and smallest swan. Two populations exist, with one wintering in the West, and the other along the East Coast. The Tundra Swan can be confused with the Trumpeter Swan, but their different calls immediately distinguish the two species.

fairly thick neck

small head and bill

eye stands out from face at close range

yellow facial skin next to eye

dark legs

all-white plumage

dull, grayish body

dirty pink bill

VOICE *Clear, high-pitched yodeling whoo-hooo calls mixed with garbles, yelping, and barking sounds.*
NESTING *Mound-shaped nest made of plant matter near water; 3–6 eggs; 1 brood; May–Sep.*
FEEDING *Aquatic vegetation, insects, and mollusks; grain.*
HABITAT *Northern tundra near lakes and pools while nesting; shallow coastal bays, ponds, and lakes in winter.*
LENGTH *4–5ft (1.2–1.5m)*
WINGSPAN *6¼–7¼ft (1.9–2.2m)*

Fulvous Whistling-Duck (S)

Dendrocygna bicolor

Although often thought of as dabbling ducks, whistling-ducks act more like swans, because they form long-term pairs, and the male helps raise the brood. Although widespread in tropical regions, the Fulvous Whistling-Duck is closely associated with rice fields in the US, where populations of these noisy birds have steadily recovered from the use of pesticides in the 1960s.

faint crest

tawny buff head and neck

white flank plumes

barred back

gray bill

tawny buff underparts

dark wings

white rump

tawny head and underparts

gray feet extend beyond tail

VOICE *High-pitched squeaky pi-teeeew; often calls in flight.*
NESTING *Simple bowl-shaped nest made of plant matter; among dense floating plants, or on ground; 6–20 eggs; 1 brood; Apr–Sep.*
FEEDING *Filter feeds on rice and other water plants, seeds, insects, worms, snails, and clams.*
HABITAT *Rice fields in the US.*
LENGTH *16½–20in (42–51cm)*
WINGSPAN *33–37in (85–93cm)*

Wood Duck (S)

Aix sponsa

The male Wood Duck is unmistakable, with its gaudy plumage, red eye and bill, and helmet-shaped profile. The Wood Duck is typically found in marshes, shallow lakes, ponds, and park settings that are surrounded by trees. When swimming, it jerks its head front to back. Of all waterfowl, this is the only species that regularly raises two broods each season.

blue wing patch

long wings

head held high ♂

complex white facial markings

red eye

helmetlike head profile ♂

burgundy flanks

black tip of bill

long, dark tail

white vertical breast stripe

white-flecked maroon breast appears black at a distance

bold, tear-shaped eye-ring

smaller crest

white-edged feathers

brownish breast ♀

VOICE *Males: wheezy upslurred whistle zweeet; females: double-note, rising oh-eek oh-eek.*
NESTING *Nests in natural tree cavities or nest boxes close to water; 10–13 eggs; 2 broods; Apr–Aug.*
FEEDING *Seeds, tree fruit, and small acorns; spiders, insects, and crustaceans.*
HABITAT *Rivers, streams, swamps, and marshes; agricultural fields.*
LENGTH *18½–21½in (47–54cm)*
WINGSPAN *26–29in (66–73cm)*

Gadwall ⓢ

Mareca strepera

Despite being common and widespread, Gadwalls are often overlooked because of their retiring behavior and relatively quiet vocalizations. This dabbling duck is slightly smaller and more delicate than the Mallard, yet female Gadwalls are often mistaken for female Mallards. Gadwalls associate with other species, especially in winter.

conspicuous white patch ♂❋

mostly white underwings

brown, rounded head

black bill

dark grayish overall ♂❋

white belly

black uppertail

orange-yellow legs

finely patterned gray flanks and breast

white wing patch

brown, scalloped back

dark eye-stripe

♀

VOICE *Low, raspy meep or reb in quick succession; females: high-pitched, nasal quack; high-pitched peep, or pe-peep; tickety-tickety-tickety chatter while feeding.*
NESTING *Bowl nest made of plant material in a scrape; 8–12 eggs; 1 brood; Apr.–Aug.*
FEEDING *Seeds, aquatic vegetation, and invertebrates, including mollusks and insects.*
HABITAT *Shallow wetlands, reservoirs, ponds, lakes, and rivers.*
LENGTH *18–22½in (46–57cm)*
WINGSPAN *33in (84cm)*

American Wigeon ⓢ

Mareca americana

Often found in mixed flocks with other ducks, the American Wigeon is a common and widespread, medium-sized dabbling duck. This bird is an opportunist that loiters around other diving ducks and coots, feeding on the vegetation they dislodge. It is more social during migration and in the nonbreeding season than when breeding. The male's cream-colored forehead is distinctive.

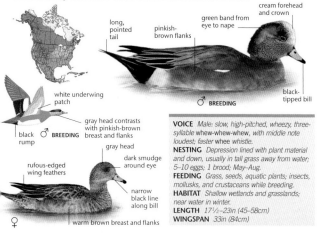

long, pointed tail

pinkish-brown flanks

green band from eye to nape

cream forehead and crown

white underwing patch

black rump ♂ BREEDING

gray head contrasts with pinkish-brown breast and flanks

black-tipped bill

♂ BREEDING

rufous-edged wing feathers

gray head

dark smudge around eye

narrow black line along bill

♀

warm brown breast and flanks

VOICE *Male: slow, high-pitched, wheezy, three-syllable whew-whew-whew, with middle note loudest; faster whee whistle.*
NESTING *Depression lined with plant material and down, usually in tall grass away from water; 5–10 eggs; 1 brood; May–Aug.*
FEEDING *Grass, seeds, aquatic plants; insects, mollusks, and crustaceans while breeding.*
HABITAT *Shallow wetlands and grasslands; near water in winter.*
LENGTH *17½–23in (45–58cm)*
WINGSPAN *33in (84cm)*

American Black Duck

Anas rubripes

The American Black Duck, a large dabbling duck, is closely related to the Mallard, and the two species often interbreed. In the past, the American Black Duck preferred forested locations, while the Mallard frequented more open habitats. Over the years, these habitats became less distinct as the East was deforested and trees were planted in the Midwest. Breeding American Black Duck males readily chase away other males to maintain their territories.

rich violet patch

dark tail

♂

white underwing

heavily streaked head and neck

♀

cinnamon-edged flank feathers

olive bill

dark cap

narrow, dark eye-line

pale head

♂

greenish-yellow bill

dark body

VOICE Male: reedy *raeb*, given once or twice; females: *quack* sounds similar to Mallard.
NESTING Scrape lined with plant material and down, usually on ground or close to water; 4–10 eggs; 1 brood; Mar–Sep.
FEEDING Plants, roots, seeds, grains, fruit, aquatic plants, fish, and amphibians.
HABITAT Hardwood forests, wooded uplands, bogs, and marshes while breeding; saltwater marshes in winter.
LENGTH 21½–23in (54–59cm)
WINGSPAN 35–37in (88–95cm)

Mallard

Anas platyrhynchos

The Mallard is perhaps the most familiar of all ducks, and occurs in the wild all across the Northern Hemisphere. It is the ancestor of most domestic ducks, and hybrids between the wild and domestic forms are frequently seen in city lakes and ponds, often with patches of white on the breast. Mating is generally a violent affair, but outside of the breeding season the wild species is strongly migratory and gregarious, sometimes forming large flocks that may join with other species. In some places, they even nest in backyards with swimming pools.

broad-based wings

♂ ❀

short, round, pale tail

heavy body

♀

whitish outer tail feathers

brown underparts

dark eye-line and cap

yellowish-brown back

♀

orange bill with blackish patch

mottled brown belly

bright yellow bill

short black curls above white tail

warm gray body

metallic-green head

blue wing patch

narrow white neck collar

♂ ❀

chestnut-brown breast

VOICE *Male: quiet raspy raab; during courtship a high-pitched whistle; females: quack.*
NESTING *Scrape lined with plant matter, usually near water or on floating vegetation; 6–15 eggs; 1 brood; Feb–Sep.*
FEEDING *Insects, crustaceans, mollusks, and earthworms when breeding; seeds, acorns, agricultural crops, and aquatic vegetation.*
HABITAT *Shallow water in marshes, ponds, and ditches; city parks and reservoirs.*
LENGTH 19½–26in (50–65cm)
WINGSPAN 32–37in (82–95cm)

Mottled Duck

D

Anas fulvigula

The Mottled Duck, American Black Duck, and Mallard Duck constitute the "Mallard complex"—the three species are closely related and interbreed easily. There is concern that the fertile hybrid ducks produced may dilute the purity of Mottled Duck populations. The Mottled Duck is a little smaller and darker than the similar female Mallard, and lacks a white edge to the blue wing patch.

iridescent blue-green wing patch

bright white underwing

♂

paler edges to dark body feathers

dark body

no white on tail

orange legs

pale, buffy head and neck

olive-yellow bill

♂

dull green to orange-yellow bill

dark eye-line

paler breast than male

duller orange legs than male

♀

VOICE *Males give a variety of raspy* raab *calls; females quack.*
NESTING *Bowl-shaped depression in dense grass; 8–12 eggs; 1 brood; Jan–Sep.*
FEEDING *Dabbles for aquatic vegetation, crustaceans, mollusks, insects, rice, seeds, and some small fish.*
HABITAT *Shallow freshwater wetlands, breeding on coastal marshes.*
LENGTH *17½–24in (44–61cm)*
WINGSPAN *33–34in (83–87cm)*

Northern Pintail

D

Anas acuta

An elegant long-necked dabbler, the Northern Pintail has distinctive markings and the longest tail of any freshwater duck. It begins nesting soon after the ice thaws. Northern Pintails were once one of the most abundant prairie breeding ducks, but droughts, combined with habitat reduction on both their wintering and breeding grounds, have resulted in a population decline.

green wing patch with buff bar

♂ ❄

black bill with gray sides

pale chocolate-brown head

gray back and flanks

outstretched head and neck

long, pointed black tail

long neck

white neck and breast

♂ ❄

black undertail with white flank patch

blackish bill

plain buff face with dark eye

pointed tail; shorter than male

♀

mottled gray-brown body

VOICE *Males: high-pitched* prrreep prrreep; *lower-pitched wheezy* wheeeee; *females: quiet, harsh quack or* kuk; *loud, repeated* gaak.
NESTING *Scrape lined with plants and down; 3–12 eggs; 1 brood; Apr–Aug.*
FEEDING *Grains, rice, seeds, aquatic weeds, insect larvae, crustaceans, and snails.*
HABITAT *Shallow wetlands or meadows in mountainous forests while breeding; tidal wetlands, saltwater habitats while migrating.*
LENGTH *20–30in (51–76cm)*
WINGSPAN *35in (89cm)*

Green-winged Teal

Ⓢ

Anas crecca

The Green-winged Teal, the smallest North American dabbling duck, is slightly smaller than the Blue-winged and Cinnamon Teals, and lacks their blue wing patch. Its population is increasing, apparently because it breeds in more pristine habitats, and farther north, than the prairie ducks. *A. c. carolinensis* males have a conspicuous vertical white bar on their wings.

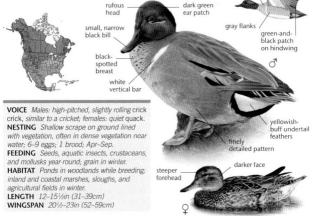

♂

short neck
gray flanks
green-and-black patch on hindwing
♂

rufous head
dark green ear patch
small, narrow black bill
black-spotted breast
white vertical bar
yellowish-buff undertail feathers
finely detailed pattern
steeper forehead
darker face
♀

VOICE Males: high-pitched, slightly rolling crick crick, similar to a cricket; females: quiet quack.
NESTING Shallow scrape on ground lined with vegetation, often in dense vegetation near water; 6–9 eggs; 1 brood; Apr–Sep.
FEEDING Seeds, aquatic insects, crustaceans, and mollusks year-round; grain in winter.
HABITAT Ponds in woodlands while breeding; inland and coastal marshes, sloughs, and agricultural fields in winter.
LENGTH 12–15½in (31–39cm)
WINGSPAN 20½–23in (52–59cm)

Blue-winged Teal

Ⓢ

Spatula discors

With a bold white crescent between bill and eye on its otherwise slate-gray head and neck, the male Blue-winged Teal is quite distinctive. The Blue-winged and Cinnamon Teals, along with the Northern Shoveler, constitute the three "blue-winged" ducks: a feature that is conspicuous in flight. The Cinnamon and the Blue-winged Teals are almost identical genetically and sometimes interbreed.

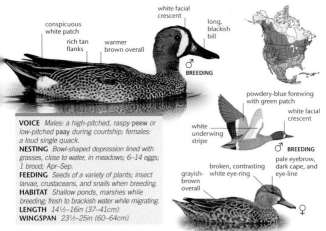

conspicuous white patch
rich tan flanks
warmer brown overall
white facial crescent
long, blackish bill
♂ **BREEDING**

powdery-blue forewing with green patch
white facial crescent
white underwing stripe
♂ **BREEDING**
pale eyebrow, dark cape, and eye-line
broken, contrasting white eye-ring
grayish-brown overall
♀

VOICE Males: a high-pitched, raspy peew or low-pitched paay during courtship; females: a loud single quack.
NESTING Bowl-shaped depression lined with grasses, close to water, in meadows; 6–14 eggs; 1 brood; Apr–Sep.
FEEDING Seeds of a variety of plants; insect larvae, crustaceans, and snails when breeding.
HABITAT Shallow ponds, marshes while breeding; fresh to brackish water while migrating.
LENGTH 14½–16in (37–41cm)
WINGSPAN 23½–25in (60–64cm)

Northern Shoveler ⓢ

Spatula clypeata

The Northern Shoveler is a common, medium-sized, dabbling duck found in North America and Eurasia. It is monogamous, and pairs remain together longer than any other dabbler species. Its distinctive long bill is highly specialized to filter food items from the water. Shovelers often form tight feeding groups, swimming close together as they sieve the water for prey.

pale blue wing patch

♂

heavy-fronted

large, dark, spatula-shaped bill

yellow eye

dark green head

white breast

chestnut belly and flanks

black-and-white rump

dark, narrow eye-line

pale-edged, brown flank feathers

♀

dusky olive-gray to orange bill

brown overall

VOICE Males: nasal, muffled thuk thuk… thuk thuk; loud, nasal paaaay; females: variety of quacks, singly or in series of 4–5 descending notes.
NESTING Scrape lined with plant matter and down, in short plants near water; 6–19 eggs; 1 brood; May–Aug.
FEEDING Seeds; small crustaceans, mollusks.
HABITAT Wetlands with nearby grasslands; fresh- and salt marshes, and ponds in winter.
LENGTH 17½–20in (44–51cm)
WINGSPAN 27–33in (69–84cm)

Canvasback ⓢ

Aythya valisineria

A large, long-billed diving duck, the Canvasback is a bird of Prairie Pothole Country with a specialized diet of aquatic plants. With legs set toward the rear, it is an accomplished swimmer and diver but is rarely seen on land. Weather conditions and brood parasitism by Redheads determine how successful the Canvasback's nesting is from year to year.

light gray forewing

♂

high, peaked black crown

rich chestnut head and neck

long neck held horizontally in flight

belly appears white

black rump and tail

bright red eye

white to pale gray back and flanks

black at both ends

black breast

♂

extended teardrop

♀

dingy brownish-gray upperparts and sides

VOICE Males: soft cooing noises during courtship; females: grating krrrrr krrrrrr krrrrr; both sexes: soft wheezing rrrr rrrr rrrr.
NESTING Platform of woven vegetation built over water or occasionally on shore; 8–11 eggs; 1 brood; Apr–Sep.
FEEDING Aquatic tubers, buds, root stalks, and shoots, particularly wild celery; snails.
HABITAT Shallow wetlands in prairies and tundra; northern forests.
LENGTH 19–22in (48–56cm)
WINGSPAN 31–35in (79–89cm)

Redhead

Ⓢ

Aythya americana

The Redhead, a medium-sized diving duck, is native only to North America.
The male's seemingly gray upperparts and flanks are actually white, with dense
black, wavy markings. The Redhead forages mostly around dusk and dawn,
drifting during the day. It lays its eggs in other duck nests more than any other
duck species, particularly those of the Canvasback and even other Redheads.

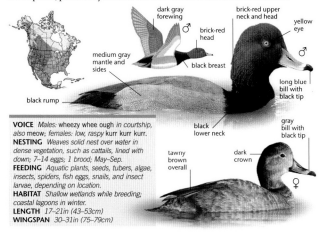

dark gray forewing ♂

brick-red head

medium gray mantle and sides

black breast

black rump

brick-red upper neck and head

yellow eye

♂

long blue bill with black tip

black lower neck

gray bill with black tip

black breast

tawny brown overall

dark crown

♀

VOICE *Males: wheezy whee ough in courtship,
also meow; females: low, raspy kurr kurr kurr.*
NESTING *Weaves solid nest over water in
dense vegetation, such as cattails, lined with
down; 7–14 eggs; 1 brood; May–Sep.*
FEEDING *Aquatic plants, seeds, tubers, algae,
insects, spiders, fish eggs, snails, and insect
larvae, depending on location.*
HABITAT *Shallow wetlands while breeding;
coastal lagoons in winter.*
LENGTH *17–21in (43–53cm)*
WINGSPAN *30–31in (75–79cm)*

Ring-necked Duck

Ⓢ

Aythya collaris

The Ring-necked Duck is a fairly common medium-sized diving duck. The
bold white band near its bill tip is easy to see, whereas the thin chestnut
ring around the neck can be very difficult to observe.
The tall, pointed head is quite distinctive, peaking
at the rear of the crown.

tall, peaked head

gray bill with white band at base and white and black tip

yellow eye

thin chestnut ring

rounded gray sides

♂

black neck and breast

dark forewing

♂

bold white underwing

dark brown back

bold white eye-ring

white band on bill

♀

VOICE *Males: normally silent; females: low
kerp kerp.*
NESTING *Floating nest built in dense aquatic
vegetation, often in marshes; 6–14 eggs;
1 brood; May–Aug.*
FEEDING *Aquatic plant tubers and seeds;
aquatic invertebrates, such as clams and snails.*
HABITAT *Shallow freshwater marshes and
bogs while breeding; swamps, lakes, estuaries,
and flooded fields in winter.*
LENGTH *15–18in (38–46cm)*
WINGSPAN *24–25in (62–63cm)*

Greater Scaup

Ⓢ

Aythya marila

Due to its more restricted range for breeding and wintering, the Greater Scaup is less numerous in North America than the Lesser Scaup. The Greater Scaup forms large, often sexually segregated flocks outside the breeding season. If both scaup species are present, they will also segregate within the flocks according to species. Correct identification is difficult.

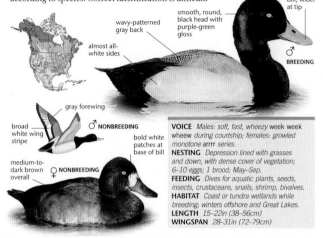

wavy-patterned gray back

smooth, round, black head with purple-green gloss

blue-gray bill, wider at tip

almost all-white sides

♂ BREEDING

gray forewing

♂ NONBREEDING

broad white wing stripe

bold white patches at base of bill

medium-to-dark brown overall

♀ NONBREEDING

VOICE *Males: soft, fast, wheezy* week week wheew *during courtship; females: growled monotone* arrrr *series.*
NESTING *Depression lined with grasses and down, with dense cover of vegetation; 6–10 eggs; 1 brood; May–Sep.*
FEEDING *Dives for aquatic plants, seeds, insects, crustaceans, snails, shrimp, bivalves.*
HABITAT *Coast or tundra wetlands while breeding; winters offshore and Great Lakes.*
LENGTH *15–22in (38–56cm)*
WINGSPAN *28–31in (72–79cm)*

Lesser Scaup

Ⓢ

Aythya affinis

The Lesser Scaup is the most abundant diving duck in North America. The two scaup species are very similar in appearance and are best identified by head shape when stationary. Lesser Scaups generally have a more pointed head than Greater Scaups, but head shape can change with position. For example, the crown feathers are flattened just before diving in both species.

dark, wavy pattern on upperparts

narrow head with bump at the rear

narrow, thin blue-gray bill

purple-green gloss on head

black rear end

♂

black breast and neck

pale flanks

VOICE *Males: mostly silent except wheezy* wheeow wheeow wheeow *during courtship; females: repetitive, grating* garrrf garrrf garrrf.
NESTING *Nest built in tall vegetation, far from water, or on islands and mats of floating vegetation; 8–11 eggs; 1 brood; May–Sep.*
FEEDING *Leeches, crustaceans, mollusks, aquatic insects, and aquatic plants and seeds.*
HABITAT *Open northern forests and forest tundra while breeding; coasts, lakes in winter.*
LENGTH *15½–17½in (39–45cm)*
WINGSPAN *27–31in (68–78cm)*

♂ whitish underwings

black head

whitish belly

white patch around base of gray bill

rich brown head and neck

brown back

brown flank feathers with gray fringes

♀

Common Eider

S

Somateria mollissima

The largest duck in North America, the Common Eider is also the most numerous, widespread, and variable of the eiders. Four of its seven subspecies occur in North America, and vary in the markings and color of their heads and bills. Male Common Eiders also have considerable seasonal plumage changes, and do not acquire their adult plumage until the third year.

♂※

black rump and tail

whitish underwing

♀

brown overall

long, sloping forehead

mottled black-and-brown upperparts

♀

black cap

greenish-olive bill

white breast with rose tinge

olive-green wash on nape

♂※

VOICE Repeated hoarse, grating notes korr-korr-korr; males: owl-like ah-WOO-ooo; females: low, guttural notes krrrr-krrrr-krrrr.
NESTING Depression on ground lined with down and plant matter, near water; 2–7 eggs; 1 brood; Jun–Sep.
FEEDING Dives in synchronized flocks for mollusks and crustaceans; consumes larger prey above the surface.
HABITAT Mostly coastal islands and peninsulas while breeding; coastal waters in winter.
LENGTH 19½–28in (50–71cm)
WINGSPAN 31–42in (80–108cm)

King Eider ⓢ

Somateria spectabilis

The scientific name of the King Eider, *spectabilis*, means "worth seeing," and its gaudy marking and coloring around the head and bill make it hard to mistake. Females resemble the somewhat larger and paler Common Eider. The female King Eider has a more rounded head, more compact body, and a longer bill than the male. King Eiders may dive down to 180ft (55m) when foraging.

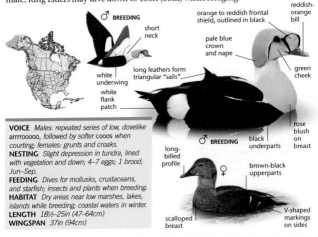

♂ BREEDING

short neck

white underwing

white flank patch

orange to reddish frontal shield, outlined in black

pale blue crown and nape

long feathers form triangular "sails"

reddish-orange bill

green cheek

rose blush on breast

♂ BREEDING

black underparts

long-billed profile

brown-black upperparts

♀

V-shaped markings on sides

scalloped breast

VOICE Males: repeated series of low, dovelike arrrrooooo, followed by softer cooos when courting; females: grunts and croaks.
NESTING Slight depression in tundra, lined with vegetation and down; 4–7 eggs; 1 brood; Jun–Sep.
FEEDING Dives for mollusks, crustaceans, and starfish; insects and plants when breeding.
HABITAT Dry areas near low marshes, lakes, islands while breeding; coastal waters in winter.
LENGTH 18½–25in (47–64cm)
WINGSPAN 37in (94cm)

Harlequin Duck Ⓓ

Histrionicus histrionicus

This small, hardy duck is a skillful swimmer, diving to forage on the bottom of fast-moving, turbulent streams for its favorite insect prey. Despite the male's unmistakable plumage at close range, it looks very dark from a distance. It can be found among crashing waves, alongside larger and bigger-billed Surf and White-winged Scoters, which feed in the same habitat.

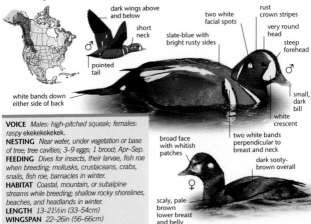

dark wings above and below

short neck

♂

pointed tail

white bands down either side of back

two white facial spots

slate-blue with bright rusty sides

rust crown stripes

very round head

steep forehead

♂

small, dark bill

white crescent

two white bands perpendicular to breast and neck

dark sooty-brown overall

broad face with whitish patches

♀

scaly, pale brown lower breast and belly

VOICE Males: high-pitched squeak; females: raspy ekekekekekek.
NESTING Near water, under vegetation or base of tree; tree cavities; 3–9 eggs; 1 brood; Apr–Sep.
FEEDING Dives for insects, their larvae, fish roe when breeding; mollusks, crustaceans, crabs, snails, fish roe, barnacles in winter.
HABITAT Coastal, mountain, or subalpine streams while breeding; shallow rocky shorelines, beaches, and headlands in winter.
LENGTH 13–21½in (33–54cm)
WINGSPAN 22–26in (56–66cm)

Surf Scoter

Ⓢ

Melanitta perspicillata

Surf Scoters migrate up and down both coasts, often with other species. They take their name from the way they dive for mollusks through heavy surf. Groups often dive and resurface in unison. Black and Surf Scoters can be difficult to tell apart; look for silvery-gray flight feathers on the Black Scoter and black wings overall on the Surf Scoter.

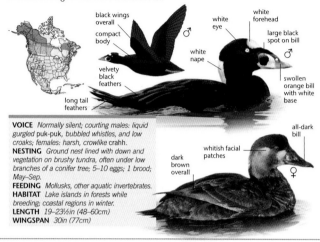

black wings overall

compact body

velvety black feathers

long tail feathers

♂

white eye

white forehead

large black spot on bill

♂

white nape

swollen orange bill with white base

all-dark bill

whitish facial patches

dark brown overall

♀

VOICE *Normally silent; courting males: liquid gurgled* puk-puk, *bubbled whistles, and low croaks; females: harsh, crowlike* crahh.
NESTING *Ground nest lined with down and vegetation on brushy tundra, often under low branches of a conifer tree; 5–10 eggs; 1 brood; May–Sep.*
FEEDING *Mollusks, other aquatic invertebrates.*
HABITAT *Lake islands in forests while breeding; coastal regions in winter.*
LENGTH *19–23½in (48–60cm)*
WINGSPAN *30in (77cm)*

White-winged Scoter

Ⓢ

Melanitta deglandi

The largest of the three scoters, the White-winged Scoter can be identified by its white wing patch. Females look similar to immature Surf Scoters and can be identified by head shape, extent of bill feathering, and shape of white areas on the face. When diving, this scoter leaps forward and up, arching its neck, and opens its wings when entering the water.

white wing patch

appears all-black in flight

upturned, white "comma" around white eye

black knob at base of bill

black, with brownish sides

♂

pinkish-red to yellow-orange bill

feathers extend onto the bill

dark brown overall

♀

VOICE *Mostly silent; courting males: whistling note; females: growly* karr.
NESTING *Depression lined with twigs and down in dense thickets, often far from water; 8–9 eggs; 1 brood; Jun–Sep.*
FEEDING *Dives for mollusks and crustaceans; sometimes fish and aquatic plants.*
HABITAT *Large freshwater or brackish lakes or ponds while breeding; coasts, bays, and inlets in winter.*
LENGTH *19–23in (48–58cm)*
WINGSPAN *31in (80cm)*

Black Scoter

Melanitta americana

Black Scoters, the most vocal of the scoters, winter along both coasts of North America. They form dense flocks on the waves, often segregated by gender. While swimming, the Black Scoter sometimes flaps its wings, and while doing so, it drops its neck low, unlike the other two scoters. This scoter breeds in two widely separated sub-Arctic breeding areas.

pale silvery-gray flight feathers

black lining on underwings

dark brown eye

♂

conspicuous yellow-orange knob on black bill

entirely black, heavily built body

black bill with small yellow patch

dark cap

pale brownish-gray cheeks

dark brown overall

♀

smaller bill

VOICE *Males: high-whistled peeew; females: low, raspy kraaa.*
NESTING *Depression lined with grass and down, often in tall grass on tundra; 5–10 eggs; 1 brood; May–Sep.*
FEEDING *Dives for mollusks, crustaceans, and plants; aquatic insects, freshwater mussels.*
HABITAT *Near shallow small lakes while breeding; shallow water over gravel or sand and offshore ledges in winter.*
LENGTH *17–21in (43–53cm)*
WINGSPAN *31–35in (79–90cm)*

Long-tailed Duck

Clangula hyemalis

The Long-tailed Duck is a small sea duck with a wide range of plumages depending on the season and the sex of the bird. The male has two extremely long tail feathers, which are often held up in the air. The male's loud calls are quite musical and, when heard from a flock, have a choruslike quality. This species can dive for a prolonged period of time, and may reach depths of 200ft (60m), making it one of the deepest-diving ducks.

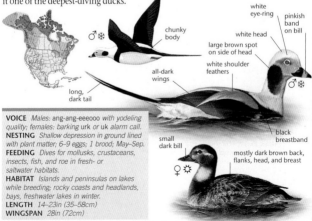

♂❄

chunky body

white eye-ring

pinkish band on bill

white head

large brown spot on side of head

white shoulder feathers

♂❄

all-dark wings

long, dark tail

black breastband

VOICE *Males: ang-ang-eeeooo with yodeling quality; females: barking urk or uk alarm call.*
NESTING *Shallow depression in ground lined with plant matter; 6–9 eggs; 1 brood; May–Sep.*
FEEDING *Dives for mollusks, crustaceans, insects, fish, and roe in fresh- or saltwater habitats.*
HABITAT *Islands and peninsulas on lakes while breeding; rocky coasts and headlands, bays, freshwater lakes in winter.*
LENGTH *14–23in (35–58cm)*
WINGSPAN *28in (72cm)*

small dark bill

♀❄

mostly dark brown back, flanks, head, and breast

Bufflehead

S

Bucephala albeola

The smallest diving duck in North America, the Bufflehead is related to the Common and Barrow's Goldeneyes. Males have a striking head pattern. In flight, males resemble the larger Common Goldeneye, except for the Bufflehead's large white patch on the head. The Bufflehead's wings are also silent in flight. The northern limit of the Bufflehead's breeding range corresponds to that of the Northern Flicker because Buffleheads usually nest in these woodpeckers' abandoned cavities.

gray underwings with white patch

♂

black-and-white outer wings

pinkish-orange legs

oval, white cheek patch

dark brown head

dark, unmarked back

all-dark wings

♀

grayish-brown sides

front part of head and neck has iridescent green-and-purple gloss

angled forehead

large triangular white patch on head

♂

small, narrow gray bill

black back

white breast and flanks

VOICE Males: low growl or squeal; chattering during breeding; females: mostly silent except during courtship or calling to chicks.
NESTING Cavity-nester, near water; 7–9 eggs; 1 brood; Apr–Sep.
FEEDING Aquatic invertebrates: usually insects in fresh water, mollusks and crustaceans in salt water; seeds.
HABITAT Woodlands near small lakes, ponds while breeding; both coasts in winter.
LENGTH 12½–15½in (32–39cm)
WINGSPAN 21½–24in (54–61cm)

Common Goldeneye

S

Bucephala clangula

The Common Goldeneye is a medium-sized, compact diving duck. It closely resembles the Barrow's Goldeneye, to which it is related along with the Bufflehead. It is aggressive and very competitive with members of its own species, as well as with other cavity-nesting ducks, regularly laying eggs in the nests of other species. Before diving, the Common Goldeneye flattens its feathers in preparation for underwater foraging. Its wings make a whirring sound in flight.

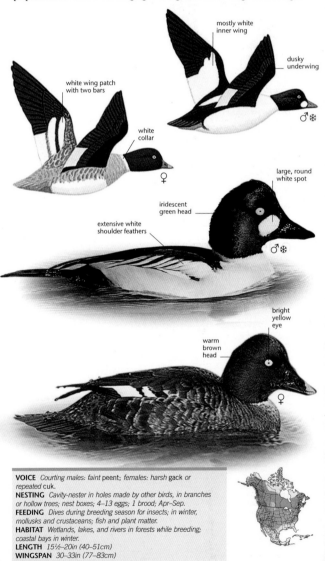

mostly white inner wing

dusky underwing

♂ ❄

white wing patch with two bars

white collar

♀

large, round white spot

iridescent green head

extensive white shoulder feathers

♂ ❄

bright yellow eye

warm brown head

♀

VOICE *Courting males: faint peent; females: harsh gack or repeated cuk.*
NESTING *Cavity-nester in holes made by other birds, in branches or hollow trees; nest boxes; 4–13 eggs; 1 brood; Apr–Sep.*
FEEDING *Dives during breeding season for insects; in winter, mollusks and crustaceans; fish and plant matter.*
HABITAT *Wetlands, lakes, and rivers in forests while breeding; coastal bays in winter.*
LENGTH *15½–20in (40–51cm)*
WINGSPAN *30–33in (77–83cm)*

Barrow's Goldeneye

Ⓓ

Bucephala islandica

Barrow's Goldeneye is a slightly larger, darker version of the Common Goldeneye. The bill color varies seasonally and geographically: eastern Barrow's have blacker bills with less yellow, and western populations have entirely yellow bills, which darken in summer. During the breeding season, the majority of Barrow's Goldeneyes are found in mountainous regions of northwest North America.

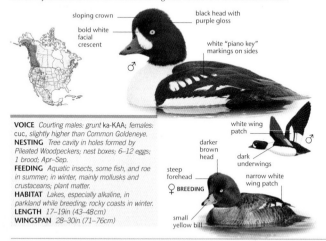

sloping crown

black head with purple gloss

bold white facial crescent

white "piano key" markings on sides

♂

white wing patch

darker brown head

♂

dark underwings

steep forehead

narrow white wing patch

♀ BREEDING

small yellow bill

VOICE *Courting males: grunt ka-KAA; females: cuc, slightly higher than Common Goldeneye.*
NESTING *Tree cavity in holes formed by Pileated Woodpeckers; nest boxes; 6–12 eggs; 1 brood; Apr–Sep.*
FEEDING *Aquatic insects, some fish, and roe in summer; in winter, mainly mollusks and crustaceans; plant matter.*
HABITAT *Lakes, especially alkaline, in parkland while breeding; rocky coasts in winter.*
LENGTH *17–19in (43–48cm)*
WINGSPAN *28–30in (71–76cm)*

Hooded Merganser

Ⓢ

Lophodytes cucullatus

The smallest of the three mergansers, Hooded Mergansers have crests that they can raise or flatten. The male's raised crest displays a gorgeous white fan, surrounded by black. The Hooded Merganser and the Wood Duck can be confused when seen in flight because they are both fairly small, with bushy heads and long tails.

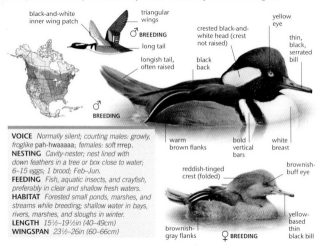

black-and-white inner wing patch

triangular wings

♂ BREEDING

long tail

longish tail, often raised

crested black-and-white head (crest not raised)

yellow eye

thin, black, serrated bill

black back

♂ BREEDING

warm brown flanks

bold vertical bars

white breast

reddish-tinged crest (folded)

brownish-buff eye

brownish-gray flanks

♀ BREEDING

yellow-based thin black bill

VOICE *Normally silent; courting males: growly, froglike pah-hwaaaaa; females: soft rrrep.*
NESTING *Cavity-nester; nest lined with down feathers in a tree or box close to water; 6–15 eggs; 1 brood; Feb–Jun.*
FEEDING *Fish, aquatic insects, and crayfish, preferably in clear and shallow fresh waters.*
HABITAT *Forested small ponds, marshes, and streams while breeding; shallow water in bays, rivers, marshes, and sloughs in winter.*
LENGTH *15½–19½in (40–49cm)*
WINGSPAN *23½–26in (60–66cm)*

Common Merganser

Mergus merganser

The Common Merganser is the largest of the three merganser species in North America. This large fish-eater is common and widespread, particularly in the northern portion of its range. It is often found in big flocks on lakes or smaller groups along rivers. It spends most of its time on the water, using its serrated bill to catch fish underwater.

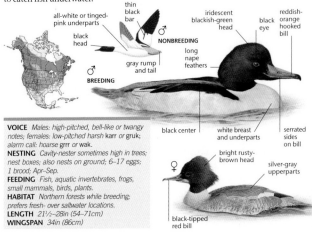

all-white or tinged-pink underparts

thin black bar

NONBREEDING ♂

iridescent blackish-green head

black eye

reddish-orange hooked bill

black head

long nape feathers

gray rump and tail

BREEDING

black center

white breast and underparts

serrated sides on bill

bright rusty-brown head

silver-gray upperparts

♀

black-tipped red bill

VOICE *Males: high-pitched, bell-like or twangy notes; females: low-pitched harsh karr or gruk; alarm call: hoarse grrr or wak.*
NESTING *Cavity-nester sometimes high in trees; nest boxes; also nests on ground; 6–17 eggs; 1 brood; Apr–Sep.*
FEEDING *Fish, aquatic invertebrates, frogs, small mammals, birds, plants.*
HABITAT *Northern forests while breeding; prefers fresh- over saltwater locations.*
LENGTH *21½–28in (54–71cm)*
WINGSPAN *34in (86cm)*

Red-breasted Merganser

Mergus serrator

The Red-breasted Merganser is somewhat smaller than the Common Merganser but larger than the Hooded. Both sexes are easily recognized by their long, sparse, ragged-looking double crest. The Red-breasted Merganser, unlike the other two mergansers, nests on the ground in loose colonies, often among gulls and terns, and is protected by its neighbors.

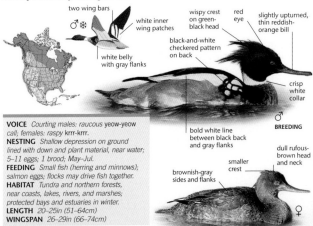

two wing bars

♂ ❄

white inner wing patches

white belly with gray flanks

wispy crest on green-black head

black-and-white checkered pattern on back

red eye

slightly upturned, thin reddish-orange bill

crisp white collar

bold white line between black back and gray flanks

♂

BREEDING

smaller crest

dull rufous-brown head and neck

brownish-gray sides and flanks

♀

VOICE *Courting males: raucous yeow-yeow call; females: raspy krrr-krrr.*
NESTING *Shallow depression on ground lined with down and plant material, near water; 5–11 eggs; 1 brood; May–Jul.*
FEEDING *Small fish (herring and minnows); salmon eggs; flocks may drive fish together.*
HABITAT *Tundra and northern forests, near coasts, lakes, rivers, and marshes; protected bays and estuaries in winter.*
LENGTH *20–25in (51–64cm)*
WINGSPAN *26–29in (66–74cm)*

Ruddy Duck

Oxyura jamaicensis

The small, spunky Ruddy Duck often holds its tail in a cocked position. During courtship displays, the male points its long tail skyward while rapidly thumping its electric-blue bill against its chest, ending the performance with an odd, bubbling sound. Large feet and legs set far back on the body make the Ruddy Duck an excellent swimmer. However, on land it is among the most awkward of diving ducks.

broad, short wings with whitish wing linings

arched dark line on cheek

dark bill

♂ **BREEDING**

pale belly

brownish upperparts

♀

paler flanks

black cap and nape

bright blue bill, slightly knobby at base

large head

large white cheek patches

♂ **BREEDING**

long tail, often erect

rich cinnamon body and neck

VOICE *Females: nasal* raanh, *high-pitched* eeek; *males: popping noises with feet.*
NESTING *Platform, bowl-shaped nest built over water in thick vegetation, rarely on land; 6–10 eggs; 1 brood; May–Sep.*
FEEDING *Aquatic insects, larvae, crustaceans, and other invertebrates, particularly when breeding; also plants during winter.*
HABITAT *Shallow wetlands while breeding; mostly freshwater habitats in winter.*
LENGTH *14–17in (35–43cm)*
WINGSPAN *22–24in (56–62cm)*

Quails, Grouse, Turkeys, and Relatives

This diverse and adaptable group of birds spends most of the time on the ground, springing loudly into the air when alarmed. Among the most terrestrial of all galliforms, quails are also renowned for their great sociability, often forming large family groups, or "coveys," of up to 100 birds. Grouse are the most diverse and widespread galliforms in North America, and often possess patterns that match their surroundings, providing camouflage from enemies both animal and human. Native to Eurasia, pheasants and partridges were introduced into North America in the 19th and 20th centuries to provide additional targets for recreational hunters. Some adapted well and now thrive in established populations.

SNOW BIRD
The Rock Ptarmigan's winter plumage camouflages it against the snow, helping it hide from predators.

Northern Bobwhite

Colinus virginianus

The Northern Bobwhite, a small, plump, chickenlike bird, is named for its cheery "bob-WHITE" call, whistled by males in the breeding season. There are many subspecies of Northern Bobwhites, widely distributed across eastern North America from southwestern Ontario down to Mexico. They vary primarily in the color and pattern of their head and the color of their plumage, which is darker in the East, grayer in the West. When flushed, these birds erupt in "coveys" of 10–20 individuals, rapidly bursting from groundcover and dispersing in multiple directions.

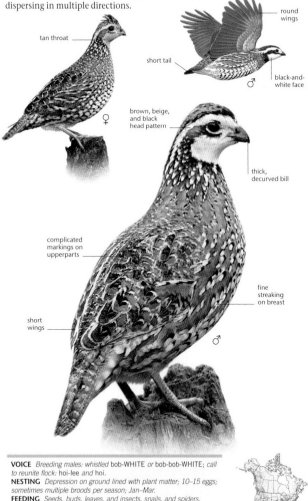

tan throat

round wings

short tail

black-and-white face

♀

brown, beige, and black head pattern

thick, decurved bill

complicated markings on upperparts

fine streaking on breast

short wings

♂

VOICE *Breeding males: whistled bob-WHITE or bob-bob-WHITE; call to reunite flock: hoi-lee and hoi.*
NESTING *Depression on ground lined with plant matter; 10–15 eggs; sometimes multiple broods per season; Jan–Mar.*
FEEDING *Seeds, buds, leaves, and insects, snails, and spiders, when available.*
HABITAT *Agricultural fields; mixed young forests, fields, and brushy hedges.*
LENGTH *8–10in (20–25cm)*
WINGSPAN *11–14in (28–35cm)*

Ring-necked Pheasant

S

Phasianus colchicus

A native of Asia, the Ring-necked Pheasant was originally introduced in North America for recreational hunting purposes, and is now widely distributed across the continent. Birds are bred in captivity and released into the wild to supplement numbers for hunting purposes. In the wild, several females may lay eggs in the same nest—a phenomenon called "egg-dumping." There is a less common dark form, which can be distinguished principally because it lacks the distinctive white band around the neck.

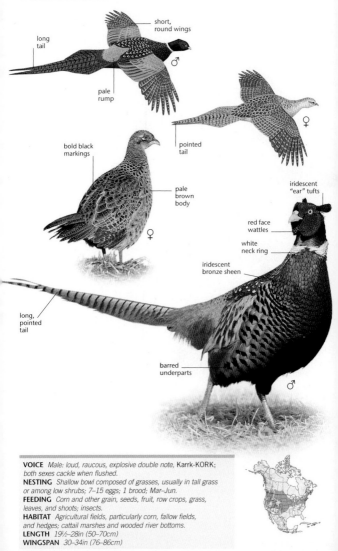

short, round wings

long tail

♂

pale rump

pointed tail

♀

bold black markings

pale brown body

♀

iridescent "ear" tufts

red face wattles

white neck ring

iridescent bronze sheen

long, pointed tail

barred underparts

♂

VOICE *Male: loud, raucous, explosive double note, Karrk-KORK; both sexes cackle when flushed.*
NESTING *Shallow bowl composed of grasses, usually in tall grass or among low shrubs; 7–15 eggs; 1 brood; Mar–Jun.*
FEEDING *Corn and other grain, seeds, fruit, row crops, grass, leaves, and shoots; insects.*
HABITAT *Agricultural fields, particularly corn, fallow fields, and hedges; cattail marshes and wooded river bottoms.*
LENGTH *19½–28in (50–70cm)*
WINGSPAN *30–34in (76–86cm)*

Ruffed Grouse

Bonasa umbellus

The Ruffed Grouse is perhaps the most widespread galliform in North America. There are two color forms, rufous and gray, both allowing the birds to remain camouflaged and undetected on the forest floor, until they eventually burst into the air in an explosion of whirring wings. The male is well known for his extraordinary wing-beating or "drumming" display, which he performs year-round, but most frequently in the spring.

RUFOUS FORM

rusty tail with black band

brown-barred underparts

heavy white spotting on brown upperparts

raised crest

dark patch on neck

feathered legs

RUFOUS FORM

spotted gray upperparts

gray-barred underparts

GRAY FORM

VOICE *Hissing notes, and soft purrt, purrt, purrt when alarmed; male's "drumming" display when heard from a distance resembles small engine starting, thump... thump... thump... thuthuthuth.*
NESTING *Shallow, leaf-lined bowl set against tree or fallen log in forest; 6–14 eggs; 1 brood; Mar–Jun.*
FEEDING *Leaves, buds, and fruit from the ground; occasionally insects.*
HABITAT *Young, mixed-habitat forests.*
LENGTH *17–20in (43–51cm)*
WINGSPAN *20–23in (51–58cm)*

Spruce Grouse

Canachites canadensis

The remoteness of their habitat and the resulting lack of human contact may contribute to the Spruce Grouse's tendency to be unafraid of humans. This bird generally avoids flying. These pine-needle specialists have an expanded intestinal tract to accommodate the large volume of food needed to compensate for the needles' low nutritional value. There are two groups of Spruce Grouse, the Taiga and the Franklin's, both of which have red and gray forms.

gray upperparts

♂ **FRANKLIN'S**

white spots
on black tail

♀
C. c. franklinii
FRANKLIN'S

heavily barred
underparts

bright
red comb
above eye

black
throat

mottled gray-
brown upperparts

black
breast

♂ *C. c. canadensis*
TAIGA

white spots
on underparts

mostly blackish
tail with rufous tip

VOICE *Mostly silent; males clap their wings during courtship display; females often utter a long cackle at dawn and dusk.*
NESTING *Lined with moss, leaves, feathers; often at tree base; 4–6 eggs; 1 brood; May–Jul.*
FEEDING *Pine and spruce needles; insects, leaves, fruit, and seeds when available.*
HABITAT *Forests dominated by conifers, including Jack and lodgepole pine, spruce, hemlock, and cedar.*
LENGTH 14–17in (36–43cm)
WINGSPAN 21–23in (53–58cm)

Willow Ptarmigan

S

Lagopus lagopus

The most common of the three ptarmigan species, the Willow Ptarmigan also undertakes the longest migration of the group from its wintering to its breeding range. The Willow Ptarmigan is an unusual galliform species, in that male and female remain bonded throughout the chick-rearing process, in which the male is an active participant.

black bill

♂ ☼

reddish-brown body

black bill ◐ ❄

all-white body

black bill

red comb

♂ ☼

rich reddish-brown body

dark scaly bars

white belly

feathered feet

VOICE *Purrs, clucks, hissing, meowing noises; Kow-Kow-Kow call given before flushing.*
NESTING *Shallow bowl scraped in soil, lined with plant matter, with overhead cover; 8–10 eggs; 1 brood; Mar–May.*
FEEDING *Mostly buds, stems, and seeds; also flowers, insects, and leaves.*
HABITAT *Arctic, sub-Arctic, and subalpine tundra; willow thickets along river corridors; low woodlands.*
LENGTH *14–17½in (35–44cm)*
WINGSPAN *22–24in (56–61cm)*

Rock Ptarmigan

Ⓢ

Lagopus muta

The Rock Ptarmigan is the most northerly of the three North American ptarmigan species. Although some birds make a short southerly winter migration, many remain on their breeding grounds year-round. This bird is known for distinctive seasonal variation in plumage, which helps helps camouflage it against its surroundings.

mostly gray upperparts

gray wing patch

♂ ☼

black line between eye and bill

♂ ❅

brown-and-black barring

white wings

mottled belly

♀ ☼

red comb

small, round head

small, delicate bill

♂ ☼

"salt-and-pepper" barring on gray upperparts

white belly

feathered feet

VOICE *Quiet; male calls a raspy krrrh, also growls and clucks.*
NESTING *Small scrape or depression lined with plants; 8–10 eggs; 1 brood; Apr–Jun.*
FEEDING *Buds, seeds, flowers, and leaves, especially birch and willow; insects in summer.*
HABITAT *Dry, rocky tundra, and shrubby ridge tops; open meadow edges and dense evergreens along rivers and streams during winter.*
LENGTH *12⅔–15½in (32–40cm)*
WINGSPAN *19½–23½in (50–60cm)*

Greater Prairie-Chicken

Tympanuchus cupido

Once common in prairies and woodlands across central North America, Greater Prairie-Chicken populations have been greatly reduced because of agriculture taking over their habitats. During the breeding season, males defend territories called leks and perform dramatic displays. They entice females by stamping their feet, "booming," and inflating the air sacs on their necks. These birds burst from cover to take flight when startled.

rounded wings

♂

display feathers against neck

♂

barred overall

no display feathers

♀

square tail

♂ **DISPLAYING**

two sets of feathers raised during display

orange skin over eye

beardlike feathers

bright orange skin of "air sac"

VOICE *Courting males emit three-part low "booming" calls; also cackling calls.*
NESTING *Depression in soil lined with vegetation and feathers, in thick grass or other cover; 10–12 eggs; 1 brood; Apr–Jul.*
FEEDING *Berries, leaves, seeds, and grain; also insects.*
HABITAT *Oak-forested river corridors, especially with areas of native tallgrass prairie; resident year-round.*
LENGTH *15½–17½in (40–45cm)*
WINGSPAN *26–29in (66–74cm)*

Wild Turkey

S

Meleagris gallopavo

Once proposed by Benjamin Franklin to be the national emblem of the US, the Wild Turkey is the largest galliform in North America. The bird's well-known gobble is uttered by males, especially during courtship. Wild Turkeys were eliminated from most of their original range by the early 1900s due to overhunting and habitat destruction. Since then, habitat restoration and subsequent reintroduction efforts have succeeded in restoring some Wild Turkey populations.

black-and-white barred wings

iridescent bronze-and-purplish body

dark overall

rusty tail with black band

♂ EAST

♀

tail fanned in display

unfeathered blue-and-red head

large red wattles

hairlike "beard" on breast

♂ WEST

dark body with bronze iridescence

VOICE *Males: gobble, especially during courtship; females: yelps, clucks, and purrs.*
NESTING *Scrape on ground lined with grass, near protective cover; 10–15 eggs; 1 brood; Mar–Jun.*
FEEDING *Omnivorous; acorns, vegetation, and insects from forest floor or agricultural fields.*
HABITAT *Mixed mature woodlands and agricultural fields; grasslands, close to swamps.*
LENGTH *2¾–4ft (0.9–1.2m)*
WINGSPAN *4–5ft (1.2–1.5m)*

Loons

Loons are almost entirely aquatic birds; their legs are positioned so far to the rear of their bodies that they must shuffle on their bellies when they go from water to land. In summer, they are found on rivers, lakes, and ponds, where they nest close to the water's edge. After breeding, they occur along coasts, often after flying hundreds of miles away from their freshwater breeding grounds. Excellent swimmers and divers, loons are unusual among birds in that their bones are less hollow than those of other groups. Consequently, they can expel air from their lungs and compress their body feathers until they slowly sink beneath the surface. They can remain submerged for several minutes.

FEEDING TIME
A Red-throated Loon gives a fish to its chick, which will gulp it down headfirst and whole.

Red-throated Loon ⓢ

Gavia stellata

This elegant loon is almost unmistakable, with a pale, slim body, upward-tilted head, and a thin, upturned bill. Unlike other loons, the Red-throated Loon can launch straight into the air from both land and water, but most of the time it tends to use a "runway." In an elaborate breeding ritual, a pair of birds races side by side upright across the surface of water.

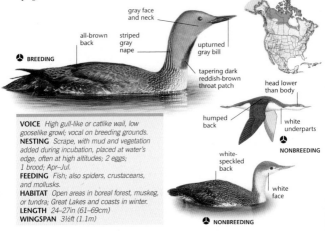

gray face and neck

all-brown back

striped gray nape

upturned gray bill

tapering dark reddish-brown throat patch

🦆 BREEDING

humped back

head lower than body

white underparts

🦆 NONBREEDING

white-speckled back

white face

🦆 NONBREEDING

VOICE High gull-like or catlike wail, low gooselike growl; vocal on breeding grounds.
NESTING Scrape, with mud and vegetation added during incubation, placed at water's edge, often at high altitudes; 2 eggs; 1 brood; Apr–Jul.
FEEDING Fish; also spiders, crustaceans, and mollusks.
HABITAT Open areas in boreal forest, muskeg, or tundra; Great Lakes and coasts in winter.
LENGTH 24–27in (61–69cm)
WINGSPAN 3½ft (1.1m)

Common Loon ⓢ

Gavia immer

The Common Loon has the largest range of all loons in North America and is the only species to nest in a few of the northern states. It is slightly smaller than the Yellow-billed Loon but larger than the other three loons. It can remain underwater for well over 10 minutes, although it usually stays submerged for 40 seconds to 2 minutes while fishing. Occasionally, it interbreeds with the Yellow-billed, Arctic, or Pacific Loon.

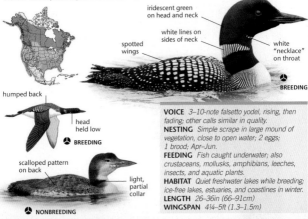

iridescent green on head and neck

white lines on sides of neck

spotted wings

white "necklace" on throat

🦆 BREEDING

humped back

head held low

🦆 BREEDING

scalloped pattern on back

light, partial collar

🦆 NONBREEDING

VOICE 3–10-note falsetto yodel, rising, then fading; other calls similar in quality.
NESTING Simple scrape in large mound of vegetation, close to open water; 2 eggs; 1 brood; Apr–Jun.
FEEDING Fish caught underwater; also crustaceans, mollusks, amphibians, leeches, insects, and aquatic plants.
HABITAT Quiet freshwater lakes while breeding; ice-free lakes, estuaries, and coastlines in winter.
LENGTH 26–36in (66–91cm)
WINGSPAN 4¼–5ft (1.3–1.5m)

Grebes

Grebes resemble loons and share many of their aquatic characteristics, including a streamlined shape and legs that are positioned far back on the body, making them awkward on land. Grebe nests are usually partially floating platforms, built on beds of water plants. They dive to catch fish with a short, forward-arching spring, using their lobed toes in a sideways motion to propel them underwater. Unusually among birds, they swallow feathers, supposedly to trap fish bones and protect their stomachs, then periodically disgorge them. Like loons, grebes can control their buoyancy by exhaling air and compressing their plumage so that they sink quietly below the surface. They are strong fliers, and migratory.

A FINE DISPLAY
A Horned Grebe reveals colorful plumes in its courtship display.

Pied-billed Grebe

Podilymbus podiceps

The widest ranging of the North American grebes, the Pied-billed Grebe is tolerant of populated areas and breeds on lakes and ponds. A powerful swimmer, it can remain submerged for 16–30 seconds when it dives. Its courtship ritual is more vocal than visual, and pairs usually duet-call in the mating season. Migration begins when its breeding area ices up and food becomes scarce. The Pied-billed Grebe is capable of sustained flights of over 2,000 miles (3,200km).

outstretched neck

BREEDING

lighter flight feathers

yellowish bill

whitish throat

NONBREEDING

whitish hooked bill with a black ring

brown eye

reddish-brown neck and breast

brownish-gray body

black throat patch

BREEDING

white undertail

VOICE *Grunts and wails; in spring, cuckoolike repeated gobble kup-kup-Kaow-Kaow-kaow.*
NESTING *Floating nest of partially decayed plants and clipped leaves, attached to vegetation in marshes and quiet waters; 4–7 eggs; 2 broods; Apr–Oct.*
FEEDING *Dives for crustaceans, fish, amphibians, and insects; picks prey from emergent vegetation, or catches them midair.*
HABITAT *Coastal brackish ponds, seasonal ponds, and marshes.*
LENGTH *12–15in (31–38cm)*
WINGSPAN *18–24in (46–62cm)*

Red-necked Grebe

Podiceps grisegena

The Red-necked Grebe is smaller than the Western and Clark's Grebes, but larger than other North American grebes. It migrates over short to medium distances and spends the winter along both coasts, where large flocks may occur. This grebe runs along the water's surface to become airborne. Like other grebes, Red-necked Grebes have the odd behavior of swallowing some of their feathers. These may line the digestive track, offering protection from sharp fish bones.

head and neck in line with body

BREEDING

white-edged inner wing

brownish cap

pale reddish-brown crescent near ear

NONBREEDING

grayish-white cheeks and throat

broad head with crest at rear

black cap

chestnut-brown neck and chest

gray flanks

brown eye

BREEDING

VOICE Nasal, gull-like call on breeding grounds, evolves into bray, ends with whinny; also honks, rattles, hisses, purrs, and ticks.
NESTING Compact, buoyant mound of vegetation in sheltered, shallow marshes and lakes; 4–5 eggs; 1 brood; May–Jul.
FEEDING Fish, crustaceans, aquatic insects, worms, mollusks, salamanders, and tadpoles.
HABITAT Large marshes and small lakes while breeding; estuaries, inlets, bays in winter.
LENGTH 16½–22in (42–56cm)
WINGSPAN 24–35in (61–88cm)

Horned Grebe

D

Podiceps auritus

The timing of the Horned Grebe's migration depends largely on the weather—this species may not leave until its breeding grounds get iced over, nor does it arrive before the ice melts. Its breeding behavior is well documented because it is approachable on nesting grounds and has an elaborate breeding ritual. This grebe's so-called "horns" are, in fact, yellowish feather patches located behind its eyes, which it can raise at will.

neck and head in line with body

flattish top of head

white cheek

white sides to neck

gold streak from eye to nape

black crown

red eye

MOLT

short, dark bill with whitish tip

rufous neck

black throat

VOICE *Descending aaanrrh call most common in winter, ends in trill; muted conversational calls when in groups.*
NESTING *Floating, soggy nest, hidden in vegetation, in small ponds and lake inlets; 3–9 eggs; 1 brood; May–Jul.*
FEEDING *Dives in open water or forages among plants for small crustaceans, insects, leeches, mollusks, amphibians, and fish.*
HABITAT *Fresh water or brackish water with emergent vegetation while breeding; coastlines or large bodies of fresh water in winter.*
LENGTH 12–15in (30–38cm)
WINGSPAN 18–24in (46–62cm)

Tubenoses

The tubenoses are characterized by the tubular nostrils for which they are named. These nostrils act like water pistols to help get rid of excess salt, and may enhance their sense of smell.

The long, narrow wings of albatrosses are perfectly suited for almost endless flight in the strong, constant ocean air currents. Although expert gliders, they need lift from wind to take off from the ground.

Smaller than albatrosses, shearwaters and gadfly petrels range over all the world's oceans, especially the Pacific. During and after storms are the best times to look for these birds, as this is when they drift in from deep sea due to wind and waves.

The smallest tubenoses in North American waters, the storm-petrels are also the most agile fliers. They spend most of their lives flying over the open sea, only visiting land in the breeding season, when they form huge colonies.

STRONG PAIR BOND
After elaborate courtship displays, albatrosses generally pair for life.

Northern Fulmar Ⓢ

Fulmarus glacialis

Possessing paddle-shaped wings and color patterns ranging from almost all-white to all-gray, the Northern Fulmar breeds at high latitudes, then disperses south to offshore waters on both coasts. The Northern Fulmar can often be seen in large mixed flocks containing albatrosses, shearwaters, and petrels. Fulmars often follow fishing boats, eager to pounce on the offal thrown overboard.

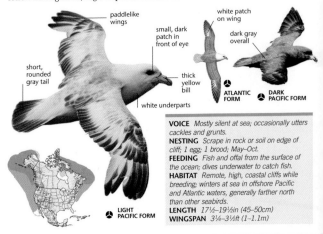

paddlelike wings

small, dark patch in front of eye

short, rounded gray tail

thick yellow bill

white underparts

white patch on wing

dark gray overall

ATLANTIC FORM

DARK PACIFIC FORM

LIGHT PACIFIC FORM

VOICE *Mostly silent at sea; occasionally utters cackles and grunts.*
NESTING *Scrape in rock or soil on edge of cliff; 1 egg; 1 brood; May–Oct.*
FEEDING *Fish and offal from the surface of the ocean; dives underwater to catch fish.*
HABITAT *Remote, high, coastal cliffs while breeding; winters at sea in offshore Pacific and Atlantic waters, generally farther north than other seabirds.*
LENGTH 17½–19½in (45–50cm)
WINGSPAN 3¼–3½ft (1–1.1m)

Cory's Shearwater Ⓢ

Calonectris diomedea

Studies of Cory's Shearwaters off the Atlantic Coast suggest the presence of two forms. The more common form, *C. d. borealis,* nests in the eastern Atlantic and is chunkier, with less white in the wing from below. The other form, *C. d. diomedea,* breeds in the Mediterranean, and has a more slender build and more extensive white under the wing.

scalloped pattern

grayish head and chin

yellow bill with dark tip

dark wingtip and trailing edge

white breast with sooty-gray sides

all-white belly

clean white underwing

long, pointed wings

pale rump

VOICE *Mostly silent at sea; descending, lamblike bleating.*
NESTING *Nests in burrow or rocky crevice; 1 egg; 1 brood; May–Sep.*
FEEDING *Dives into water or picks at surface for small schooling fish, and marine invertebrates, such as squid.*
HABITAT *Breeds mostly in the Mediterranean and on islands of the eastern Atlantic; winters widely over the Atlantic Ocean.*
LENGTH 18in (46cm)
WINGSPAN 3½ft (1.1m)

Manx Shearwater Ⓢ

Puffinus puffinus

Most shearwaters are little known, but the Manx is an exception. It is common in the British Isles, with more than 330,000 pairs breeding in colonies there. These birds are most often seen singly or in small flocks with other shearwater species. Long-term banding programs revealed one bird that flew over 3,000 miles (4,800km) from Massachusetts to its nesting burrow in Wales in just 12½ days.

dark upperwings

short tail

small head

black edge of wing

dark, hooked bill

white throat

white undertail feathers

snow-white underparts

long, pointed wings

crisp white underwings

VOICE *Usually silent at sea; loud and raucous kah-kah-kah-kah-kah-HOWW at breeding sites.*
NESTING *In burrow, in peaty soil, or rocky crevice; 1 egg; 1 brood; Apr–Oct.*
FEEDING *Dives into water, often with open wings and stays underwater, or picks at surface for small schooling fish and squid.*
HABITAT *Islands in the eastern North Atlantic while breeding; rarely seen from shore during migration and winter.*
LENGTH *13½in (34cm)*
WINGSPAN *33in (83cm)*

Audubon's Shearwater Ⓢ

Puffinus lherminieri

Audubon's Shearwater is much smaller and more slender than other regularly occurring shearwaters in North American waters. Its short wings and small size render its flight similar to that of alcids (auks, murres, and puffins). Audubon's Shearwater is rare on land, spending most of its life at sea.

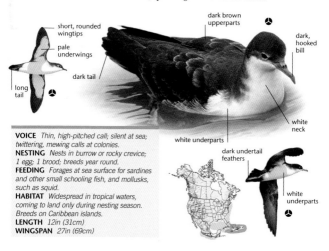

short, rounded wingtips

pale underwings

dark tail

long tail

dark brown upperparts

dark, hooked bill

white neck

white underparts

dark undertail feathers

white underparts

VOICE *Thin, high-pitched call; silent at sea; twittering, mewing calls at colonies.*
NESTING *Nests in burrow or rocky crevice; 1 egg; 1 brood; breeds year round.*
FEEDING *Forages at sea surface for sardines and other small schooling fish, and mollusks, such as squid.*
HABITAT *Widespread in tropical waters, coming to land only during nesting season. Breeds on Caribbean islands.*
LENGTH *12in (31cm)*
WINGSPAN *27in (69cm)*

Great Shearwater ⓢ

Ardenna gravis

The Great Shearwater is similar in size to Cory's Shearwater and the birds scavenge together for scraps around fishing boats. However, while the Cory's Shearwater has slow, labored wing beats and glides high on broad, swept-back wings, Great Shearwaters keep low, flapping hurriedly between glides on straight, narrow wings. The brown smudges on the belly and paler underwings of the Great Shearwater also help distinguish the species.

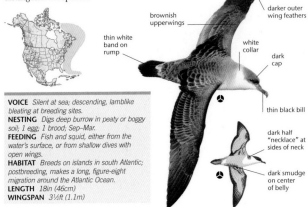

brownish upperwings

darker outer wing feathers

thin white band on rump

white collar

dark cap

thin black bill

dark half "necklace" at sides of neck

dark smudge on center of belly

VOICE *Silent at sea; descending, lamblike bleating at breeding sites.*
NESTING *Digs deep burrow in peaty or boggy soil; 1 egg; 1 brood; Sep–Mar.*
FEEDING *Fish and squid, either from the water's surface, or from shallow dives with open wings.*
HABITAT *Breeds on islands in south Atlantic; postbreeding, makes a figure-eight migration around the Atlantic Ocean.*
LENGTH *18in (46cm)*
WINGSPAN *3½ft (1.1m)*

Sooty Shearwater ⓢ

Ardenna grisea

Sooty Shearwaters are extremely long-distance migrants. Pacific populations, in particular, travel as far as 300 miles (480km) per day and an extraordinary 45,000 miles (72,500km) or more per year. It is fairly easy to identify off the East Coast of North America because it is the only all-dark shearwater found there.

all-dark underparts

silvery-white patch along underwing

long, slender wings

sooty head

all-dark upperparts

long, hooked bill

VOICE *Silent at sea; occasionally gives varied, agitated vocalizations when feeding, very loud calls at breeding colonies.*
NESTING *In burrow or rocky crevice; 1 egg; 1 brood; Oct–May.*
FEEDING *Dives and picks at surface for small schooling fish and mollusks, such as squid.*
HABITAT *Islands in southern oceans while breeding; open ocean off both coasts in nonbreeding season.*
LENGTH *18in (46cm)*
WINGSPAN *3¼ft (1m)*

Wilson's Storm-Petrel Ⓢ

Oceanites oceanicus

Wilson's Storm-Petrel is the quintessential small oceanic petrel. After breeding in the many millions on the Antarctic Peninsula and various islands there, it moves north to spend the summer off the Atlantic Coast of North America and is a familiar sight to fishermen and birders at sea. By August, individuals can be seen lingering, but by October they have flown south.

dark wings and body

small black "tube nose"

yellow webbing between toes

pale bar on upperwing

short, square tail

white rump and lower flanks

broad, pointed wings

"walking" on water

VOICE At sea, soft rasping notes; variety of coos, churrs, and twitters during the night at breeding sites.
NESTING In rock crevices; also burrows where there is peaty soil; 1 egg; 1 brood; Nov–Mar.
FEEDING Patters on the water's surface, legs extended, picking up tiny crustaceans; also carrion, oil droplets, and cetacean feces.
HABITAT Rocky islets, cliffs, and boulder scree while breeding; Apr–Sep off the Atlantic coasts.
LENGTH 6¾in (17cm)
WINGSPAN 16in (41cm)

Leach's Storm-Petrel Ⓢ

Hydrobates leucorhous

Leach's Storm-Petrel is widespread in both the Atlantic and Pacific Oceans. It breeds in colonies on islands off the coasts, coming to land at night and feeding offshore during the day, often many miles from the colony. This storm-petrel has both geographical and individual variation; most populations show a white rump, but others have a rump that is the same color as the rest of the body.

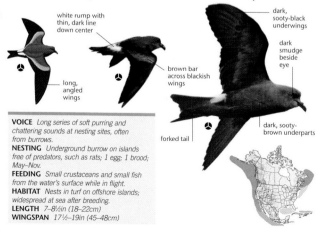

white rump with thin, dark line down center

long, angled wings

brown bar across blackish wings

dark, sooty-black underwings

dark smudge beside eye

forked tail

dark, sooty-brown underparts

VOICE Long series of soft purring and chattering sounds at nesting sites, often from burrows.
NESTING Underground burrow on islands free of predators, such as rats; 1 egg; 1 brood; May–Nov.
FEEDING Small crustaceans and small fish from the water's surface while in flight.
HABITAT Nests in turf on offshore islands; widespread at sea after breeding.
LENGTH 7–8½in (18–22cm)
WINGSPAN 17½–19in (45–48cm)

Storks

Storks are long-legged, primarily wetland birds, ranging in height from 2 to 5ft (60–150cm). All or part of the head and neck may be brightly colored and bare of feathers. Storks are nearly voiceless; however, they may clatter their bills when excited. They fly with their long necks extended and their feet trailing behind them. Their wings are "fingered" at the tips, which aids them in soaring flight by providing extra lift. Storks feed in marshes and open grasslands, preying on amphibians, small reptiles, rodents, and insects.

BARE HEADS
Wood Storks have bare heads with wrinkled, blackish skin, and bills that are tapered and drooped.

Frigatebirds, Gannets, Cormorants, and Anhingas

Frigatebirds are large seabirds with long, angular wings, deeply forked tails, and sharply hooked bills. They feed by catching flying fish or forcing other birds to disgorge food. Gannets and boobies have pointed bills, long wings, and fully webbed feet. Cormorants and Anhingas also have four fully webbed toes. Anhingas, or darters, have narrow heads and long, pointed bills that give them a snakelike appearance.

SEEKING ATTENTION
A male Magnificent Frigatebird inflates his red gular pouch to attract a female.

Wood Stork

Mycteria americana

The Wood Stork is the largest wading bird in the US and the only stork that breeds here. It formerly bred mostly in southern Florida, but as foraging conditions deteriorated, Wood Stork breeding populations moved north to North Carolina. During hot weather, Wood Storks use an extraordinary cooling method that involves defecating on their own legs. Wood Storks often feed by stirring the bottom with their feet, and feeling for prey movement with their bills.

black-and-white wings

dark head

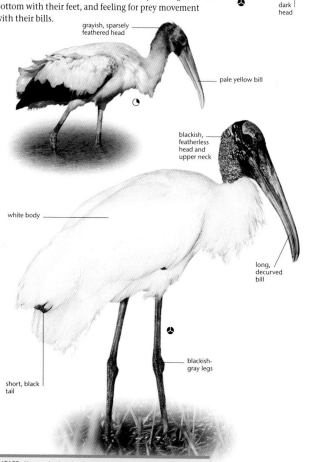

grayish, sparsely feathered head

pale yellow bill

blackish, featherless head and upper neck

white body

long, decurved bill

blackish-gray legs

short, black tail

VOICE *Young give braying begging calls; adults clatter bills during courtship.*
NESTING *Large twig nest usually in swamps; colonial nesters, usually in trees over water for protection from predators; 2–4 eggs; 1 brood; Dec–Aug.*
FEEDING *Aquatic prey, including fish, crabs, and insects.*
HABITAT *Forested freshwater and coastal areas, swamps and marshes; feeds in shallow wetlands.*
LENGTH *3¼ft (1m)*
WINGSPAN *5ft (1.5m)*

Magnificent Frigatebird

Fregata magnificens

One of North America's most skilled aerialists, the Magnificent Frigatebird perches only when nesting in mangroves or roosting on buoys. Usually spotted soaring gracefully over open water, this bird never alights on the surface or gets wet. Magnificent Frigatebirds are well known for their aggressive food piracy, and for the breeding males' display of their inflated, gaudy throat pouches.

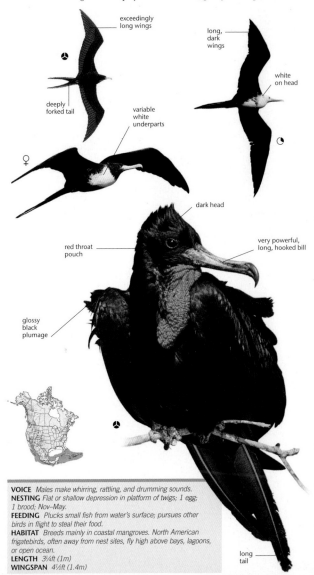

exceedingly long wings

long, dark wings

white on head

deeply forked tail

variable white underparts

♀

dark head

red throat pouch

very powerful, long, hooked bill

glossy black plumage

long tail

VOICE *Males make whirring, rattling, and drumming sounds.*
NESTING *Flat or shallow depression in platform of twigs; 1 egg; 1 brood; Nov–May.*
FEEDING *Plucks small fish from water's surface; pursues other birds in flight to steal their food.*
HABITAT *Breeds mainly in coastal mangroves. North American frigatebirds, often away from nest sites, fly high above bays, lagoons, or open ocean.*
LENGTH *3¼ft (1m)*
WINGSPAN *4½ft (1.4m)*

Northern Gannet

Morus bassanus

The Northern Gannet is known for its spectacular headfirst dives during frantic, voracious foraging in flocks of hundreds to thousands for surface-schooling fish. In North America, this bird nests in just six locations in northeastern Canada. It was the first species to have its total world population estimated—there were 83,000 birds in 1939. Numbers have since increased.

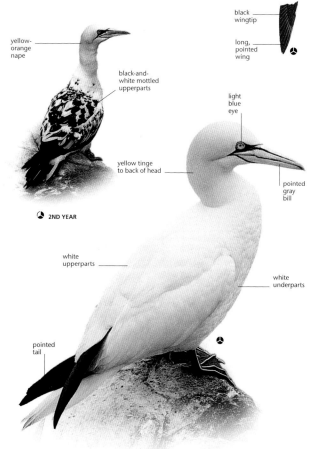

yellow-orange nape

black-and-white mottled upperparts

black wingtip

long, pointed wing

light blue eye

yellow tinge to back of head

pointed gray bill

2ND YEAR

white upperparts

white underparts

pointed tail

VOICE *Loud landing call* arrrr, arrah, *or* urrah rah rah; *hollow groan* oh-ah *during takeoff;* krok *call at sea.*
NESTING *Large pile of mud, seaweed, and trash, glued with guano, on bare rock or soil; 1 egg; 1 brood; Apr–Nov.*
FEEDING *Plunge-dives headfirst into water and often swims with its wings underwater to catch mackerel, herring, capelin, and cod.*
HABITAT *Isolated rock stacks on small islands or cliffs while breeding; continental shelf waters in winter.*
LENGTH *2¾–3½ ft (0.8–1.1m)*
WINGSPAN *5½ ft (1.7m)*

Brown Booby

D

Sula leucogaster

The Brown Booby, a sooty-brown-and-white bird, is distinguishable from other boobies by the sharp border between its dark chest and white belly. This long-lived species overlaps with Masked and Red-footed Boobies and often nests in mixed colonies with them. Unlike other ground-nesting boobies, it often builds a substantial nest. Like other boobies, it feeds with spectacular plunges into the sea. The oldest known Brown Booby was 26 years old.

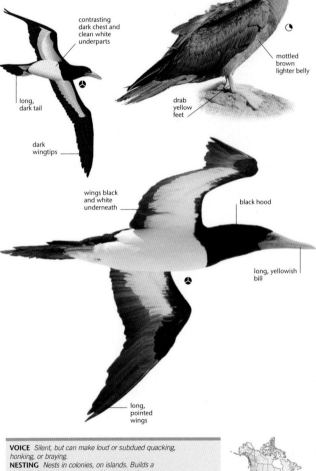

contrasting dark chest and clean white underparts

mottled brown lighter belly

long, dark tail

drab yellow feet

dark wingtips

wings black and white underneath

black hood

long, yellowish bill

long, pointed wings

VOICE Silent, but can make loud or subdued quacking, honking, or braying.
NESTING Nests in colonies, on islands. Builds a mound of branches, grass, and human trash, on sunny, flat ground.
FEEDING Feeds on squid and fish, particularly flying fish.
HABITAT Breeds on a variety of tropical islands; at sea in nonbreeding season. Rare on Atlantic and Pacific Coasts.
LENGTH 30in (76cm)
WINGSPAN 4½ft (1.4m)

Double-crested Cormorant

Nannopterum auritum

This species is the most widespread of the North American cormorants. It often flies high over land in V-shaped flocks, but is mostly seen swimming low in the water with its head and neck visible, or resting on trees and rocks, sometimes with its wings spread to dry and drain their flight feathers after fishing bouts. When fishing, it dives from the surface of the water and chases fish underwater, using its webbed toes for propulsion.

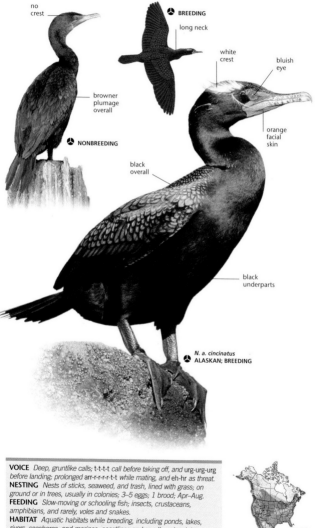

no crest

♠ BREEDING

long neck

browner plumage overall

♠ NONBREEDING

white crest

bluish eye

orange facial skin

black overall

black underparts

N. a. cincinatus
♠ ALASKAN; BREEDING

VOICE *Deep, gruntlike calls; t-t-t-t call before taking off, and urg-urg-urg before landing; prolonged arr-r-r-r-r-t-t while mating, and eh-hr as threat.*
NESTING *Nests of sticks, seaweed, and trash, lined with grass; on ground or in trees, usually in colonies; 3–5 eggs; 1 brood; Apr–Aug.*
FEEDING *Slow-moving or schooling fish; insects, crustaceans, amphibians, and rarely, voles and snakes.*
HABITAT *Aquatic habitats while breeding, including ponds, lakes, rivers, seashores, and marinas; coastlines and sandbars in winter.*
LENGTH *28–35in (70–90cm)*
WINGSPAN *3½–4ft (1.1–1.2m)*

Great Cormorant

Phalacrocorax carbo

As its name suggests, the Great Cormorant is the largest North American cormorant. It is also the most widely distributed cormorant species in the world. It sometimes breeds in mixed colonies with Double-crested Cormorants; it is distinguishable by its stouter bill, larger size, and white throat in summer. Like other cormorants, its plumage retains water, which reduces buoyancy for easier diving—often to depths of 115ft (35m)—to catch prey. Flocks often fly in a V-shape.

brown neck

mostly white underparts

outstretched head

neck kinked in flight

thick bill with hooked tip

large head with flat forehead

orange-yellow patch of skin near bill

long, black neck

white throat

BREEDING

glossy black underparts with greenish scalloping

long body with glossy black upperparts

short, black legs and webbed feet

long, broad tail

VOICE *Deep, guttural calls at nesting and roosting site; otherwise silent.*
NESTING *Mound of seaweed, sticks, and debris, on cliff ledges and flat rocks above high-water mark; 3–5 eggs; 1 brood; Apr–Aug.*
FEEDING *Fish and small crustaceans; smaller prey swallowed underwater, while larger prey brought to surface.*
HABITAT *Cliff ledges on rocky coasts while breeding; shallow coastal waters in winter.*
LENGTH *33–35in (84–90cm)*
WINGSPAN *4¼–5¼ft (1.3–1.6m)*

Anhinga

Ⓢ

Anhinga anhinga

Anhingas may be found swimming in murky swamps, roosting in tall trees, or soaring high overhead. The species is also known as the "snake bird" due to its habit of swimming with its body immersed so deeply that only its long, thin, sinuous neck, pointed head, and daggerlike bill stick out above the water. Although Anhingas superficially resemble cormorants, they can be distinguished by their sharply pointed bills and long tails with horizontally ridged feathers. Lacking waterproof plumage, Anhingas spend a lot of time perched above the water with wings outstretched.

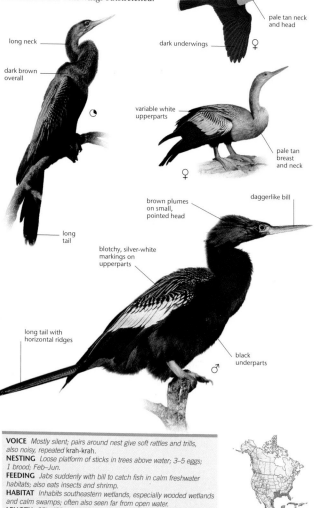

pale tan neck and head

dark underwings

♀

long neck

dark brown overall

☽

variable white upperparts

pale tan breast and neck

♀

brown plumes on small, pointed head

daggerlike bill

long tail

blotchy, silver-white markings on upperparts

long tail with horizontal ridges

black underparts

♂

VOICE Mostly silent; pairs around nest give soft rattles and trills, also noisy, repeated *krah-krah*.
NESTING Loose platform of sticks in trees above water; 3–5 eggs; 1 brood; Feb–Jun.
FEEDING Jabs suddenly with bill to catch fish in calm freshwater habitats; also eats insects and shrimp.
HABITAT Inhabits southeastern wetlands, especially wooded wetlands and calm swamps; often also seen far from open water.
LENGTH 35in (89cm)
WINGSPAN 3½ft (1.1m)

Pelicans, Herons, Ibises, and Relatives

Pelicans are large, fish-eating birds, bulky but buoyant on the water. Flocks can be seen soaring to great heights on migration and when flying to feeding grounds. Brown Pelicans dive headfirst to catch fish, while White Pelicans work together to herd fish into shallow bays, then scoop them into pouches beneath their long bills.

Herons, egrets, and bitterns are waterside birds with long toes that enable them to walk on wet mud and provide greater balance as they lean forward to catch fish. Herons and egrets have slender necks with a distinct kink. They make bulky nests in treetop colonies, whereas bitterns nest on the ground in marshes.

Ibises and related spoonbills are long-legged, waterside or dryland birds. Ibises have long, decurved bills well adapted for picking insects, worms, small mollusks, and crustaceans from wet mud. Spoonbills have a unique flat, spatula-shaped bill that they sweep from side to side in shallow water to catch aquatic prey.

WATER BIRD
Webbed feet help the Brown Pelican negotiate water with ease, while strong wings enable easy takeoffs.

American White Pelican

(S)

Pelecanus erythrorhynchos

This colossal white bird, with its distinctive, oversized bill, is a social inhabitant of large lakes and marshes in western North America. It is a colonial bird, with most of its population concentrated in a handful of large colonies in isolated wetlands in deserts and prairies. The American White Pelican forms cooperative foraging flocks, which beat their wings to herd fish into shallow water, where they can be caught more easily.

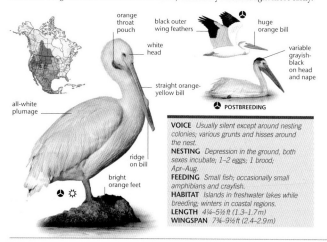

orange throat pouch

black outer wing feathers

huge orange bill

white head

variable grayish-black on head and nape

straight orange-yellow bill

POSTBREEDING

all-white plumage

ridge on bill

bright orange feet

VOICE *Usually silent except around nesting colonies; various grunts and hisses around the nest.*
NESTING *Depression in the ground, both sexes incubate; 1–2 eggs; 1 brood; Apr–Aug.*
FEEDING *Small fish; occasionally small amphibians and crayfish.*
HABITAT *Islands in freshwater lakes while breeding; winters in coastal regions.*
LENGTH *4¼–5½ ft (1.3–1.7m)*
WINGSPAN *7¾–9½ ft (2.4–2.9m)*

Brown Pelican

(S)

Pelecanus occidentalis

This enormous and conspicuous inhabitant of warm coastal regions is ungainly on land but surprisingly graceful in flight. Brown Pelican numbers plummeted in the 1960s due to widespread DDT use, but the species has recovered rapidly in recent decades. Their range is now expanding northward along both coasts. These social birds are often seen roosting in groups. The Brown Pelican's throat color varies with geographic location.

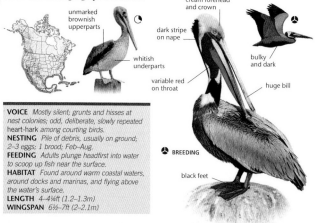

cream forehead and crown

unmarked brownish upperparts

dark stripe on nape

whitish underparts

bulky and dark

variable red on throat

huge bill

VOICE *Mostly silent; grunts and hisses at nest colonies; odd, deliberate, slowly repeated heart-hark among courting birds.*
NESTING *Pile of debris, usually on ground; 2–3 eggs; 1 brood; Feb–Aug.*
FEEDING *Adults plunge headfirst into water to scoop up fish near the surface.*
HABITAT *Found around warm coastal waters, around docks and marinas, and flying above the water's surface.*
LENGTH *4–4¼ft (1.2–1.3m)*
WINGSPAN *6½–7ft (2–2.1m)*

BREEDING

black feet

American Bittern

Botaurus lentiginosus ⓢ

The American Bittern's camouflaged plumage and secretive behavior help it blend into its thick reed habitat. It is heard much more often than it is seen; its call is unmistakable and has given rise to many evocative colloquial names, such as "thunder pumper."

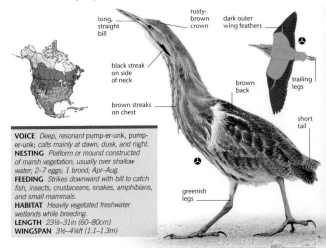

long, straight bill

rusty-brown crown

dark outer wing feathers

black streak on side of neck

brown streaks on chest

brown back

trailing legs

short tail

greenish legs

VOICE *Deep, resonant pump-er-unk, pump-er-unk; calls mainly at dawn, dusk, and night.*
NESTING *Platform or mound constructed of marsh vegetation, usually over shallow water; 2–7 eggs; 1 brood; Apr–Aug.*
FEEDING *Strikes downward with bill to catch fish, insects, crustaceans, snakes, amphibians, and small mammals.*
HABITAT *Heavily vegetated freshwater wetlands while breeding.*
LENGTH *23½–31in (60–80cm)*
WINGSPAN *3½–4¼ft (1.1–1.3m)*

Least Bittern

Ixobrychus exilis ⓣ

The smallest heron in North America, the Least Bittern is also one of the most colorful, but its secretive nature makes it easy to overlook in its densely vegetated marsh habitat. A dark color form, which was originally described in the 1800s as a separate species named Cory's Bittern, has rarely been reported in recent decades.

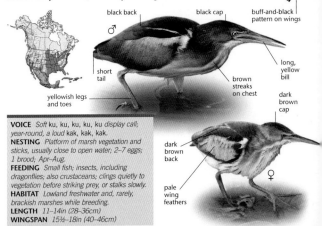

black back

black cap

♂

buff-and-black pattern on wings

short tail

yellowish legs and toes

brown streaks on chest

long, yellow bill

dark brown cap

dark brown back

pale wing feathers

♀

VOICE *Soft ku, ku, ku, ku, ku display call; year-round, a loud kak, kak, kak.*
NESTING *Platform of marsh vegetation and sticks, usually close to open water; 2–7 eggs; 1 brood; Apr–Aug.*
FEEDING *Small fish; insects, including dragonflies; also crustaceans; clings quietly to vegetation before striking prey, or stalks slowly.*
HABITAT *Lowland freshwater and, rarely, brackish marshes while breeding.*
LENGTH *11–14in (28–36cm)*
WINGSPAN *15½–18in (40–46cm)*

Great Blue Heron

Ardea herodias

This is one of the world's largest herons, slightly smaller than Africa's Goliath Heron but of similar stature to the more closely related Gray Heron of Eurasia and Cocoi Heron of South America. Unlike the Great White Heron, which is found only in southern Florida, the Great Blue Heron is a common inhabitant of a variety of North American waterbodies, from marshes to swamps, as well as along sea coasts. Opportunistic feeders, they sometimes kill and swallow ducklings and small mammals.

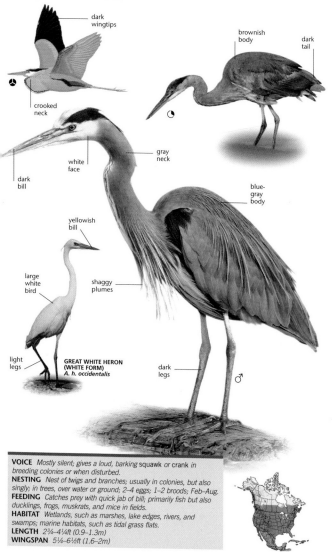

dark wingtips

crooked neck

brownish body

dark tail

gray neck

white face

dark bill

blue-gray body

yellowish bill

large white bird

shaggy plumes

light legs

GREAT WHITE HERON (WHITE FORM)
A. h. occidentalis

dark legs

♂

VOICE *Mostly silent; gives a loud, barking squawk or crank in breeding colonies or when disturbed.*
NESTING *Nest of twigs and branches; usually in colonies, but also singly; in trees, over water or ground; 2–4 eggs; 1–2 broods; Feb–Aug.*
FEEDING *Catches prey with quick jab of bill; primarily fish but also ducklings, frogs, muskrats, and mice in fields.*
HABITAT *Wetlands, such as marshes, lake edges, rivers, and swamps; marine habitats, such as tidal grass flats.*
LENGTH *2¾–4¼ft (0.9–1.3m)*
WINGSPAN *5¼–6½ft (1.6–2m)*

Cattle Egret (S)

Bubulcus ibis

Unlike most other herons, the Cattle Egret is a grassland species that rarely wades in water, and is often seen with livestock, feeding on the insects disturbed by their feet. It was first seen in Florida in 1941, but expanded rapidly and has now bred in over 40 US states and up into the southern provinces of Canada.

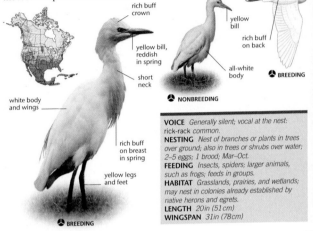

rich buff crown

yellow bill

yellow bill, reddish in spring

rich buff on back

short neck

all-white body

NONBREEDING

white body and wings

rich buff on breast in spring

yellow legs and feet

BREEDING

VOICE *Generally silent; vocal at the nest: rick-rack common.*
NESTING *Nest of branches or plants in trees over ground; also in trees or shrubs over water; 2–5 eggs; 1 brood; Mar–Oct.*
FEEDING *Insects, spiders; larger animals, such as frogs; feeds in groups.*
HABITAT *Grasslands, prairies, and wetlands; may nest in colonies already established by native herons and egrets.*
LENGTH *20in (51cm)*
WINGSPAN *31in (78cm)*

Great Egret (S)

Ardea alba

Unlike other egrets, the Great Egret apparently prefers to forage alone; it maintains space around itself, defending a territory of 10ft (3m) in diameter from other wading birds. This territory "moves" with the bird as it feeds. In years of scarce food supplies, a nestling may kill a sibling, permitting the survival of at least one bird.

large size

white overall

long yellow bill

lime-green patch between eye and bill

all-white plumage

long, S-curved neck

BREEDING

VOICE *Vocal during courtship and breeding; otherwise, kraak or cuk-cuk-cuk when disturbed or in a combative encounter.*
NESTING *Nest of twigs in trees, over land or water; 2–4 eggs; 1 brood; Mar–Jul.*
FEEDING *Aquatic prey: fish and crustaceans; stands quietly in shallow water then catches prey with quick thrust of bill.*
HABITAT *Freshwater and marine wetlands, such as marshes, ponds, and rivers.*
LENGTH *3¼ft (1m)*
WINGSPAN *6ft (1.8m)*

black legs and feet

long black plumes

NONBREEDING

Snowy Egret

D

Egretta thula

The highly adaptable Snowy Egret is widespread throughout North America in both estuarine and freshwater habitats. This egret's white plumes were once coveted by the fashion industry, and hunting endangered the species until early conservationists successfully rallied to protect it. Snowy Egrets use a variety of foraging behaviors, including wing-flicking, and stirring mud with their brilliant yellow feet to get their prey moving, making capture easier.

paler patch of skin at base of bill

greenish-yellow legs

long, extended legs

plumes on head

all-white plumage

black bill

yellow patch between eye and bill

wispy breast plumes

black legs

BREEDING

yellow feet

VOICE *High-pitched* aargaarg *when flushed; low-pitched* aarg *and* raah *calls during attacks.*
NESTING *Small sticks, branches, and rushes over water, on ground, and in shrubs and mangroves; 3–5 eggs; 1 brood; Mar–Aug.*
FEEDING *Aquatic prey, including amphibians, insects, shrimp, prawns, small fish, and snakes.*
HABITAT *Shallow coastal wetlands ranging from Florida mangroves to New England and western marshlands.*
LENGTH *24in (62cm)*
WINGSPAN *3½ft (1.1m)*

Little Blue Heron

S

Egretta caerulea

The shy Little Blue Heron is often overlooked because of its blue-gray color and secretive habits. No other heron species undergoes such a drastic change from an all-white first-year juvenile to all-dark adult plumage. Adults feed alone, wading slowly in shallow waters to stalk prey in swamps and thick wetlands, marshes, lakes, streams, rivers, flooded fields, lagoons, and tidal flats.

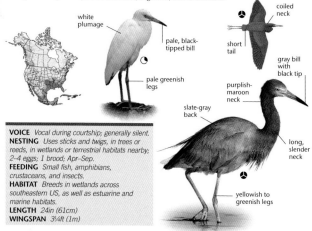

white plumage

pale, black-tipped bill

pale greenish legs

coiled neck

short tail

gray bill with black tip

purplish-maroon neck

slate-gray back

long, slender neck

yellowish to greenish legs

VOICE *Vocal during courtship; generally silent.*
NESTING *Uses sticks and twigs, in trees or reeds, in wetlands or terrestrial habitats nearby; 2–4 eggs; 1 brood; Apr–Sep.*
FEEDING *Small fish, amphibians, crustaceans, and insects.*
HABITAT *Breeds in wetlands across southeastern US, as well as estuarine and marine habitats.*
LENGTH *24in (61cm)*
WINGSPAN *3¼ft (1m)*

Tricolored Heron
Ⓓ

Egretta tricolor

Formerly called the Louisiana Heron due to its southeastern US habitat, the Tricolored Heron has spread along the East Coast and over much of the interior since the 1940s. More recently, populations have been declining. The oldest recorded Tricolored Heron was nearly 18. Like other herons, they fly with their legs trailing behind, but swing them downward as they land.

reddish neck with light throat

white underwings

dark wings

NONBREEDING

dark neck and head

greenish-yellow legs

blue bill with dark tip

gray back

pale line down throat and neck

golden plumes on lower back

BREEDING

white belly

pinkish legs

VOICE *Generally nonvocal; males make unh call during courtship; aaah in aggressive encounters; both sexes call culh-culh; scaah when approaching nest with food.*
NESTING *Nest of twigs and branches, usually over water, singly or in small colonies; 2–4 eggs; 1 brood; Jan–Aug.*
FEEDING *Mainly small fish.*
HABITAT *Breeds mainly in estuaries, but also in inland freshwater marshes.*
LENGTH *26in (66cm)*
WINGSPAN *36in (92cm)*

Reddish Egret
Ⓣ

Egretta rufescens

The Reddish Egret occurs in two colors: an all-white form resembling other egrets, and a dark form with a rufous head and neck that gives the species its name. This bird's unique feeding habits include running back and forth in shallow mudflats, halting occasionally to stretch its wings overhead, apparently to lure small fish into their shadow. This hunting method is called "canopy feeding."

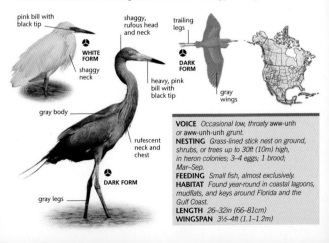

pink bill with black tip

shaggy, rufous head and neck

trailing legs

WHITE FORM

DARK FORM

shaggy neck

heavy, pink bill with black tip

gray wings

gray body

rufescent neck and chest

DARK FORM

gray legs

VOICE *Occasional low, throaty aww-unh or aww-unh-unh grunt.*
NESTING *Grass-lined stick nest on ground, shrubs, or trees up to 30ft (10m) high, in heron colonies; 3–4 eggs; 1 brood; Mar–Sep.*
FEEDING *Small fish, almost exclusively.*
HABITAT *Found year-round in coastal lagoons, mudflats, and keys around Florida and the Gulf Coast.*
LENGTH *26–32in (66–81cm)*
WINGSPAN *3½–4ft (1.1–1.2m)*

Green Heron

Butorides virescens

A small, solitary, and secretive bird of dense, thicketed wetlands, the Green Heron can be difficult to observe. This dark, crested heron is most often seen flying away from a perceived threat, emitting a loud squawk. While the Green Heron of North and Central America has now been recognized as a separate species, it was earlier grouped with what is now the Striated Heron (*B. striata*), which is found in the tropics and subtropics throughout the world.

greenish back

BREEDING

long back plumes

BREEDING

glossy orange legs

paler bill

white speckles on wings

greenish-black cap

short rufous neck

white chin

cream streak extends from throat to belly

yellowish legs and feet

NONBREEDING

VOICE *Squawking* keow *when flying from disturbance.*
NESTING *Nest of twigs in bushes or trees, often over water but also on land; 1–2 broods; 3–5 eggs; Mar–Jul.*
FEEDING *Fish; also frogs, insects, and spiders; stands quietly on the shore or in shallow water and strikes quickly; wades less often than larger herons.*
HABITAT *Swampy thickets, or dry land close to water; coastal wetlands in winter.*
LENGTH *14½–15½in (37–39cm)*
WINGSPAN *25–27in (63–68cm)*

Black-crowned Night-Heron ⓢ

Nycticorax nycticorax

The Black-crowned Night-Heron is chunky and squat. It is also one of the most common and widespread herons in the world, but because it is mainly active at twilight and at night, many people have never seen one. However, its distinctive barking call can be heard at night—even at the center of large cities.

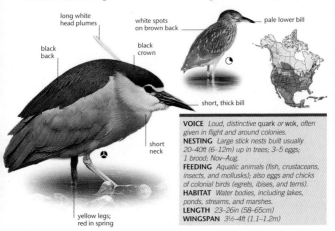

gray wings

long white head plumes

black back

white spots on brown back

black crown

pale lower bill

short, thick bill

short neck

yellow legs; red in spring

VOICE *Loud, distinctive* quark *or* wok, *often given in flight and around colonies.*
NESTING *Large stick nests built usually 20–40ft (6–12m) up in trees; 3–5 eggs; 1 brood; Nov–Aug.*
FEEDING *Aquatic animals (fish, crustaceans, insects, and mollusks); also eggs and chicks of colonial birds (egrets, ibises, and terns).*
HABITAT *Water bodies, including lakes, ponds, streams, and marshes.*
LENGTH *23–26in (58–65cm)*
WINGSPAN *3½–4ft (1.1–1.2m)*

Yellow-crowned Night-Heron ⓢ

Nyctanassa violacea

The elegant Yellow-crowned Night-Heron was unaffected by the plume-hunting that once decimated many heron species. It expanded northward in the 20th century, but has recently retreated from northern areas. Like other herons, it flies with its neck drawn in and legs trailing. It forages both by day and night, standing motionless or slowly stalking prey and then lunging.

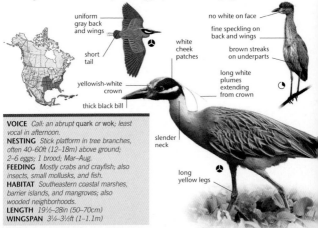

uniform gray back and wings

no white on face

fine speckling on back and wings

white cheek patches

brown streaks on underparts

short tail

yellowish-white crown

long white plumes extending from crown

thick black bill

slender neck

long yellow legs

VOICE *Call: an abrupt* quark *or* wok; *least vocal in afternoon.*
NESTING *Stick platform in tree branches, often 40–60ft (12–18m) above ground; 2–6 eggs; 1 brood; Mar–Aug.*
FEEDING *Mostly crabs and crayfish; also insects, small mollusks, and fish.*
HABITAT *Southeastern coastal marshes, barrier islands, and mangroves; also wooded neighborhoods.*
LENGTH *19½–28in (50–70cm)*
WINGSPAN *3¼–3½ft (1–1.1m)*

White Ibis

Eudocimus albus

The White Ibis has a pink face, bill, and legs set against its white plumage. When breeding, however, the face, legs, and bill turn vivid red. The 20,000–30,000 birds living in the southeastern US move around within this area, depending on the water level. White Ibises are extremely social birds, flying, breeding, feeding, and roosting in large flocks.

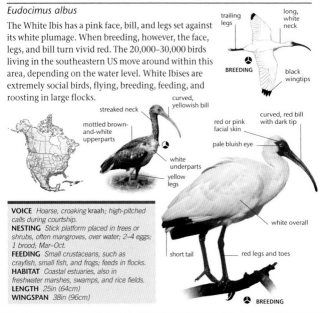

VOICE *Hoarse, croaking* kraah; *high-pitched calls during courtship.*
NESTING *Stick platform placed in trees or shrubs, often mangroves, over water; 2–4 eggs; 1 brood; Mar–Oct.*
FEEDING *Small crustaceans, such as crayfish, small fish, and frogs; feeds in flocks.*
HABITAT *Coastal estuaries, also in freshwater marshes, swamps, and rice fields.*
LENGTH *25in (64cm)*
WINGSPAN *38in (96cm)*

Glossy Ibis

Plegadis falcinellus

Glossy Ibises are dark, long-legged, and have a long, curved bill. Well known for their wandering tendencies, they can also be found in southern Europe, Asia, Australia, and Africa. Confined to Florida until the mid-20th century, this species then started spreading northward, eventually as far as New England and southeastern Canada.

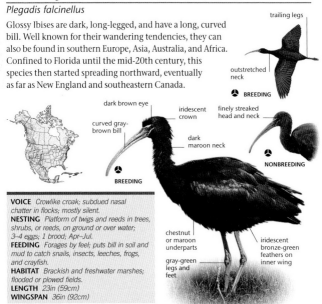

VOICE *Crowlike croak; subdued nasal chatter in flocks; mostly silent.*
NESTING *Platform of twigs and reeds in trees, shrubs, or reeds, on ground or over water; 3–4 eggs; 1 brood; Apr–Jul.*
FEEDING *Forages by feel; puts bill in soil and mud to catch snails, insects, leeches, frogs, and crayfish.*
HABITAT *Brackish and freshwater marshes; flooded or plowed fields.*
LENGTH *23in (59cm)*
WINGSPAN *36in (92cm)*

Roseate Spoonbill

Platalea ajaja

Of the six spoonbills that occur around the world, the North American species is the only one that is bright pink, deriving its color from its diet of of crustaceans. Its spectacular color has inspired local names, including "Flame Bird," "Banjo-bill," and simply "Pink." This wading bird swings its unique bill from side to side to strain small food items out of the water. The oldest known Roseate Spoonbill was nearly 16 when captured and released.

light, pink-tinted body

pink wings

red rump

dark legs

yellowish-green naked skin

long white neck

pinkish-red patch on wing

long, spoon-shaped bill

pink back

mostly pink underparts

pink tail

reddish legs

VOICE *Generally silent; huh-huh-huh-huh greeting and alarm calls at nesting colony.*
NESTING *Nest of large sticks in mangroves, small trees, or on ground; 3–4 eggs; 1 brood; Apr–Aug.*
FEEDING *Small aquatic prey, such as small fish, shrimp, insects, and spiders.*
HABITAT *Shallow wetlands: estuarine, brackish, and freshwater lagoons in flocks, often near the southern coasts.*
LENGTH *32in (82cm)*
WINGSPAN *4¼ft (1.3m)*

New World Vultures

New World vultures are not related to Old World vultures, although they look somewhat similar, with long, broad wings with "fingered" tips. All the birds in this group have exceptional eyesight and find their food by sight while soaring high over open ground. The Turkey Vulture, a common sight in many areas, also has a keen sense of smell and can even find dead animals inside woodland.

WEAK TOOL
In spite of its sharp beak, the Turkey Vulture cannot always break the skin of carcasses.

Hawks, Eagles, and Relatives

These diurnal birds of prey include several loosely related groups. All have hooked bills and large eyes, but their shapes and lifestyles are varied. The sole member of the Pandionidae family, the Osprey catches fish in a headlong dive from a hover. It has long, curved claws and toes equipped with sharp scales to give extra grip. The Accipitridae family covers a range of raptors—such as kites, harriers, eagles, and hawks—with much variation in shape, size, and habitat.

DOUBLE SHOT
With lots of fish running in a tight school, this Osprey has the strength and skill to catch two with one dive.

Black Vulture

Coragyps atratus

Common in southern and eastern states, Black Vultures often spend evenings in large communal roosts that act as meeting places and perhaps information centers where food locations are communicated. Black Vulture pairs remain together year-round; parents continue to feed fledglings for up to eight months. Black Vultures are found soaring above the landscape in search of carrion, or feeding on roadkills along highways, often displacing less aggressive Turkey Vultures.

yellowish tip of bill

broad wings, spread at roost

silvery-white patch on wing

short, rounded tail

naked wrinkled gray skin

black upperparts

black underparts

long grayish legs and feet

VOICE *Usually silent; occasionally hisses and barks.*
NESTING *No nest; lays eggs on ground in thickets, old buildings, or rock piles; 2 eggs; 1 brood; Jan–Aug.*
FEEDING *Often eats large mammal carrion on the ground; sometimes live prey.*
HABITAT *Breeds in dense woodlands and caves; roosts in tall tree stands; forages in open habitats and near roads.*
LENGTH *24–27in (61–68cm)*
WINGSPAN *4½–5ft (1.4–1.5m)*

Turkey Vulture

Cathartes aura

The most widely distributed vulture in North America, the Turkey Vulture is found in most of the US and has expanded its range into southern Canada. It possesses a better sense of smell than the Black Vulture, which often follows it and displaces it from carcasses. The Turkey Vulture's habit of defecating down its legs may serve to cool it or to kill bacteria with its ammonia content.

long wings

silvery-gray flight feathers

blackish back feathers, edged brown

brownish-gray head

naked skin

small red head

brownish back

black underparts

pink legs

long tail

VOICE *Silent, but will hiss at intruders; also grunts.*
NESTING *Dark recesses under large rocks or stumps, on rocky ledges in caves, in mammal burrows, and abandoned buildings; 1–3 eggs; 1 brood; Mar–Aug.*
FEEDING *Wild and domestic carrion: mammals, birds, reptiles, amphibians, fish; occasionally live prey (nestlings or trapped birds).*
HABITAT *Mixed farmland, forests, beaches, and urban areas; forested hillsides and abandoned structures while nesting.*
LENGTH *25–32in (64–81cm)*
WINGSPAN *5½–6ft (1.7–1.8m)*

Osprey

Pandion haliaetus

Sometimes referred to as the "fish hawk" or "fish eagle," the Osprey is the only bird of prey in North America that feeds almost exclusively on live fish. The Osprey plunges into the water feet first, and sharp spicules (tiny, spikelike growths) on the pads of its feet, reversible outer toes, and an ability to lock its talons in place enable it to hold onto slippery fish.

dark band running across wing

barred tail

finely barred underwings

wingtips at slight backward angle

dark brown upperparts

wings crooked while soaring

black eyestripe

yellow eyes

crest on head

black mask on face

speckled chest

black bill

white underparts

pale gray legs and feet

VOICE *Slow, whistled notes, falling in pitch: tiooop, tioooop, tiooop; also screams by displaying male.*
NESTING *Twig nest on tree, cliff, rock pinnacles, ground, hydro towers, channel markers; 1–4 eggs; 1 brood; Mar–Aug.*
FEEDING *Dives as deep as 3ft (90cm) to catch fish.*
HABITAT *Forests near water, such as lakes, rivers, coastal waters, estuaries.*
LENGTH *21–23in (53–58cm)*
WINGSPAN *5–6ft (1.5–1.8m)*

Swallow-tailed Kite

Elanoides forficatus

The Swallow-tailed Kite's black-and-white plumage, deeply forked tail, and amazingly graceful flight make it easy to identify. Rarely flapping its wings, it continuously rotates its tail to maintain its course, making sharp turns and circles while feeding on the wing. Unlike most soaring hawks, the Swallow-tailed Kite can hang motionless into the wind. This bird needs both tall trees for nesting and open areas for foraging.

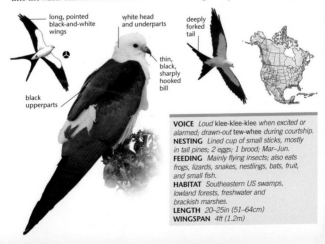

long, pointed black-and-white wings

white head and underparts

deeply forked tail

thin, black, sharply hooked bill

black upperparts

VOICE *Loud klee-klee-klee when excited or alarmed; drawn-out tew-whee during courtship.*
NESTING *Lined cup of small sticks, mostly in tall pines; 2 eggs; 1 brood; Mar–Jun.*
FEEDING *Mainly flying insects; also eats frogs, lizards, snakes, nestlings, bats, fruit, and small fish.*
HABITAT *Southeastern US swamps, lowland forests, freshwater and brackish marshes.*
LENGTH *20–25in (51–64cm)*
WINGSPAN *4ft (1.2m)*

Mississippi Kite

Ⓢ

Ictinia mississippiensis

The Mississippi Kite is more common and more colonial in the Great Plains region than elsewhere. It forages in flocks of several dozen; smaller groups roost near nests. These long-distance migrants winter in South America. Urban kites can be aggressive, even attacking humans who venture too close to their nests. Mississippi Kites are often seen soaring gracefully, rather than perched.

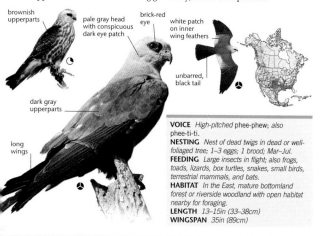

brownish upperparts

pale gray head with conspicuous dark eye patch

brick-red eye

white patch on inner wing feathers

unbarred, black tail

dark gray upperparts

long wings

VOICE *High-pitched* phee-phew; *also* phee-ti-ti.
NESTING *Nest of dead twigs in dead or well-foliaged tree; 1–3 eggs; 1 brood; Mar–Jul.*
FEEDING *Large insects in flight; also frogs, toads, lizards, box turtles, snakes, small birds, terrestrial mammals, and bats.*
HABITAT *In the East, mature bottomland forest or riverside woodland with open habitat nearby for foraging.*
LENGTH *13–15in (33–38cm)*
WINGSPAN *35in (89cm)*

Bald Eagle

Ⓢ

Haliaeetus leucocephalus

The Bald Eagle, although an opportunist, prefers to scavenge on carrion and steal prey from other birds, including Ospreys. Its reproductive failure, caused by DDT use, as well as bounties, led to it being declared endangered in 1967. Now frequenting landfill sites, its numbers have since rebounded, especially on the East and West Coasts.

white head

brown body

white tail

dark brown overall

yellow hooked bill

all-white head with yellow eyes

dark chocolate-brown overall

dark bill starting to turn yellow at base

Ⓒ **1ST YEAR**

long, wedge-shaped white tail

yellow legs and feet

VOICE *Surprisingly high-pitched voice, 3–4 notes followed by a rapidly descending series.*
NESTING *Huge stick nest, usually in tallest tree; 1–3 eggs; 1 brood; Mar–Sep.*
FEEDING *Carrion, especially fish; birds, mammals; steals fish from Ospreys.*
HABITAT *Forested areas near water while breeding; along major rivers and coastal areas in winter.*
LENGTH *28–38in (71–96cm)*
WINGSPAN *6½ft (2m)*

Northern Harrier

Circus hudsonius

The Northern Harrier is most often seen flying low in search of food. A white rump, V-shaped wings, and tilting flight make this species easily identifiable. The blue-gray males are strikingly different from the dark brown females. The bird has an owl-like face, which contains stiff feathers to help channel in sounds from prey.

white ring around owl-like face

♀

brown upperparts

black wingtips

♂

white rump

bluish-gray head

dark bill with yellow skin near bluish base

bluish-gray upperparts

♂

white underparts with reddish-brown markings

gray uppertail with light undertail feathers

VOICE *Kek* in rapid succession at nest, becoming more high-pitched in alarm.
NESTING Platform of sticks on ground in open, wet field; 4–6 eggs; 1 brood; Apr–Sep.
FEEDING Rodents, such as mice and muskrats; also birds, frogs, reptiles; occasionally larger prey, such as rabbits.
HABITAT Open wetlands while breeding; open habitats, such as deserts, coastal sand dunes, and grasslands, in winter.
LENGTH 18–20in (46–51cm)
WINGSPAN 3½–4ft (1.1–1.2m)

Sharp-shinned Hawk

Accipiter striatus

This small, swift hawk is quite adept at capturing songbirds in flight, occasionally even taking species larger than itself. The Sharp-shinned Hawk's short, rounded wings and long tail allow it to make abrupt turns and fast dashes in thick woods and dense, shrubby terrain. Its prey is plucked before being consumed or fed to nestlings.

grayish-blue upperparts

♂

yellow legs and toes

slightly browner upperparts than male

grayish-blue crown

reddish-yellow eye

wide, dark, horizontal bars on gray tail

reddish-brown bars on underparts

♀

white, fluffy undertail feathers

VOICE High-pitched, repeated *kiu kiu kiu*; squealing sound when disturbed at nest.
NESTING Sturdy nest of sticks lined with twigs or pieces of bark; 3–4 eggs; 1 brood; Mar–Jun.
FEEDING Small birds, such as sparrows and wood warblers, caught either on the wing or while perched.
HABITAT Coniferous forests and mixed hardwood-conifer woodlands.
LENGTH 11in (28cm)
WINGSPAN 23in (58cm)

Cooper's Hawk Ⓢ

Accipiter cooperii

A secretive bird, the Cooper's Hawk is capable of quickly maneuvering through dense vegetation. It is now numerous in urban areas, mainly taking pigeons, doves, and birds at feeders. Should a human approach its nest, the brooding adult will quietly glide down and away from the nest tree rather than attack the intruder.

grayish-blue overall

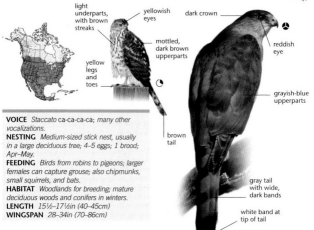

light underparts, with brown streaks

yellowish eyes

dark crown

mottled, dark brown upperparts

reddish eye

yellow legs and toes

grayish-blue upperparts

brown tail

gray tail with wide, dark bands

white band at tip of tail

VOICE Staccato ca-ca-ca-ca; many other vocalizations.
NESTING Medium-sized stick nest, usually in a large deciduous tree; 4–5 eggs; 1 brood; Apr–May.
FEEDING Birds from robins to pigeons; larger females can capture grouse; also chipmunks, small squirrels, and bats.
HABITAT Woodlands for breeding; mature deciduous woods and conifers in winters.
LENGTH 15½–17½in (40–45cm)
WINGSPAN 28–34in (70–86cm)

Northern Goshawk Ⓢ Ⓣ

Accipiter gentilis

The Northern Goshawk is secretive by nature and not easily observed, even where it is common. Nesting in both coniferous and deciduous trees, it is a fierce and noisy defender of its territories, nests, and young and will even attack humans. Spring hikers occasionally discover Northern Goshawks by wandering into their territory, only to be driven off by the angry occupants.

long tail

fairly short, rounded wings

slate-gray upperparts

conspicuous white stripe above eye

slate-gray tail

yellow to red eye

conspicuous dark barring on underparts

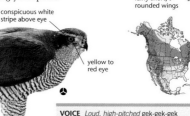

speckled back

light yellow iris

yellow legs and feet

buff underparts with vertical streaks

VOICE Loud, high-pitched gek-gek-gek when agitated.
NESTING Large stick structures lined with bark and plant matter in the mid- to lower region of trees; 1–3 eggs; 1 brood; May–Jun.
FEEDING Birds as large as grouse and pheasants; mammals, including hares and squirrels; waits on perch before diving rapidly.
HABITAT Deciduous, coniferous, and mixed woodlands, mature tree farms while breeding.
LENGTH 21in (53cm)
WINGSPAN 3½ft (1.1m)

Red-shouldered Hawk

S

Buteo lineatus

The Red-shouldered Hawk has widespread populations in the East and northeast, and in the Midwest Great Plains and West Coast. Eastern birds are divided into four subspecies; western populations belong to the subspecies *B. l. elegans*. The red shoulder patches are not always evident, but the striped tail and translucent "windows" in the wings are easily identifiable.

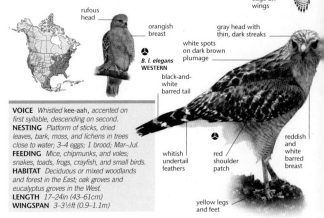

reddish leading edge on wings

rufous head

orangish breast

B. l. elegans
WESTERN

black-and-white barred tail

gray head with thin, dark streaks

white spots on dark brown plumage

whitish undertail feathers

red shoulder patch

reddish and white barred breast

yellow legs and feet

VOICE Whistled kee-aah, accented on first syllable, descending on second.
NESTING Platform of sticks, dried leaves, bark, moss, and lichens in trees close to water; 3–4 eggs; 1 brood; Mar–Jul.
FEEDING Mice, chipmunks, and voles; snakes, toads, frogs, crayfish, and small birds.
HABITAT Deciduous or mixed woodlands and forest in the East; oak groves and eucalyptus groves in the West.
LENGTH 17–24in (43–61cm)
WINGSPAN 3–3½ft (0.9–1.1m)

Broad-winged Hawk

S

Buteo platypterus

Broad-winged Hawks migrate in huge flocks or "kettles," soaring on rising thermals. The majority log more than 4,000 miles (6,500km) before ending up in Brazil, Bolivia, and some of the Caribbean islands. Adults are easily identified by a broad white-and-black band on their tails. Broad-winged Hawks have two color forms, the light one being more common than the dark, sooty-brown one.

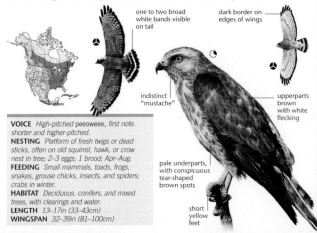

one to two broad white bands visible on tail

dark border on edges of wings

indistinct "mustache"

upperparts brown with white flecking

pale underparts, with conspicuous tear-shaped brown spots

short yellow feet

VOICE High-pitched peeoweee, first note shorter and higher-pitched.
NESTING Platform of fresh twigs or dead sticks, often on old squirrel, hawk, or crow nest in tree; 2–3 eggs; 1 brood; Apr–Aug.
FEEDING Small mammals, toads, frogs, snakes, grouse chicks, insects, and spiders; crabs in winter.
HABITAT Deciduous, conifers, and mixed trees, with clearings and water.
LENGTH 13–17in (33–43cm)
WINGSPAN 32–39in (81–100cm)

Red-tailed Hawk

S

Buteo jamaicensis

The Red-tailed Hawk is the most widely distributed hawk in North America. As many as 16 subspecies have been described to date, varying in coloration, tail markings, and size. The very dark Harlan's Hawk, which breeds in Alaska and northwestern Canada, is considered to be a subspecies of the Red-tailed Hawk. While it occasionally swoops on prey, the Red-tailed Hawk usually adopts a sit-and-wait approach.

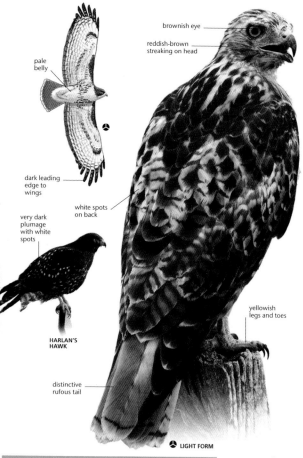

brownish eye

reddish-brown streaking on head

pale belly

dark leading edge to wings

white spots on back

very dark plumage with white spots

HARLAN'S HAWK

yellowish legs and toes

distinctive rufous tail

🔻 LIGHT FORM

VOICE Kee-eee-arrr *that rises then descends over a period of 2–3 seconds.*
NESTING *Large platform of sticks, twigs on top of tall tree, cliff, building, or billboard; 2 eggs; 1 brood; Feb–Sep.*
FEEDING *Small mammals, such as mice and rats; birds, including pheasants, quail; small reptiles; carrion.*
HABITAT *Open areas in scrub desert, grasslands, agricultural fields, and woodlands; occasionally in urban areas.*
LENGTH *18–26in (46–65cm)*
WINGSPAN *3½–4¼ft (1.1–1.3m)*

Rough-legged Hawk

Buteo lagopus

The Rough-legged Hawk exhibits extensive variation in plumage, ranging from almost completely black to nearly cream or whitish. The year-to-year fluctuation in numbers of breeding pairs in a given region strongly suggests that this species is nomadic, moving around in response to the availability of its prey.

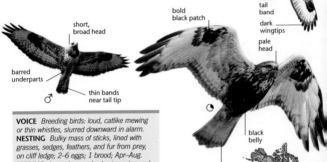

dark wrist patches

dark tail band

dark wingtips

pale head

short, broad head

bold black patch

barred underparts

thin bands near tail tip

♂

black belly

white tail with faint black band at tip

VOICE Breeding birds: loud, catlike mewing or thin whistles, slurred downward in alarm.
NESTING Bulky mass of sticks, lined with grasses, sedges, feathers, and fur from prey, on cliff ledge; 2–6 eggs; 1 brood; Apr–Aug.
FEEDING Lemmings and voles in spring and summer; mice and shrews in winter; birds, ground squirrels, and rabbits year-round.
HABITAT Rough, open country with cliffs while breeding; edges of forests, treeless tundra.
LENGTH 19–20in (48–51cm)
WINGSPAN 4¼–4½ft (1.3–1.4m)

Golden Eagle

Aquila chrysaetos

Perhaps the most formidable of all North American birds of prey, the Golden Eagle is found mostly in the western part of the continent. It defends large territories of 8–12 square miles (20–30 square kilometers). Although it appears sluggish, it is swift and agile, and employs a variety of hunting techniques to catch specific prey.

dark brown underparts

dark plumage with variable white

pale head

flat, broad head merges into heavy bill

golden feathers on long neck

large, powerful bill

brown overall

white tail feathers

heavy feathering on legs

VOICE High-pitched far-carrying yelps and deep liquid babbling notes.
NESTING Large pile of sticks and vegetation on cliffs, in trees, and on artificial structures; 1–3 eggs; 1 brood; Apr–Aug.
FEEDING Hares, rabbits, ground squirrels, prairie dogs, marmots, foxes, coyotes; also birds.
HABITAT Grasslands, wetlands, and rocky areas; tundra, shrublands, grasslands, and coniferous forests while breeding.
LENGTH 28–33in (70–84cm)
WINGSPAN 6–7¼ft (1.8–2.2m)

Rails, Cranes, and Relatives

These birds of the marshes and wetlands include many groups. The Rallidae, or rail family, is a diverse group of small- to medium-sized marsh birds. The cranes, or Gruidae, include very large to huge birds, superficially similar to storks and the largest of the herons and egrets.

Rails are mostly secretive, solitary, and inconspicuous in dense marsh vegetation, while coots and gallinules are seen on open water. Rails have stubby tails and short, rounded wings. The rails of the genus *Rallus* have excellent camouflage, and are long-legged, long-toed, long-billed, and narrow-bodied. The short-billed species are similar, but with shorter necks and stout, stubby bills. The gallinules are more colorful, and have long, slender toes. The two North American species of cranes have long necks, small heads, and short bills. The long plumes on their inner wing feathers form a bustle, cloaking the tail on a standing crane, thereby giving them a different profile than any heron.

CRANE RALLY
Large numbers of Sandhill Cranes gather on feeding grounds in winter, groups arriving in V-formation.

Yellow Rail

Ⓢ

Coturnicops noveboracensis

The secretive, nocturnal Yellow Rail is extremely difficult
to observe in its dense, grassy habitat, and is detected
mainly by its voice. It has a small head, almost no neck,
a stubby bill, a plump, almost tail-less body, and short legs.
The bill of the male turns yellow in the breeding season.

dangling legs

white patch on inner wing feathers

dark brown crown

stubby yellow to olive-gray bill

long tan stripes on blackish background

dark stripe runs from cheek to bill

buff or yellow breast

short tail

VOICE *Males: clicking calls, also descending cackles, quiet croaking, and soft clucking.*
NESTING *Small cup of grasses and sedges, on the ground or in a plant tuft above water, concealed by overhanging vegetation; 8–10 eggs; 1 brood; May–Jun.*
FEEDING *Seeds, aquatic insects, small crustaceans, freshwater snails.*
HABITAT *Brackish and freshwater marshes, and wet sedge meadows while breeding.*
LENGTH *7¼in (18.5cm)*
WINGSPAN *11in (28cm)*

Black Rail

Ⓢ

Laterallus jamaicensis

This mouse-sized, highly secretive rail is so elusive
that few birders have ever seen it; consequently, much
remains unknown about its life history. It is usually
detected by its territorial breeding call, given from the
cover of marsh grass. The best chance to see a Black Rail
is when high tides force it to higher ground—where,
unfortunately, this reluctant flier can fall prey to herons.

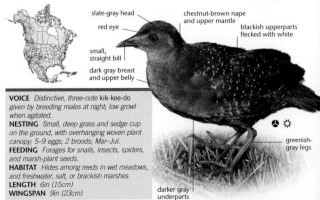

dark overall

white-spotted back

reddish-brown nape

slate-gray head

red eye

chestnut-brown nape and upper mantle

blackish upperparts flecked with white

small, straight bill

dark gray breast and upper belly

greenish-gray legs

darker gray underparts

VOICE *Distinctive, three-note kik-kee-do given by breeding males at night; low growl when agitated.*
NESTING *Small, deep grass and sedge cup on the ground, with overhanging woven plant canopy; 5–9 eggs; 2 broods; Mar–Jul.*
FEEDING *Forages for snails, insects, spiders, and marsh-plant seeds.*
HABITAT *Hides among reeds in wet meadows, and freshwater, salt, or brackish marshes.*
LENGTH *6in (15cm)*
WINGSPAN *9in (23cm)*

Clapper Rail

Rallus crepitans

The Clapper Rail is common and widespread on the Atlantic and Gulf Coasts, where it is closely tied to brackish and saltwater marshes dominated by spartina cord grass; in southern Florida, it prefers mangrove swamps. Its distinctive, insistent calls are the best way to detect its presence because it is rarely seen. It flies low with its neck outstretched and legs dangling.

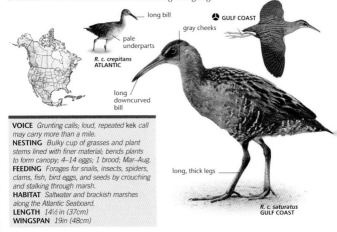

long bill

pale underparts

R. c. crepitans ATLANTIC

GULF COAST

gray cheeks

long downcurved bill

long, thick legs

R. c. saturatus GULF COAST

VOICE *Grunting calls; loud, repeated kek call may carry more than a mile.*
NESTING *Bulky cup of grasses and plant stems lined with finer material; bends plants to form canopy; 4–14 eggs; 1 brood; Mar–Aug.*
FEEDING *Forages for snails, insects, spiders, clams, fish, bird eggs, and seeds by crouching and stalking through marsh.*
HABITAT *Saltwater and brackish marshes along the Atlantic Seaboard.*
LENGTH *14½ in (37cm)*
WINGSPAN *19in (48cm)*

King Rail

Rallus elegans

A scattered and localized breeder in the East and Midwest, the King Rail depends on extensive freshwater marshy habitats with tall, emergent reeds and cattails. Concealed by this vegetation, this chickenlike bird is rarely seen and is most often detected by its distinctive calls.

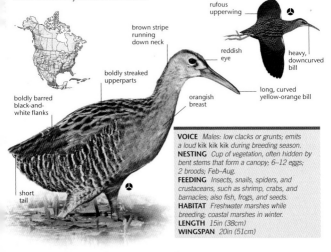

rufous upperwing

brown stripe running down neck

reddish eye

heavy, downcurved bill

boldly streaked upperparts

orangish breast

long, curved yellow-orange bill

boldly barred black-and-white flanks

short tail

VOICE *Males: low clacks or grunts; emits a loud kik kik kik during breeding season.*
NESTING *Cup of vegetation, often hidden by bent stems that form a canopy; 6–12 eggs; 2 broods; Feb–Aug.*
FEEDING *Insects, snails, spiders, and crustaceans, such as shrimp, crabs, and barnacles; also fish, frogs, and seeds.*
HABITAT *Freshwater marshes while breeding; coastal marshes in winter.*
LENGTH *15in (38cm)*
WINGSPAN *20in (51cm)*

Virginia Rail

S

Rallus limicola

A smaller version of the King Rail, this freshwater marsh-dweller is more often heard than seen. Distributed across a wide range, the Virginia Rail spends most of its time in thick, reedy vegetation, which it pushes apart using its "rail-thin" body and flexible vertebrae. Although it spends most of its life walking, it can swim and dive to escape danger. It is a partial migrant that leaves its northern breeding grounds in the winter.

rufous upperwing

BREEDING

dark outer wing feathers

diffused streaking

dark bill

dark, blotchy breast

NONBREEDING

streaked, black-and-brown upperparts

gray cheeks

curved red bill

reddish-brown breast

BREEDING

white undertail

black-and-white barring on flanks

reddish legs and toes

VOICE Series of piglike grunting oinks, loud and sharp, then steadily softer; also emits a series of double notes ka-dik ka-dik.
NESTING Substantial cup of plant material, concealed by bent-over stems; 5–12 eggs; 1–2 broods; Apr–Jul.
FEEDING Stalks prey or waits and dives into water; snails, insects, and spiders, also seeds.
HABITAT Freshwater habitats while breeding; saltwater and freshwater marshes in winter.
LENGTH 9½ in (24cm)
WINGSPAN 13in (33cm)

Sora

Porzana carolina

The Sora is widely distributed but rarely seen. It breeds in freshwater marshes and migrates hundreds of miles south in winter, despite its weak and hesitant flight. It swims well, with a characteristic head-bobbing action. The Sora can be spotted walking at the edge of emergent vegetation—its yellow bill and black mask distinguish it from other rails.

long, trailing legs

white markings on back

BREEDING

yellow bill

brown cheek patch

black mask

gray breast

short tail

yellowish-green legs

BREEDING

reduced black on face

white barring on flanks

NONBREEDING

VOICE *Long, high, and loud descending, horselike whinny ko-wee-hee-hee-hee-hee; upslurred whistle.*
NESTING *Loosely woven basket of vegetation above water or in clumps of vegetation on water's surface; 8–11 eggs; 1 brood; May–Jun.*
FEEDING *Seeds of wetland plants, insects, spiders, and snails.*
HABITAT *Freshwater marshes with emergent vegetation while breeding.*
LENGTH *8½in (22cm)*
WINGSPAN *14in (36cm)*

Purple Gallinule

Porphyrio martinicus

This vibrantly colored rail is conspicuous for its purple head and neck, red bill, and yellow legs. Purple Gallinules are well known for long-distance wandering outside their normal breeding range, from as far away as Labrador, South Georgia, and South Africa. The Purple Gallinule's long toes enable it to walk across floating vegetation, where it turns over lily pads to find aquatic insects.

blue wings

long, trailing legs

BREEDING

brownish upperparts

greenish frontal shield

grayish breast

pale blue frontal shield

yellow-tipped red bill

iridescent green back and rump

dark blue breast and belly

BREEDING

yellow legs and feet with very large toes

VOICE *Call: a chickenlike clucking; also grunts and higher-pitched single notes.*
NESTING *Bulky cup of plant material built in marsh vegetation slightly above the water's surface; 5–10 eggs; 1 brood; Apr–Aug.*
FEEDING *Omnivorous diet; seeds, leaves, insects, spiders, and worms.*
HABITAT *Freshwater marshes in the southeastern US. Breeds in lush wetlands containing emergent vegetation.*
LENGTH *13in (33cm)*
WINGSPAN *22in (56cm)*

Common Gallinule

Gallinula galeata

The Common Gallinule is fairly widespread in the eastern US, and more scattered in the western states. It is similar in behavior and habitat to both true rails and coots. Equally at home on land and water, its long toes allow it to walk easily over floating vegetation and soft mud. When walking or swimming, the Common Gallinule bobs its head and nervously jerks its short tail, revealing its white undertail feathers.

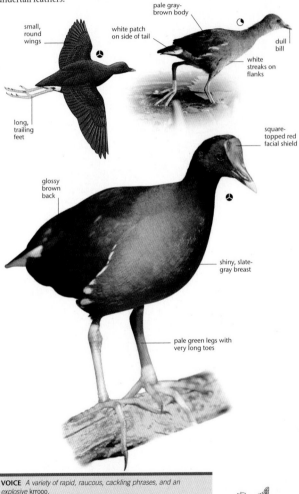

small, round wings

white patch on side of tail

pale gray-brown body

dull bill

white streaks on flanks

long, trailing feet

square-topped red facial shield

glossy brown back

shiny, slate-gray breast

pale green legs with very long toes

VOICE *A variety of rapid, raucous, cackling phrases, and an explosive krrooo.*
NESTING *Bulky platform of aquatic vegetation with growing plants pulled over to conceal it; 5–11 eggs, 1–3 broods; May–Aug.*
FEEDING *Mainly aquatic and terrestrial plants; also eats snails, spiders, and insects.*
HABITAT *Freshwater habitats in the eastern US and Canada; more localized in the West.*
LENGTH *14in (36cm)*
WINGSPAN *21in (53cm)*

American Coot

Fulica americana

The most abundant and widely distributed of North American rails, this ducklike bird commonly bobs its head forward and backward while swimming. Its lobed toes make it well adapted to swimming and diving, but they are somewhat of an impediment on land. Its flight is clumsy; it becomes airborne with difficulty, running along the water's surface before taking off. American Coots form large flocks on open water in winter, often associating with ducks—an unusual trait for a member of the rail family.

dull grayish plumage

white-edged feathers

white bill

BREEDING

dark gray body

black head

red eye

black ring on bill

BREEDING

long greenish-yellow legs

lobed toes

VOICE *Raucous clucks, grunts, and croaks and an explosive keek.*
NESTING *Bulky cup of plant material placed in aquatic vegetation on or near water; 5–15 eggs; 1–2 broods; Apr–Jul.*
FEEDING *Forages on or under shallow water and feeds on land; primarily herbivorous; also snails, insects, spiders, tadpoles, fish, and carrion.*
HABITAT *Open-water habitats while breeding and in winter; ponds, marshes, reservoirs, lake edges, and saltwater inlets.*
LENGTH *15½in (40cm)*
WINGSPAN *24in (61cm)*

Limkin

D

Aramus guarauna

Limpkins inhabit southeastern waterways, eating during the daylight, but remaining active at night. Relatives of cranes, coots, and rails, Limpkins tend to move slowly and deliberately, occasionally erupting into animated motions and wild wailing. Limpkins often hide in vegetation, but sometimes wander into open water, foraging mainly for apple snails, their preferred food source.

dark wings

long, curved neck

curved bill

white speckles on neck

sparse white spotting on back

chocolate-brown overall

long gray legs

VOICE *Short whistles, abrupt barks, and wails; often with an eerie quality.*
NESTING *Vegetation placed on ground or in tree; 5–6 eggs; 1–3 broods; Feb–Jul.*
FEEDING *Apple snails in shallow water; also insects and spiders.*
HABITAT *Limited to quiet waterways inhabited by apple snails, including marshes and swamp forests; also ranges into ditches, canals, and parks.*
LENGTH 26in (66cm)
WINGSPAN 3¼in (100cm)

Sandhill Crane

S

Antigone canadensis

Sandhill Cranes are famous for their elaborate courtship dances, far-carrying vocalizations, and remarkable migrations. Their bodies are sometimes stained with a rusty color, supposedly because they probe into mud that contains iron and then preen, transferring color from bill to plumage. Sandhill Cranes are broadly grouped into "Lesser" and "Greater" populations that differ in the breeding-ground locations and migration routes.

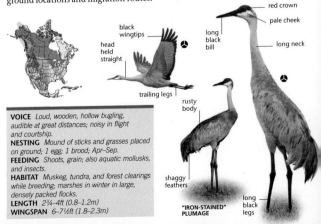

red crown

pale cheek

black wingtips

head held straight

long black bill

long neck

trailing legs

rusty body

shaggy feathers

"IRON-STAINED" PLUMAGE

long black legs

VOICE *Loud, wooden, hollow bugling, audible at great distances; noisy in flight and courtship.*
NESTING *Mound of sticks and grasses placed on ground; 1 egg; 1 brood; Apr–Sep.*
FEEDING *Shoots, grain; also aquatic mollusks, and insects.*
HABITAT *Muskeg, tundra, and forest clearings while breeding; marshes in winter in large, densely packed flocks.*
LENGTH 2¾–4ft (0.8–1.2m)
WINGSPAN 6–7½ft (1.8–2.3m)

Whooping Crane

Grus americana

Large-scale habitat protection, captive breeding and release, and public education efforts enabled the colossal, majestic Whooping Crane to rebound from just a few dozen birds in the mid-1900s to hundreds of individuals today—one of the US Endangered Species Act's most compelling success stories. However, because this crane reproduces slowly and in a restricted range, additional intervention measures are required to help this still-endangered species to continue its recovery.

black wingtips

head held straight

trailing legs

very dark red "mask"

long, dark bill

long neck

brownish head

scattered brown feathers

white overall

gray-black legs

VOICE *Piercing and trumpeting, kerloo! and kerleeyew, audible from afar; bugling calls during courtship dances.*
NESTING *Mound of vegetation placed on ground; 2 eggs; 1 brood; Apr–Aug.*
FEEDING *Animal and plant matter (frogs, mollusks, berries, and seeds) from the ground.*
HABITAT *Marshy country with scattered ponds and prairies while breeding; coastal estuaries in winter.*
LENGTH 4–4½ft (1.2–1.4m)
WINGSPAN 7¼ft (2.2m)

Plovers, Sandpipers, and Auks

The diverse shorebird and auk families together form the order Charadriiformes. They are small to medium-sized, mostly migratory birds, associated with aquatic habitats.

The shorebirds include oystercatchers, avocets and stilts, plovers, sandpipers, and phalaropes. They have long legs in proportion to their bodies, and a variety of bills, ranging from short to long, thin, thick, straight, downcurved, and upcurved.

Auks, murres, and puffins are denizens of the northern oceans. These birds come to land only to breed. Most nest in colonies on sheer seaside cliffs overlooking the ocean, but puffins excavate burrows in the ground, and some murrelets nest inland, high up in treetops, away from predators.

ON THE MOVE
Dunlins and other sandpipers gather in large, highly coordinated flocks on migration.

Black-necked Stilt

Himantopus mexicanus

This tall, slender, elegant, black-and-white shorebird is a familiar sight at ponds and lagoons in the southern US. Even for a shorebird, it is remarkably long-legged; in flight, it often crosses its trailing feet as if for extra support. Breeding takes place in small colonies. In winter, small flocks of about 25 individuals feed quietly in sheltered areas or aggressively drive visitors away with raucous calls, doglike yips, and noisy communal protests.

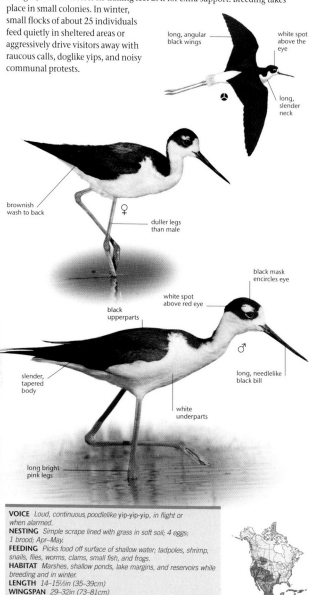

long, angular black wings

white spot above the eye

long, slender neck

brownish wash to back

♀

duller legs than male

black mask encircles eye

white spot above red eye

black upperparts

long, needlelike black bill

slender, tapered body

♂

white underparts

long bright pink legs

VOICE Loud, continuous, poodlelike yip-yip-yip, in flight or when alarmed.
NESTING Simple scrape lined with grass in soft soil; 4 eggs; 1 brood; Apr–May.
FEEDING Picks food off surface of shallow water; tadpoles, shrimp, snails, flies, worms, clams, small fish, and frogs.
HABITAT Marshes, shallow ponds, lake margins, and reservoirs while breeding and in winter.
LENGTH 14–15½in (35–39cm)
WINGSPAN 29–32in (73–81cm)

American Avocet

Recurvirostra americana

With its long, thin, and upturned bill, this graceful, long-legged shorebird is unmistakable when foraging. When it takes off, its striking plumage pattern is clearly visible. It is the only one of the four avocet species in the world that changes plumage when breeding. Breeding birds have a cinnamon head and neck, and bold patterns on their black-and-white wings and upperparts. The American Avocet forms large flocks during migration and in winter.

white plumage

no cinnamon color on head and neck

striking black-and-white pattern

NONBREEDING

BREEDING

less upturned bill

♂

white eye-ring

dark eye

cinnamon-colored head

long, thin upturned bill

bold shoulder feathers

cinnamon-colored neck

♀

white underparts

long, bluish legs

VOICE *Variable melodic* kleet, *loud and repetitive, when alarmed and while foraging.*
NESTING *Simple, shallow scrape; 4 eggs; 1 brood; May–Jun.*
FEEDING *Uses specialized bill to probe or jab at a variety of aquatic invertebrates, small fish, and seeds; walks in belly-deep water to chase its prey.*
HABITAT *Temporary wetlands in dry to arid regions while breeding; shallow-water habitats in winter.*
LENGTH *17–18½in (43–47cm)*
WINGSPAN *29–32in (74–81cm)*

American Oystercatcher

Haematopus palliatus

The large, noisy American Oystercatcher is conspicuous on Atlantic beachfronts.
Heaviest of all North American shorebirds, the Oystercatcher makes swift, short
forays using its long, powerful wings, and runs on its thick,
strong legs to escape danger. It uses its long, powerful bill to
pry open or smash bivalve mollusks on rocks. Up to 8 birds
perform synchronized courtship flights together, with their
heads and necks bowed and wings arched upward.

prominent
white wing
bar

white
rump

powerful
wings

pale fringes
on upperpart
feathers

dull orange
eye-ring

dark eye

black tip to
orange bill

yellow eye

orange
eye-ring

black head

dark brown
upperparts

large, bulky
body

long, carrotlike
orange bill

white underparts

thick, pinkish
legs

VOICE *Whistled, loud, clear descending* wheeu *call; alarm call
sharp* wheep.
NESTING *Simple scrape with shell debris on coastal sandy beaches,
dunes, and salt marshes; 2–3 eggs; 1 brood; Apr–May.*
FEEDING *Forages for mollusks in slightly submerged shellfish beds
and subsoil.*
HABITAT *Exclusive to saltwater coastal habitats along the Atlantic
and Gulf coastlines; expanding northward.*
LENGTH 15½–17½in (40–44cm)
WINGSPAN 29–32in (73–81cm)

Black-bellied Plover

Ⓢ

Pluvialis squatarola

The Black-bellied Plover is the largest and most common of the three North American *Pluvialis* plovers. Its preference for open feeding habitats, its bulky structure, and very upright stance make it a fairly conspicuous species. The Black-bellied Plover's black underwing patches, visible in flight, are present in both its breeding and nonbreeding plumages and distinguish it from the other *Pluvialis* plovers, along with its larger size.

white rump

♂ BREEDING

white wing stripe

diffused streaks to upper breast

whitish underparts

🔷 NONBREEDING

darker crown

duller plumage than male

♀ MOLTING TO BREEDING PLUMAGE

whitish crown

checkered black-and-white upperparts

black cheeks

black belly

♂ BREEDING

VOICE *Clear, plaintive, whistled whEE-er-eee, with middle note lower; breeding males: softer, with accent on second syllable.*
NESTING *Shallow depression lined with mosses and lichens in moist to dry lowland tundra; 1–5 eggs; 1 brood; May–Jul.*
FEEDING *Forages along coasts in typical run-pause-and-pluck style; insects, worms, bivalves, and crustaceans.*
HABITAT *High-Arctic habitats while breeding; coastal areas in winter.*
LENGTH *10½–12in (27–30cm)*
WINGSPAN *29–32in (73–81cm)*

American Golden-Plover

Pluvialis dominica

The American Golden-Plover is seen in North America only during lengthy migrations between its high-Arctic breeding grounds and wintering locations in southern South America. Its annual migration route includes a 1,550–1,860-mile (2,494–2,993-km) flight over the Atlantic Ocean. This elegant, slender, yet large plover prefers inland grassy habitats and plowed fields to coastal mudflats. Breeding American Golden-Plovers may feign injury to distract predators away from eggs or chicks.

black-and-white face

dark tail

BREEDING

dark cap

brownish upperparts

small, thin bill

uniformly dusky underparts

NONBREEDING

white stripe from forehead to nape

BREEDING

tan-and-black spangled upperparts

black underparts

black legs

VOICE *Whistled two-note queE-dle or klee-u in flight; males: strong, melodious whistled kid-eek, or kid-EEp in flight.*
NESTING *Shallow depression lined with lichens in dry tundra; 4 eggs; 1 brood; May–Jul.*
FEEDING *Insects, mollusks, crustaceans, and worms; also berries and seeds.*
HABITAT *Arctic tundra while breeding; prairies, farmlands, golf courses, pastures, mudflats, and shorelines while migrating.*
LENGTH *9½–11in (24–28cm)*
WINGSPAN *23–28in (59–72cm)*

Snowy Plover

Charadrius nivosus

The smallest, palest North American plover, the Snowy Plover's cryptic coloration blends in so well with its sandy habitat that it often remains unnoticed. These birds run faster and cover longer distances than other beach plovers, sprinting along the sand for extended spurts. They construct new nests after habitat loss or predation, even up to six times. Nevertheless, Snowy Plover populations are shrinking.

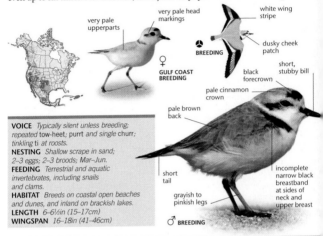

very pale upperparts

very pale head markings

white wing stripe

BREEDING

dusky cheek patch

♀
GULF COAST BREEDING

black forecrown

short, stubby bill

pale cinnamon crown

pale brown back

short tail

grayish to pinkish legs

incomplete narrow black breastband at sides of neck and upper breast

♂ BREEDING

VOICE *Typically silent unless breeding; repeated* tow-heet; purrt *and single* churr; *tinkling* ti *at roosts.*
NESTING *Shallow scrape in sand; 2–3 eggs; 2–3 broods; Mar–Jun.*
FEEDING *Terrestrial and aquatic invertebrates, including snails and clams.*
HABITAT *Breeds on coastal open beaches and dunes, and inland on brackish lakes.*
LENGTH *6–6½in (15–17cm)*
WINGSPAN *16–18in (41–46cm)*

Wilson's Plover

Charadrius wilsonia

Named after ornithologist Alexander Wilson, this plover is one of the largest North American *Charadrius* species. The Wilson's Plover's round belly gives it an upright posture when it pauses, and it has the distinctive habit of running horizontally low to the ground as it forages during low tide. It was listed as a species of high concern in 2000.

prominent white wing bar

dusky tail band

brownish upperparts

less contrast in head pattern

white eyebrow narrows behind eye

often incomplete brownish breastband with little or no black color

white forehead

heavy black bill

♀

black breastband

♂

brownish upperparts

white underparts

pinkish legs

VOICE *Flight call a short* pip; *alarm calls include short whistled* peet; *distraction call a series of descending buzzy rattles.*
NESTING *Simple scrape in sand dunes; 3–4 eggs; 1 brood; Apr–Jun.*
FEEDING *Mainly crustaceans, including fiddler crabs; also insects.*
HABITAT *Prefers open beaches, vegetated sand dunes, coastal lagoons, and saltwater flats.*
LENGTH *6½–8in (16–20cm)*
WINGSPAN *15½–19½in (39–49cm)*

Semipalmated Plover

(S)

Charadrius semipalmatus

The Semipalmated Plover is a small bird with a tapered shape. They are common in a wide variety of habitats during migration and in winter, when these birds gather in loose flocks. Walking down a sandy beach between fall and spring might awaken up to 100 Semipalmated Plovers, sleeping in slight depressions in the sand; flocks may number up to 1,000 birds.

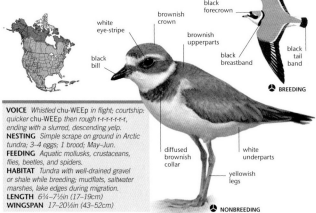

pointed wings

black forecrown

black breastband

black tail band

♠ BREEDING

white eye-stripe

brownish crown

brownish upperparts

black bill

diffused brownish collar

white underparts

yellowish legs

♠ NONBREEDING

VOICE Whistled *chu-WEEp* in flight; courtship: quicker *chu-WEEp* then rough *r-r-r-r-r-r*, ending with a slurred, descending yelp.
NESTING Simple scrape on ground in Arctic tundra; 3–4 eggs; 1 brood; May–Jun.
FEEDING Aquatic mollusks, crustaceans, flies, beetles, and spiders.
HABITAT Tundra with well-drained gravel or shale while breeding; mudflats, saltwater marshes, lake edges during migration.
LENGTH 6¾–7½in (17–19cm)
WINGSPAN 17–20½in (43–52cm)

Piping Plover

Charadrius melodus

With its pale gray back, the Piping Plover is well camouflaged along beaches or in dunes. The fragile nature of their preferred nesting sites due to eroding coastlines, human disturbance, and predation by foxes, raccoons, and cats, has led to this species becoming endangered. Conservation measures, such as fencing off nesting beaches and controlling predators, can help restore populations.

stubby bill

prominent white wing stripe

♂ **BREEDING**

dusky tail band

dark breastband

pale gray upperparts

black forecrown

black-tipped orange bill

♂ **BREEDING**

orange legs

thin white collar throughout the year

mostly black bill with slight orange base

indistinct, partial breastband

♠ NONBREEDING

VOICE Clear, whistled *peep* call in flight; quiet *peep-lo* during courtship; high-pitched *pipe-pipe-pipe* song.
NESTING Shallow scrape in sand, gravel, dunes, or salt flats; 4 eggs; 1 brood; Apr–May.
FEEDING Diet includes marine worms, insects, and mollusks.
HABITAT Found along beaches, saline sand flats, and adjacent mudflats.
LENGTH 6½–7in (17–18cm)
WINGSPAN 18–18½in (45–47cm)

Killdeer

Charadrius vociferus

This loud, vocal shorebird is the most widespread plover in North America, nesting in all southern Canadian provinces and across the US. The Killdeer's piercing, penetrating "dee-ee" call carries for long distances, sometimes causing other birds to take flight, fearing imminent danger. These birds often nest near human habitation, allowing a close observation of their vigilant parental nature—sometimes even feigning a broken wing to distract predators away from their young chicks.

white wing bar

reddish-orange tail and rump

long wings

single black breastband

red eye-ring

brownish crown

black collar encircling neck

brownish upperparts

rufous wash to back and wings

small, thin black bill

long tail

second neck band crosses upper breast ♂

white underparts

pinkish legs, sometimes with yellowish tinge

VOICE *Rising, drawn out* deeee *in flight; loud* dee-ee *in alarm, given repetitively; series of* dee *notes, followed by rising trill in agitation.*
NESTING *Scrape on ground; 4 eggs; 1 brood (north); Mar–Jul.*
FEEDING *Run-pause-and-pluck foraging; worms, snails, grasshoppers, and beetles; also small vertebrates and seeds.*
HABITAT *Shorelines, mudflats, lakes, sparsely grassy fields, golf courses, and roadsides.*
LENGTH *9–10in (23–26cm)*
WINGSPAN *23–25in (58–63cm)*

Spotted Sandpiper

Actitis macularius

This small, short-legged sandpiper is the most widespread shorebird in North America. It is characterized by its quick walking pace, its habit of constantly teetering and bobbing its tail, and its unique style of flying low over water. Spotted Sandpipers have an unusual mating behavior, in which the females take an aggressive role—defending territories and serially mating with three or more males per season.

white wing stripe

darker flight feathers

BREEDING

plain brownish-gray upperparts

straight, dark bill

white wedge on breast

NONBREEDING

brownish-gray upperparts

buff barring on wings and back

bold white eye-ring

thin white eyestripe

straight orange bill with dark tip

brownish-gray upperparts

dark barring on back

BREEDING

white underparts with bold dark spots

orange-yellow legs

VOICE Clear, ringing tee-tee-tee-tee; monotonous cree-cree-cree in flight.
NESTING Nest cup shaded by or scrape built under herbaceous vegetation; 3 eggs; 1–3 broods; May–Jun.
FEEDING Many items, including adult and larval insects, mollusks, small crabs, and worms.
HABITAT Variety of grassy, brushy, forested habitats near water while breeding; freshwater habitats (lakeshores, rivers, beaches) in winter.
LENGTH 7¼–8in (18.5–20cm)
WINGSPAN 15–16in (38–41cm)

Solitary Sandpiper

Tringa solitaria

This aptly named sandpiper seldom associates with other shorebirds as it moves nervously along margins of wetlands. When feeding, it constantly bobs its head like the Spotted Sandpiper. When disturbed, the Solitary Sandpiper often flies directly upward, and when landing, it keeps its wings upright briefly, flashing the white underneath, before carefully folding them to its body.

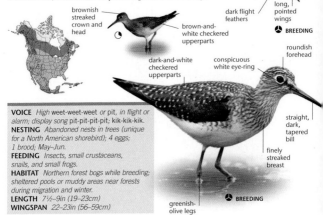

long, pointed wings

dark flight feathers

BREEDING

brownish streaked crown and head

brown-and-white checkered upperparts

dark-and-white checkered upperparts

conspicuous white eye-ring

roundish forehead

straight, dark, tapered bill

finely streaked breast

greenish-olive legs

BREEDING

VOICE *High weet-weet-weet or pit, in flight or alarm; display song pit-pit-pit-pit; kik-kik-kik.*
NESTING *Abandoned nests in trees (unique for a North American shorebird); 4 eggs; 1 brood; May–Jun.*
FEEDING *Insects, small crustaceans, snails, and small frogs.*
HABITAT *Northern forest bogs while breeding; sheltered pools or muddy areas near forests during migration and winter.*
LENGTH *7½–9in (19–23cm)*
WINGSPAN *22–23in (56–59cm)*

Greater Yellowlegs

Tringa melanoleuca

This fairly large shorebird often runs frantically in many directions while pursuing small prey. It is one of the first northbound shorebird migrants in the spring, and one of the first to return south in late June or early July. Its plumage is more streaked during the breeding season and its bill is slightly upturned.

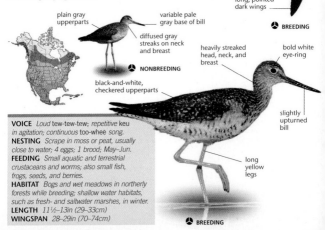

long, pointed dark wings

BREEDING

plain gray upperparts

variable pale gray base of bill

diffused gray streaks on neck and breast

NONBREEDING

black-and-white, checkered upperparts

heavily streaked head, neck, and breast

bold white eye-ring

slightly upturned bill

long yellow legs

BREEDING

VOICE *Loud tew-tew-tew; repetitive keu in agitation; continuous too-whee song.*
NESTING *Scrape in moss or peat, usually close to water; 4 eggs; 1 brood; May–Jun.*
FEEDING *Small aquatic and terrestrial crustaceans and worms; also small fish, frogs, seeds, and berries.*
HABITAT *Bogs and wet meadows in northerly forests while breeding; shallow water habitats, such as fresh- and saltwater marshes, in winter.*
LENGTH *11½–13in (29–33cm)*
WINGSPAN *28–29in (70–74cm)*

Willet

Tringa semipalmata

The two distinct subspecies of the Willet, Eastern (*T. s. semipalmata*) and Western (*T. s. inornata*), differ in breeding habit, plumage coloration, vocalizations, and migratory habits. The Eastern Willet leaves North America from September to March, whereas the Western Willet winters along southern North American shorelines south to South America.

long, grayish, straight bill

plain gray upperparts

pale underparts

bold black-and-white wing pattern

unpatterned pale underparts **WESTERN** ❉

T. s. inornata **WESTERN** ❉

heavily streaked brownish head and neck

brownish upperparts with dense dark feathers

straight, thick bill with pinkish base

bold dark barring on underside

grayish legs

T. s. semipalmata **EASTERN BREEDING**

VOICE Kyah-yah *in flight; repeated* kleep *when alarmed; rapid* pill-will-willet *song.*
NESTING *Depression in vegetated dunes, wetlands, prairies, or salt marshes; 4 eggs; 1 brood; Apr–Jun.*
FEEDING *Picks, probes, or swishes for crustaceans (fiddler and mole crabs), aquatic insects, marine worms, small mollusks, fish.*
HABITAT *Eastern birds breed in coastal salt water; western, in prairie wetlands.*
LENGTH 12½–16½in (32–42cm)
WINGSPAN 21½–28½in (54–72cm)

Lesser Yellowlegs

Tringa flavipes

The Lesser Yellowlegs has a smaller head, thinner bill, and smoother body shape than the Greater Yellowlegs. It prefers smaller freshwater or brackish pools to open saltwater habitats, and it walks quickly and methodically while feeding. Although this species is a solitary feeder, it is often seen in small to large loose flocks in migration and winter.

small head

long, pointed, dark wings

BREEDING

black-and-brown upperparts with white spotting

heavily streaked head, neck, and breast

long yellow-orange legs

gray back with delicate scalloping pattern

dark, slender bill

BREEDING

white underparts

diffused, pale streaks on breast

yellow legs

NONBREEDING

VOICE *Low, whistled* tu, *or* tu-tu; *series of* tu *or* cuw *when agitated; display song* pill-e-wee, pill-e-wee, pill-e-wee.
NESTING *Depression in ground lined with grass and leaves; 4 eggs; 1 brood; May–Jun.*
FEEDING *Insects, especially flies and beetles, mollusks, and crustaceans; also seeds.*
HABITAT *Northerly forests with clearings and forest/tundra borders while breeding; shallow wetlands, such as flooded pastures, in winter.*
LENGTH 9–10in (23–25cm)
WINGSPAN 23–25in (58–64cm)

Upland Sandpiper Ⓢ

Bartramia longicauda

Unlike other sandpipers, the graceful Upland Sandpiper spends most of its life away from water, in grassland habitats, where its coloration helps it camouflage itself, especially while nesting in the grass. It is well known for landing on wooden fence posts and raising its wings while giving its tremulous, whistling call.

long, narrow wings

long tail

pale head

speckled breast

small, pigeonlike head

large, dark eye

mostly brownish upperparts

short, straight, mostly yellow bill

buff feather fringes

long tail extends beyond wings

yellow legs

BREEDING

VOICE *Flight call a low* qui-pi-pi-pi; *song consists of gurgling notes followed by long, descending "wolf whistle"* whooooleeeeee, wheeelooooo-ooooo.
NESTING *Depression in ground among grass clumps; 4 eggs; 1 brood; May.*
FEEDING *Adult and larval insects, spiders, worms, centipedes; occasionally seeds.*
HABITAT *Native tallgrass or mixed-grass prairies while breeding.*
LENGTH *11–12½in (28–32cm)*
WINGSPAN *25–27in (64–68cm)*

Whimbrel Ⓢ

Numenius phaeopus

This large, conspicuous shorebird is the most widespread of the curlew species, with four subspecies across North America and Eurasia. Its bold head stripes and clearly streaked face, neck, and breast make the species distinctive. The Whimbrel's fairly long, decurved bill allows it to probe into fiddler crab burrows, a favorite food item.

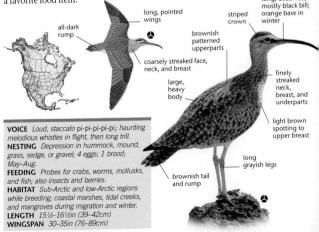

long, pointed wings

all-dark rump

long, decurved, mostly black bill; orange base in winter

striped crown

brownish patterned upperparts

coarsely streaked face, neck, and breast

large, heavy body

finely streaked neck, breast, and underparts

light brown spotting to upper breast

long grayish legs

brownish tail and rump

VOICE *Loud, staccato* pi-pi-pi-pi-pi; *haunting melodious whistles in flight, then long trill.*
NESTING *Depression in hummock, mound, grass, sedge, or gravel; 4 eggs; 1 brood; May–Aug.*
FEEDING *Probes for crabs, worms, mollusks, and fish; also insects and berries.*
HABITAT *Sub-Arctic and low-Arctic regions while breeding; coastal marshes, tidal creeks, and mangroves during migration and winter.*
LENGTH *15½–16½in (39–42cm)*
WINGSPAN *30–35in (76–89cm)*

Marbled Godwit ⓢ

Limosa fedoa

The largest godwit in North America, this shorebird is a familiar sight at its coastal wintering areas. Its distinctive brown-and-cinnamon plumage and its choice of open habitats, such as mudflats and floodplains, to feed and roost, make the Marbled Godwit a conspicuous species.

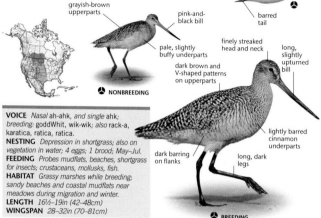

cinnamon underwing

barred tail

grayish-brown uppperparts

pink-and-black bill

pale, slightly buffy underparts

NONBREEDING

finely streaked head and neck

long, slightly upturned bill

dark brown and V-shaped patterns on upperparts

lightly barred cinnamon underparts

dark barring on flanks

long, dark legs

BREEDING

VOICE *Nasal ah-ahk, and single ahk; breeding: goddWhit, wik-wik; also rack-a, karatica, ratica, ratica.*
NESTING *Depression in shortgrass; also on vegetation in water; 4 eggs; 1 brood; May–Jul.*
FEEDING *Probes mudflats, beaches, shortgrass for insects; crustaceans, mollusks, fish.*
HABITAT *Grassy marshes while breeding; sandy beaches and coastal mudflats near meadows during migration and winter.*
LENGTH 16½–19in (42–48cm)
WINGSPAN 28–32in (70–81cm)

Hudsonian Godwit ⓣ

Limosa haemastica

This sandpiper undertakes a remarkable annual migration from its tundra breeding grounds in Alaska and Canada all the way to extreme southern South America—a distance probably close to 10,000 miles (16,000km) in each direction, with very few stopovers. During migration, North American stops are few and occur only in the spring, along a mid-continental route.

white wing stripe

white rump

NONBREEDING

brownish streaked head and neck

white-feathered chestnut breast

♀ **BREEDING**

long orange-based bill

black-and-white upperparts

unpatterned brownish wing feathers

black tail

rich chestnut underparts with black barring

♂ **BREEDING**

VOICE *Emphatic peed-wid in flight; high peet or kwee; display song to-wida to-wida to-wida, or to-wit, to-wit, to-wit.*
NESTING *Saucer-shaped depression on dry hummock; 4 eggs; 1 brood; May–Jul.*
FEEDING *Probes for insects, grubs, worms, crustaceans, and mollusks; plant tubers in fall.*
HABITAT *Sedge meadows and bogs in tundra while breeding; Atlantic Coast near fresh water in fall; flooded fields, reservoirs in spring.*
LENGTH 14–16in (35–41cm)
WINGSPAN 27–31in (68–78cm)

Red Knot

Calidris canutus

The Red Knot is the largest North American shorebird in the genus *Calidris*. There are two North American subspecies— *C. c. rufa* and *C. c. roselaari*. *C. c. rufa* flies about 9,300 miles (15,000km) between its high-Arctic breeding grounds and the wintering area in South America. Recent declines in its population are attributed to overharvesting of horseshoe crab eggs—its critical food source.

white eyebrow

white wing stripe

boldly marked black, rust, and white upperparts

white lower belly with dark V-shaped marks

salmon-colored face and breast

dark, straight, stocky bill

short, dark legs

mostly pale gray upperparts

pale underparts

yellowish-green legs

gray spots on upper breast

VOICE *Soft kuEEt or kuup in flight; display song por-meeee por-meeee, por-por por-por.*
NESTING *Simple scrape in grassy or barren tundra, often lined; 4 eggs; 1 brood; Jun.*
FEEDING *Probes mud or sand for insects, plant material, small mollusks, crustaceans, small snails, worms, and other invertebrates.*
HABITAT *Flat, barren tundra on islands and peninsulas while breeding; coastal sandbars and tidal flats during migration and winter.*
LENGTH *9–10in (23–25cm)*
WINGSPAN *23–24in (58–61cm)*

Ruddy Turnstone

Arenaria interpres

A common visitor along the shorelines of North and South America, the Ruddy Turnstone is aggressive on its high-Arctic breeding grounds, driving off predators as large as the Glaucous Gull and the Parasitic Jaeger. It was named for its reddish back color and its habit of overturning items like mollusk shells and pebbles, looking for small crustaceans and other prey.

dark flight feathers

bold red patches on back and wings

BREEDING

brownish upperparts

variably streaked, whitish face

brownish head markings

NONBREEDING

short, dark, chisel-like bill

black breast

black-and-white head and breast pattern

bright white underparts, at all ages

short orange legs

BREEDING

VOICE *TIT-wooo TIT-woooRITitititititit on breeding ground; low, rapid kut-a-kut in flight.*
NESTING *Scrape lined with lichens and grasses in dry, open areas; 4 eggs; 1 brood; Jun.*
FEEDING *Forages along shoreline for crustaceans, insects, including beetles, spiders; also plants.*
HABITAT *Open, barren, grassy habitats near water and rocky coasts while breeding; beaches and rocky shorelines in winter.*
LENGTH *8–10½in (20–27cm)*
WINGSPAN *20–22½in (51–57cm)*

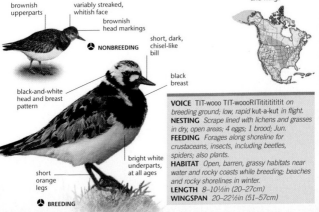

Stilt Sandpiper

(S)

Calidris himantopus

The slender Stilt Sandpiper is uncommon and unique to North America, where it breeds in several small northern tundra areas. It favors shallow, freshwater habitats, where it feeds in a distinctive style—walking slowly through belly-deep water with its neck outstretched and bill pointed downward. It then either picks at the surface, or submerges itself, while keeping its tail raised. During migration, it forms dense, rapidly moving flocks, which sometimes include other sandpipers.

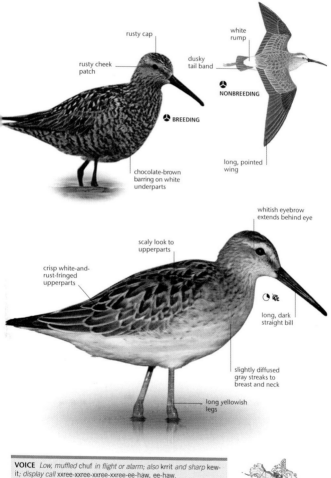

rusty cap

white rump

rusty cheek patch

dusky tail band

NONBREEDING

BREEDING

long, pointed wing

chocolate-brown barring on white underparts

whitish eyebrow extends behind eye

scaly look to upperparts

crisp white-and-rust-fringed upperparts

long, dark straight bill

slightly diffused gray streaks to breast and neck

long yellowish legs

VOICE *Low, muffled* chuf *in flight or alarm; also* krrit *and sharp* kew-it; *display call* xxree-xxree-xxree-xxree-ee-haw, ee-haw.
NESTING *Shallow depression on raised knolls or ridges in tundra; 4 eggs; 1 brood; Jun.*
FEEDING *Mostly adult and larval insects; also some snails, mollusks, and seeds.*
HABITAT *Moist to wet tundra while breeding; freshwater habitats, such as flooded fields and marsh pools, during migration and winter.*
LENGTH *8–9in (20–23cm)*
WINGSPAN *17–18½in (43–47cm)*

Sanderling

S D

Calidris alba

The Sanderling is among the best-known shorebirds in the world. It breeds in remote, high-Arctic habitats, from Greenland to Siberia, but occupies just about every temperate and tropical shoreline in the Americas when not breeding. Its wintering range spans coasts, from Canada to Argentina. Feeding flocks, constantly on the move at the water's edge, are a common sight in winter on sandy beaches. In many places though, the bird is declining rapidly—with pollution of the sea and shore and habitat disturbance being the main causes.

mostly grayish upperparts

bold white wing stripe

NONBREEDING

white face and neck

pearl-gray upperparts

clean white underparts

NONBREEDING

black-centered back feathers with buff edges

black, rust, and white upperparts

rust-and-black-streaked crown

dark, stocky bill

rust wash on breast with black markings

short black legs

BREEDING

VOICE Squeaky *pweet in flight, sew-sew-sew threat call; display song harsh, buzzy notes and chattering cher-cher-cher.*
NESTING Small, shallow depression on dry, stony ground; 4 eggs; 1–3 broods; Jun–Jul.
FEEDING Probes along the surf-line in sand for insects, small crustaceans, small mollusks, and worms.
HABITAT Barren high-Arctic coastal tundra while breeding; coastlines and sandy beaches during migration and winter.
LENGTH 7½–8in (19–20cm)
WINGSPAN 16–18in (41–46cm)

Dunlin   Ⓢ

Calidris alpina

The Dunlin is one of the most abundant and widespread of North America's shorebirds. Three subspecies breed in North America: *C. a. arcticola*, *C. a. pacifica*, and *C. a. hudsonia*. The Dunlin is unmistakable in its striking red-backed, black-bellied breeding plumage. In winter, it sports much more drab colors but is conspicuous by gathering in flocks of many thousands of birds on coastal mudflats.

thin white wing bar

white sided rump

dull gray-brown head and back

long, tapered, black bill

dull gray-streaked breast

NONBREEDING

rich chestnut-and-black back

fine dark streaks on whitish breast

large, squarish black belly patch

BREEDING

VOICE *Accented trill, drurr-drurr; jeeezp in flight; wrraah-wrraah song.*
NESTING *Cup lined with grasses and lichens in moist tundra; 4 eggs; 1 brood; Jun–Jul.*
FEEDING *Marine, freshwater, terrestrial invertebrates; clams, worms, insect larvae, crustaceans; also plants and small fish.*
HABITAT *Wet tundra near ponds while breeding; coastal areas with mudflats and beaches during migration and winter.*
LENGTH *6½–8½in (16–22cm)*
WINGSPAN *12½–17½in (32–44cm)*

Purple Sandpiper   Ⓢ

Calidris maritima

A medium-sized, stocky bird, the Purple Sandpiper shares the most northerly wintering distribution of all North American shorebirds with its close relative in the West, the Rock Sandpiper. The dark plumage and low, squat body often disguise its presence on dark tidal rocks, until a crashing wave causes a previously invisible flock to explode into flight.

thin, white wing stripe

brownish-gray upperparts

NONBREEDING

grayish wash to head and neck

compact body shape overall

gray inner wing feathers

bill yellow at base, dark at drooping tip

white belly and flanks, with thin streaking

yellow legs and toes

NONBREEDING

long bill with drooping tip

heavily streaked head

short, thick neck

BREEDING

VOICE *Low kweesh in flight; eh-eh-eh when disturbed; breeding kwi-ti-ti-ti-bli-bli-bli followed by dooree-dooree-dooree.*
NESTING *Simple lined scrape in Arctic tundra; 4 eggs; 1 brood; Jun.*
FEEDING *Invertebrates, including crustaceans, snails, insects, spiders, and worms.*
HABITAT *Barren Arctic and alpine tundra while breeding; rocky, wave-pounded shores during migration and winter.*
LENGTH *8–8½in (20–21cm)*
WINGSPAN *16½–18½in (42–47cm)*

Baird's Sandpiper

Ⓢ

Calidris bairdii

Baird's Sandpiper is less well known than the other North American *Calidris* sandpipers. From its high-Arctic tundra habitat, Baird's Sandpiper migrates across North America and the western US into South America, and all the way to Tierra del Fuego—a remarkable journey of 6,000–9,000 miles (9,700–14,500km), twice a year.

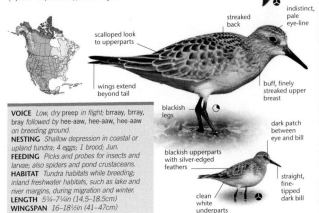

long, pointed wings

finely streaked head

indistinct, pale eye-line

streaked back

scalloped look to upperparts

buff, finely streaked upper breast

wings extend beyond tail

blackish legs

dark patch between eye and bill

blackish upperparts with silver-edged feathers

straight, fine-tipped dark bill

clean white underparts

VOICE *Low, dry* preep *in flight;* brraay, brray, bray *followed by* hee-aaw, hee-aaw, hee-aaw *on breeding ground.*
NESTING *Shallow depression in coastal or upland tundra; 4 eggs; 1 brood; Jun.*
FEEDING *Picks and probes for insects and larvae; also spiders and pond crustaceans.*
HABITAT *Tundra habitats while breeding; inland freshwater habitats, such as lake and river margins, during migration and winter.*
LENGTH *5¾–7¼in (14.5–18.5cm)*
WINGSPAN *16–18½in (41–47cm)*

Least Sandpiper

Ⓓ

Calidris minutilla

With its muted brown or brownish-gray plumage, the tiny Least Sandpiper virtually disappears in the landscape when feeding crouched down on wet margins of waterbodies. These birds are often found in small to medium flocks at the edge of other shorebird flocks. They are often nervous when foraging, and frequently burst into flight, only to alight a short way off.

faint tail band

uniform brownish-gray upperparts

pale whitish eyebrow

NONBREEDING

yellow to yellowish-green legs

white chin and belly

streaked brownish breast and head

small, rounded head

short tail and wings

short yellowish legs

BREEDING

VOICE *Kreeeep, rising in pitch, often repeated two-syllable* kree-eep *in flight; trilled* b-reeee, b-reeee, b-reeee *display call.*
NESTING *Depression in open, sub-Arctic habitat near water; 4 eggs; 1 brood; May–Jun.*
FEEDING *Small terrestrial and aquatic prey, especially sand fleas, mollusks, and flies.*
HABITAT *Wet, low-Arctic areas while breeding; muddy areas on lakeshores, riverbanks, fields, and tidal flats during migration and winter.*
LENGTH *4¾in (12cm)*
WINGSPAN *13–14in (33–35cm)*

White-rumped Sandpiper ⓢ

Calidris fuscicollis

The White-rumped Sandpiper has one of the longest migrations of any bird in the Western Hemisphere. From its high-Arctic breeding grounds, it migrates in several long jumps to extreme southern South America—about 9,000–12,000 miles (14,500–19,300km), twice a year. Almost the entire population migrates through the central US and Canada in spring, with several stopovers. Its insectlike call and white rump aid identification.

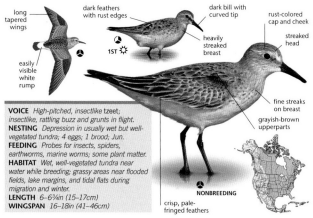

long tapered wings

dark feathers with rust edges

dark bill with curved tip

rust-colored cap and cheek

streaked head

heavily streaked breast

easily visible white rump

1ST ☀

fine streaks on breast

grayish-brown upperparts

VOICE *High-pitched, insectlike tzeet; insectlike, rattling buzz and grunts in flight.*
NESTING *Depression in usually wet but well-vegetated tundra; 4 eggs; 1 brood; Jun.*
FEEDING *Probes for insects, spiders, earthworms, marine worms; some plant matter.*
HABITAT *Wet, well-vegetated tundra near water while breeding; grassy areas near flooded fields, lake margins, and tidal flats during migration and winter.*
LENGTH *6–6¾in (15–17cm)*
WINGSPAN *16–18in (41–46cm)*

NONBREEDING

crisp, pale-fringed feathers

Buff-breasted Sandpiper ⓓ

Calidris subruficollis

This sandpiper has a unique mating system among North American shorebirds. On the ground in the Arctic, each male flashes his white underwings to attract females. After mating, the female leaves to perform all nest duties alone, while the male continues to display and mate with other females. These birds migrate an astonishing 16,000 miles (26,000km) from their breeding grounds to winter in temperate South America.

pale central band

streaked and spotted brown hind neck

buff head and face with spotted brown crown

buff-edged brown upperparts

short, dark bill

dark rump

bright yellowish-orange legs

BREEDING

NONBREEDING

scaly upperparts

more white-fringed upperpart feathers than adults

rich buff wash to breast

dull yellow legs

VOICE *Soft, short gert in flight, or longer, rising grriit.*
NESTING *Simple depression on well-drained moss or grass hummock; 4 eggs; 1 brood; Jun.*
FEEDING *Forages on land for insects, insect larvae, and spiders; occasionally seeds.*
HABITAT *Moist to wet, grassy or sedgy coastal tundra while breeding; shortgrass areas, such as pastures and meadows, during migration.*
LENGTH *7¼–8½in (18.5–20cm)*
WINGSPAN *17–18½in (43–47cm)*

Pectoral Sandpiper ⓢ

Calidris melanotos

From their breeding grounds in the high Arctic to their
wintering grounds in South America, some Pectoral Sandpipers
travel up to 30,000 miles (48,000km) each year. Males keep
harems of females in guarded territories and mate with as many
as they can attract, but they take no part in nest duties and
migrate earlier than females.

long, graceful, pointed wings

darker flight feathers

brownish upperparts, with buff fringes

streaked crown and face

curved bill with orange base

medium-length, stocky bill

heavily streaked breast

rust crown and cheeks with black streaks

white belly

yellowish legs

rust-edged, dark-centered feathers

VOICE Low, trilled chrrk in flight; deep,
hollow whoop, whoop, whoop in display.
NESTING Shallow depression on ridges
in moist to wet sedge tundra; 4 eggs;
1 brood; Jun.
FEEDING Probes or jabs mud for larvae,
and forages for insects and spiders on tundra.
HABITAT Wet, grassy tundra near coasts while
breeding; wet pastures, grassy lake margins,
and salt marshes during migration and winter.
LENGTH 7½–9in (19–23cm)
WINGSPAN 16½–19½in (42–49cm)

Semipalmated Sandpiper ⓢ

Calidris pusilla

This abundant sandpiper breeds in Canada's Arctic tundra.
Flocks of up to 300,000 birds gather at migration staging areas.
It can be difficult to identify, due to plumage variation
between juveniles and breeding adults, and a bill that varies in size
and shape. Semipalmated Sandpipers may fly from their
northeasterly breeding grounds nonstop to their South
American wintering grounds in the fall.

white eyebrow

pale wing stripe along flight feathers

streaked black-and-rust crown

slightly paler, grayish nape

dark-centered back feathers with buff fringes

wingtips extend to tail tip

short, dark bill

lightly streaked breast

crisp, pale-fringed feathers

pale grayish-black legs

short, straight bill with blunt tip

VOICE Chrrk or higher, sharper chit flight
call; display song monotonous, droning trill.
NESTING Shallow, lined scrape in shortgrass
habitat; 4 eggs; 1 brood; May–Jun.
FEEDING Probes mud for aquatic and
terrestrial invertebrates, such as mollusks,
worms, and spiders.
HABITAT Arctic and sub-Arctic tundra near
water while breeding; shallow waters and open
muddy areas during migration.
LENGTH 5¼–6in (13.5–15cm)
WINGSPAN 13½–15in (34–38cm)

Western Sandpiper

Calidris mauri

During spring migration, flocks of millions of Western Sandpipers are seen at several Pacific Coast locations. Many of these migrate over relatively short distances to winter along US coastlines, so the timing of their molt in fall is earlier than that of the similar Semipalmated Sandpiper, which migrates later in winter.

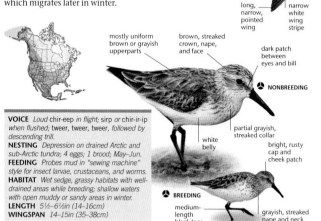

white tail

dusky tail band

long, narrow, pointed wing

narrow white wing stripe

mostly uniform brown or grayish upperparts

brown, streaked crown, nape, and face

dark patch between eyes and bill

NONBREEDING

partial grayish, streaked collar

white belly

bright, rusty cap and cheek patch

VOICE Loud chir-eep in flight; sirp or chir-ir-ip when flushed; tweer, tweer, tweer, followed by descending trill.
NESTING Depression on drained Arctic and sub-Arctic tundra; 4 eggs; 1 brood; May–Jun.
FEEDING Probes mud in "sewing machine" style for insect larvae, crustaceans, and worms.
HABITAT Wet sedge, grassy habitats with well-drained muddy or sandy areas in winter.
LENGTH 5½–6½in (14–16cm)
WINGSPAN 14–15in (35–38cm)

white belly

medium-length black legs

BREEDING

grayish, streaked nape and neck

Short-billed Dowitcher

Limnodromus griseus

The Short-billed Dowitcher is a common visitor along the Atlantic, Gulf, and Pacific Coasts. There are three subspecies (*L. g. griseus*, *L. g. hendersoni*, and *L. g. caurinus*), which differ in plumage, size, and respective breeding areas. Recent knowledge about shape and structure has helped birders distinguish between Short-billed and Long-billed Dowitchers.

slightly larger bill

L. g. hendersoni

long, pointed wings

white slash from rump to mid-back

orange wash to face, neck, breast, and underparts

BREEDING

long, stout bill

dark-centered upperpart feathers

VOICE Low tu-tu-tu or tu-tu, tu-tu, toodle-ee, tu-tu, ending with low anh-anh-anh in flight.
NESTING Simple depression, typically in sedge hummock; 4 eggs; 1 brood; May–Jun.
FEEDING Probes in "sewing machine" style in belly-deep water for mollusks, crustaceans, and insects.
HABITAT Sedge meadows or bogs with spruce and tamaracks while breeding; coastal mudflats and salt marshes in winter.
LENGTH 9–10in (23–25cm)
WINGSPAN 18–20in (46–51cm)

variable spotting on upper breast

streaked flanks

greenish-yellow legs

L. g. griseus

Long-billed Dowitcher ⓢ

Limnodromus scolopaceus

The Long-billed Dowitcher is usually slightly larger, longer-legged, and heavier in the chest and neck than the Short-billed Dowitcher. The breeding ranges of the two species are separate, but their migration and stopover areas overlap. The Long-billed Dowitcher is usually found in freshwater wetlands, and in the fall most of its population occurs west of the Mississippi River.

VOICE Sharp, whistled *keek* in flight; song buzzy *pipipipipipi-chi-drrr*.
NESTING Deep sedge or grass-lined depression in sedge or grass; 4 eggs; 1 brood; May–Jun.
FEEDING Probes in "sewing-machine" style for spiders, snails, worms, insects, and seeds.
HABITAT Wet, grassy meadows or coastal sedge tundra near freshwater pools while breeding; freshwater and saltwater habitats in winter.
LENGTH 9½–10in (24–26cm)
WINGSPAN 18–20½in (46–52cm)

Wilson's Snipe ⓢ

Gallinago delicata

Wilson's Snipe is a well-camouflaged member of the sandpiper family. On its breeding grounds, it produces eerie sounds during its aerial, mainly nocturnal, display flights. The birds fly up silently from the ground and, from about 330ft (100m) up, they descend quickly with tail feathers spread, producing a loud and vibrating sound through modified feathers.

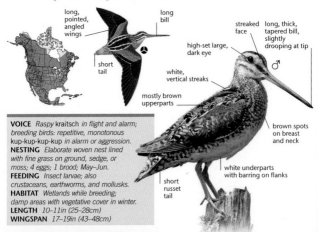

VOICE Raspy *kraitsch* in flight and alarm; breeding birds: repetitive, monotonous *kup-kup-kup-kup* in alarm or aggression.
NESTING Elaborate woven nest lined with fine grass on ground, sedge, or moss; 4 eggs; 1 brood; May–Jun.
FEEDING Insect larvae; also crustaceans, earthworms, and mollusks.
HABITAT Wetlands while breeding; damp areas with vegetative cover in winter.
LENGTH 10–11in (25–28cm)
WINGSPAN 17–19in (43–48cm)

American Woodcock (S)

Scolopax minor

This forest-dwelling member of the sandpiper family bears little resemblance in behavior to its water-favoring relatives, but slightly resembles Wilson's Snipe and the dowitchers. Although widespread, the American Woodcock is largely nocturnal and seldom seen, except during its impressive twilight courtship displays. It feeds in mature fields or woodlands. Its noisy, repetitive display flights are a sign of spring in northern breeding areas.

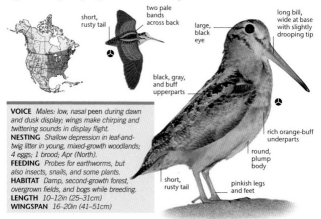

short, rusty tail

two pale bands across back

large, black eye

long bill, wide at base with slightly drooping tip

black, gray, and buff upperparts

rich orange-buff underparts

round, plump body

short, rusty tail

pinkish legs and feet

VOICE Males: low, nasal peen during dawn and dusk display; wings make chirping and twittering sounds in display flight.
NESTING Shallow depression in leaf-and-twig litter in young, mixed-growth woodlands; 4 eggs; 1 brood; Apr (North).
FEEDING Probes for earthworms, but also insects, snails, and some plants.
HABITAT Damp, second-growth forest, overgrown fields, and bogs while breeding.
LENGTH 10–12in (25–31cm)
WINGSPAN 16–20in (41–51cm)

Wilson's Phalarope (S)

Phalaropus tricolor

The largest of the three phalarope species, Wilson's Phalarope breeds in the shallow wetlands of western North America and winters mainly in Bolivia and Argentina. It feeds by spinning in shallow water to churn up insects, or chasing insects on muddy wetland edges with its head held low.

reddish-brown markings on sides of back

grayish-brown wings

♀ BREEDING

gray and reddish-brown back

white cheek

white eyebrow

black stripe from bill to nape

fairly long, straight bill

♀ BREEDING

rust neck and throat

paler head markings

plain gray-and-black upperparts

♂

VOICE Low, nasal werpf in flight; also higher, repetitive emf, emf, emf, emf, or luk, luk, luk.
NESTING Simple scrape lined with grass; 4 eggs; 1 brood; May–Jun.
FEEDING Brine shrimp, various insects, and insect larvae.
HABITAT Shallow, grassy wetlands while breeding; salty lakes and ponds and inland water bodies during migration.
LENGTH 8½–9½in (22–24cm)
WINGSPAN 15½–17in (39–43cm)

Red-necked Phalarope

Phalaropus lobatus

This aquatic sandpiper spends nine months in deep ocean waters feeding on tiny plankton before coming to nest in the Arctic. Unlike most bird species, the female phalarope is more brightly colored and slightly larger than the male; after competing savagely for a male, she migrates right after laying her eggs and leaves the male to care for them.

pointed wings

narrow white wing stripe

♀ BREEDING

needlelike, dark bill

dark gray crown and face

dark upperparts with buff or rust feather edges

♀ BREEDING

white throat

rust neck and upper breast

dark upperparts with buff stripes

VOICE Hard, squeaky pwit or kit in flight; variations of the same vocalizations on breeding grounds.
NESTING Depression in wet sedge or grass; 3–4 eggs; 1–2 broods; May–Jun.
FEEDING Plankton; also insects, brine shrimp, and mollusks.
HABITAT Wet tundra on raised ridges or hummocks while breeding; far out to sea during migration.
LENGTH 7–7½in (18–19cm)
WINGSPAN 12½–16in (32–41cm)

Red Phalarope

Phalaropus fulicarius

The Red Phalarope spends more than ten months each year over deep ocean waters. It also migrates across the ocean; few birds of this species are ever seen inland. During migration over Alaskan waters, flocks feed on crustaceans in the mud plumes created during foraging by gray and bowhead whales on the ocean floor.

broad, pointed wings

white rump with black line in center and white edges

bold white wing bar

♀ BREEDING

tan-fringed feathers on upperparts

bold white cheek patch

black crown

stout yellow bill with black tip

♀ BREEDING

deep brick-red neck, throat, and underparts

black cheek patch and nape

white neck and head

VOICE Sharp psip or pseet in flight, often in rapid succession; drawn-out, two-syllabled sweet in alarm.
NESTING Depression on ridge or hummock in coastal sedge; 3–4 eggs; 1 brood; Jun.
FEEDING Marine crustaceans, fish eggs, larval fish; adult or larval insects.
HABITAT Coastal Arctic tundra while breeding; deep ocean waters during migration and winter.
LENGTH 8–8½in (20–22cm)
WINGSPAN 16–17½in (41–44cm)

mostly gray upperparts

white underparts

NONBREEDING

Pomarine Jaeger

Stercorarius pomarinus

The Pomarine Jaeger uses its size and strength to overpower larger seabirds, such as gulls and shearwaters, in order to steal their food. Nesting only when populations of lemmings are at their peak to provide food for its young, it is readily driven away from breeding territories by the more dynamic Parasitic Jaeger. Research suggests that the Pomarine Jaeger is actually more closely related to the large skuas than to other jaegers.

prominent white "flash" in feathers

BREEDING; PALE FORM

white wing flash

DARK FORM

blunt tail spike

dark overall

NONBREEDING; PALE FORM

blackish cap

pale-based, thick bill

cream cheeks

gray-brown back

barred flanks

dusky breastband

twisted, spoonlike central tail feathers

dusky breastband

BREEDING; PALE FORM

VOICE Nasal *cow-cow-cow* and various sharp, low whistles.
NESTING Shallow, unlined depression on a rise or hummock in open tundra; 2 eggs; 1 brood; Jun–Aug.
FEEDING Lemmings and other rodents; fish; scavenges refuse from fishing boats during nonbreeding season; steals fish from other seabirds.
HABITAT Open tundra while breeding; coasts and far offshore during migration; more common on the West Coast.
LENGTH 17–20in (43–51cm)
WINGSPAN 4ft (1.2m)

Parasitic Jaeger

Stercorarius parasiticus

The Parasitic Jaeger routinely seeks food by chasing, bullying, and forcing other seabirds to drop or regurgitate fish or other food they have caught. Unlike most jaegers, the Parasitic Jaeger is adaptable in its feeding habits so that it can forage and raise its young under a wide range of environmental conditions. Breeding on the Arctic tundra, it migrates to offshore areas during the nonbreeding season.

white wing patch

PALE FORM

pale cheek

dark cap

dark upperparts

gray breastband

long, pointed, central feathers

PALE FORM

dark legs and toes

white wing patch

pale cheek patch

mostly dark brown overall

DARK FORM

VOICE *Terrierlike yelps and soft squeals, often during interactions with other jaegers or predators, usually around nesting territories.*
NESTING *Shallow, unlined depression on a rise in open tundra; 2 eggs; 1 brood; May–Aug.*
FEEDING *Steals fish and other aquatic prey from gulls and terns; small birds, eggs, or small rodents on breeding grounds.*
HABITAT *Tundra while breeding; near- and offshore waters during migration and winter.*
LENGTH *16–18½in (41–47cm)*
WINGSPAN *3¼–3½ft (1–1.1m)*

Long-tailed Jaeger

Stercorarius longicaudus

This elegant species is a surprisingly fierce Arctic and marine predator. The Long-tailed Jaeger occasionally steals food from small gulls and terns, but usually hunts for its own food. In years when lemming numbers dip so low as to become unavailable for feeding its nestlings, this jaeger may not even attempt to nest.

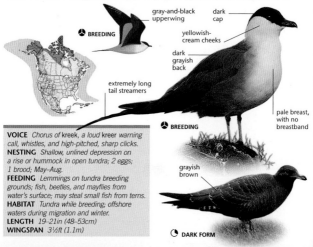

gray-and-black upperwing

dark cap

BREEDING

yellowish-cream cheeks

dark grayish back

extremely long tail streamers

BREEDING

pale breast, with no breastband

grayish brown

DARK FORM

VOICE *Chorus of kreek, a loud kreer warning call, whistles, and high-pitched, sharp clicks.*
NESTING *Shallow, unlined depression on a rise or hummock in open tundra; 2 eggs; 1 brood; May–Aug.*
FEEDING *Lemmings on tundra breeding grounds; fish, beetles, and mayflies from water's surface; may steal small fish from terns.*
HABITAT *Tundra while breeding; offshore waters during migration and winter.*
LENGTH *19–21in (48–53cm)*
WINGSPAN *3½ft (1.1m)*

Dovekie

Alle alle

Also known as the Little Auk, the Dovekie is a bird of the high Arctic. Most Dovekies breed in Greenland in large, noisy, crowded colonies, but some breed in northeastern Canada, and others on a few islands in the Bering Sea, off Alaska. Vast flocks of Dovekies winter on the low-Arctic waters off the Northeastern Seaboard of North America. Severe onshore gales may cause entire flocks to become stranded along the East Coast of North America.

short, dark tail

dark wings

BREEDING

dark back

white collar at back of head

dark crown

small bill

white throat

white undertail

NONBREEDING

dark head and upper breast

white triangle on side of breast

BREEDING

VOICE High-pitched trilling that rises and falls at breeding ground; silent at sea.
NESTING Pebble nest in crack or crevice in boulder field or rocky outcrop; 1 egg; 1 brood; Apr–Aug.
FEEDING Tiny crustaceans from just below the sea's surface.
HABITAT Islands while breeding; just south of Arctic ice pack and Northeastern Seaboard in winter.
LENGTH 8½in (21cm)
WINGSPAN 15in (38cm)

Common Murre

Uria aalge

Penguinlike Common Murres are often seen standing upright on cliffs. They are strong fliers and adept divers—to a depth of 500ft (150m). Their large nesting colonies, on rocky sea-cliff ledges, are so crowded that incubating adults may actually touch each other on both sides. Common Murre eggs are pointed at one end—perhaps to reduce the chance of the egg rolling off the ledge, but more likely to help maximize contact with the brood patch.

black wing

slender head and bill

BREEDING

curved black line droops behind eye

white face and throat

NONBREEDING

black head

long, straight black bill

white underparts

black back

grayish legs and feet

BREEDING

VOICE Low-pitched, descending call, reminiscent of trumpeting elephant.
NESTING On bare rock near shore, on cliff ledge, or in crevice; 1 egg; 1 brood; May–Jul.
FEEDING Small schooling fish, such as herring, sand lance, and haddock; also crustaceans, marine worms, and squid.
HABITAT Close to rocky shorelines, on cliff ledges or on top of sea stacks while breeding; winters at sea.
LENGTH 17½in (44cm)
WINGSPAN 26in (65cm)

Thick-billed Murre ⓢ

Uria lomvia

The Thick-billed Murre is one of the most abundant seabirds
in all of the Northern Hemisphere, breeding in dense, coastal
cliff colonies of around a million birds each. Young leave the
colony when they are only about 25 percent of the adult
weight, completing their growth at sea while being fed by
the male parent alone. This murre can dive to 600ft (180m)
to catch fish and squid.

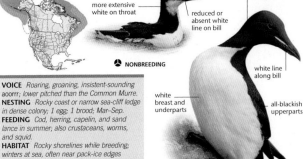

short black tail

Ⓑ BREEDING

hunched in flight

more extensive white on throat

reduced or absent white line on bill

Ⓝ NONBREEDING

brownish-black sides of head

white line along bill

white breast and underparts

all-blackish upperparts

Ⓑ BREEDING

VOICE *Roaring, groaning, insistent-sounding
aoorrr; lower pitched than the Common Murre.*
NESTING *Rocky coast or narrow sea-cliff ledge
in dense colony; 1 egg; 1 brood; Mar–Sep.*
FEEDING *Cod, herring, capelin, and sand
lance in summer; also crustaceans, worms,
and squid.*
HABITAT *Rocky shorelines while breeding;
winters at sea, often near pack-ice edges
or openings.*
LENGTH *18in (46cm)*
WINGSPAN *28in (70cm)*

Razorbill ⓢ

Alca torda

The Razorbill is the closest living relative of the extinct Great Auk.
One of the rarest breeding seabirds in North America, it is a strong
and agile flier. Razorbills typically feed at depths of about 20ft (6m),
but can dive to depths of more than 450ft (140m). Onshore,
Razorbills walk upright like penguins. Initially, both parents
carry small fish to their young; later, male Razorbills escort their
flightless young to the sea to feed.

thick black bill

long, pointed black tail

Ⓑ BREEDING

bill smaller than in breeding birds

brownish head

white underparts up to chin

Ⓝ NONBREEDING

large, round head

thin white line extends from bill to eye

short neck

black upperparts

snowy-white underparts

blackish legs and feet

Ⓑ BREEDING

VOICE *Deep, guttural, resonant croak, hey al.*
NESTING *Enclosed sites often built in
crevices, among boulders, or in abandoned
burrows; 1 egg; 1 brood; May–Jul.*
FEEDING *Schooling fish (capelin, herring, sand
lance); also marine worms and crustaceans;
sometimes steals fish from other auks.*
HABITAT *Rocky islands and shorelines, or
steep mainland cliffs while breeding; ice-free
coastal waters in winter.*
LENGTH *17in (43cm)*
WINGSPAN *26in (65cm)*

Black Guillemot

Cepphus grylle

Black Guillemots have a distinctive black plumage with white wing patches in summer, which molts to mottled gray and black in winter. Their striking scarlet legs and mouth lining help attract a mate. These birds "fly" under water with partly opened wings, and their scarlet webbed feet serve as a rudder. Black Guillemots are residents of shallow, inshore waters. They nest in rock crevices on remote islands, seeking safety from predators such as mink.

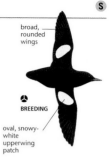

broad, rounded wings

BREEDING

oval, snowy-white upperwing patch

gray bars on white wing patch

gray cap

gray neck

large white patch

BREEDING

thin, straight bill

dark belly

round black body

scarlet legs and feet

VOICE High-pitched whistles and squeaks, near nesting habitat, that resonate like an echo.
NESTING Shallow scrape in soil or pebbles within cave or crevice; 1–2 eggs; 1 brood; May–Aug.
FEEDING Small, bottom-dwelling fish, such as rock eels, sand lance, and sculpin; feeds close to nesting islands.
HABITAT Remote, rocky islands and cliffs while breeding; shallow waters near rocky coasts.
LENGTH 13in (33cm)
WINGSPAN 21in (53cm)

Atlantic Puffin

S

Fratercula arctica

With its black-and-white "tuxedo," ungainly upright posture, and enormous, colorful bill, the Atlantic Puffin is often known as the "clown of the sea." It is seen in summer, when large breeding colonies gather on remote, rocky islands. To feed itself and its young, it can dive to 200ft (60m) with partly folded wings in pursuit of small schooling fish. One bird was seen holding 62 sand eels in its beak at once.

short tail

🌙 BREEDING

blue-gray, orange, and red stripes on bill

dull bill

dusky gray face

black back, collar, and underwings

🌙 BREEDING

🌙 NONBREEDING

orange legs and feet

red eye-ring

large, colorful, triangular bill

gray face

thick black line

stocky, rounded body

white breast

🌙 BREEDING

VOICE Rising and falling buzzy growl, resembling a chainsaw.
NESTING Underground burrow or deep rock crevice lined with grass and feathers; 1 egg; 1 brood; Jun–Aug.
FEEDING Dives for capelin, herring, hake, and sand lance, and other small fish, swallowing underwater, or storing crosswise in its bill to take back to its young.
HABITAT Small, rocky offshore islands while breeding; high seas far offshore in nonbreeding season.
LENGTH 12½in (32cm)
WINGSPAN 21in (53cm)

Gulls and Terns

The family Laridae, which includes the gulls, terns, and Black Skimmer, is part of the order Charadriiformes, together with the shorebird and auk families. Gulls and terns are found worldwide; there are more than 20 gull species found in North America, and more than 10 terns. Gulls all share similar stout body shapes, sturdy bills, and webbed toes, and nearly all are scavengers. Most large gulls have white heads and underparts, as well as long dark wings and a bright, sturdy bill. Closely associated with coastal areas, few gulls venture far out to sea. Some species are seen around fishing ports and harbors, or inland, especially in urban areas and garbage dumps.

Terns are specialized long-billed predators that dive for fish. More slender and elegant than gulls, nearly all are immediately recognizable when breeding, with their black caps, gray-and-white plumage, and long, pointed bills. The related Black Skimmer also catches fish, but by "skimming" the surface of the water with its long lower bill.

PROMINENT EYES
In all plumages, Franklin's Gull has much more prominent white eye-crescents than similar species.

Black-legged Kittiwake

S

Rissa tridactyla

A kittiwake nesting colony may have thousands of birds lined up along steep, narrow cliff ledges by the sea. Kittiwakes have sharper claws than other gulls, probably to give them a better grip on their ledges. In the late 20th century, the Black-legged Kittiwake population expanded greatly in the Canadian Maritime Provinces, with numbers doubling in the Gulf of St. Lawrence.

pale outer wing feathers

pale gray upperparts

black wingtip

white head

pale gray back feathers

yellow bill

black legs and feet

dark neck collar

dark wing bar

VOICE *Repeated nasal kit-ti-wake, kit-ti-wake call; vocal near nests; usually silent in winter.*
NESTING *Mound of mud and vegetation on narrow cliff ledge; 1–3 eggs; 1 brood; Apr–Aug.*
FEEDING *Small marine fish and invertebrates from water's surface or just below; feeds in flocks.*
HABITAT *Sea cliffs with ledges and offshore waters while breeding; winters at sea.*
LENGTH *15–16in (38–41cm)*
WINGSPAN *3–4ft (0.9–1.2m)*

Sabine's Gull

S

Xema sabini

This gull was discovered in 1818 in Greenland by English scientist Edward Sabine during John Ross's search for the Northwest Passage. The distinctive wing pattern and notched tail make it unmistakable in all plumages. This species breeds in the Arctic and winters at sea, off the coasts of the Americas and Africa.

gray hood

yellow-tipped black bill

red eye-ring

black border

gray back

white triangle on wing

white underparts

black legs

BREEDING

barring on gray-brown back

black bill

VOICE *Harsh, ternlike kyeer, kyeer, kyeer.*
NESTING *Shallow depression in marsh or tundra vegetation near water, lined with grass or unlined; 3–4 eggs; 1 brood; May–Aug.*
FEEDING *Aquatic insects from the water's surface during breeding season; winter diet: crustaceans, small fish, and plankton.*
HABITAT *Wet tundra near fresh or salt water while breeding; widespread in the Pacific and Atlantic Oceans during migration.*
LENGTH *13–14in (33–36cm)*
WINGSPAN *35–39in (90–100cm)*

Bonaparte's Gull

Chroicocephalus philadelphia

Lighter and more delicate than the other North American gulls, Bonaparte's Gull is commonly distinguished in winter by the blackish smudge behind each eye and the large white wing patch. It is one of North America's most common and widespread gulls. This species was named after 19th-century French ornithologist Charles Lucien Bonaparte (nephew of Napoleon).

black wingtips

white flash on outer wings

NONBREEDING

white head

blackish "ear" spot

gray neck

NONBREEDING

black hood

short bill

gray back and wings

white wedge on wing

BREEDING

orange-red legs

white underparts have rosy glow when breeding

VOICE Harsh keek, keek; kew, kew, kew while feeding.
NESTING Stick nest of twigs, bark, lined with mosses or lichens; in conifers or rushes over water; 1–4 eggs; 1 brood; May–Jul.
FEEDING Insects; crustaceans, mollusks, small fish from water's surface; also plunge-dives.
HABITAT Northern forests, in lakes, ponds, or bogs while feeding; near water during migration; Great Lakes, coasts in winter.
LENGTH 11–12in (28–30cm)
WINGSPAN 35–40in (90–100cm)

Black-headed Gull

Chroicocephalus ridibundus

An abundant breeder in Eurasia, the Black-headed Gull colonized North America in the 20th century. It has become common in Newfoundland after being found nesting there in 1977, and has nested as far south as Cape Cod. However, it has not spread far to the West and remains an infrequent visitor or vagrant over most of the continent.

white flash on outer wings

black trailing edge of wing

black-tipped red bill

NONBREEDING

white nape

very pale gray back

chocolate-brown hood

dark red bill

gray back

dark red legs

BREEDING

brownish "crown-collar"

reddish bill

dark "ear" spot

white underparts

bright red legs

NONBREEDING

VOICE Loud laughing or a chattering kek kek keeaar; vocal at breeding sites.
NESTING Loose mass of vegetation, on ground or on top of other vegetation; 2–3 eggs; 1 brood; Apr–Aug.
FEEDING Insects, small crustaceans, and mollusks; some vegetation; forages in plowed fields; raids garbage dumps.
HABITAT Harbors, inlets, bays, rivers, lakes, and garbage dumps.
LENGTH 13½–14½in (34–37cm)
WINGSPAN 3¼–3½ft (1–1.1m)

Little Gull

Hydrocoloeus minutus

A Eurasian species, the Little Gull is the smallest gull in the world. It was first recorded in North America in the early 1800s, but a nest was not found until 1962, in Ontario. Known nesting areas are still few, but winter numbers have been increasing steadily in recent decades.

black underwings **NONBREEDING**

pale wingtips

pale gray back

pale head, with dark markings

thin dark bill

NONBREEDING

black hood and bill

red legs

BREEDING

VOICE *Nasal kek, kek, kek, kek, reminiscent of a small tern.*
NESTING *Thick, floating mass of dry cattails, reeds, or other vegetation, in marshes and ponds; 3 eggs; 1 brood; May–Aug.*
FEEDING *Flying insects, aquatic invertebrates, such as shrimp, and small fish.*
HABITAT *Extensive freshwater marshes while breeding; sea coasts and sewage outfalls in winter.*
LENGTH *10–12in (25–30cm)*
WINGSPAN *23½–26in (60–65cm)*

Laughing Gull

Leucophaeus atricilla

The distinctive call of the Laughing Gull is a familiar sound in spring and summer along the East Coast. Greatly reduced in the 19th century by egg collectors and the millinery trade, its numbers increased in the 1920s, following protection.

dark gray wings

gray nape

black head

long, slightly drooped bill

broken white eye-ring

white neck

dark gray back

black wingtips

white underparts

long, dark legs

BREEDING

VOICE *Strident laugh, ha...ha...ha...ha...ha; vocal in breeding season; quiet in winter.*
NESTING *Mass of grass on dry land with heavy vegetation, sand, rocks, or salt marshes; 2–4 eggs, 1 brood; Apr–Jul.*
FEEDING *Insects, worms, squid, crabs, crab eggs, larvae; also small fish, garbage, berries.*
HABITAT *Near salt water while breeding; coasts, bays, estuaries, and lakes during migration and winter.*
LENGTH *15½–18in (39–46cm)*
WINGSPAN *3¼–4ft (1–1.2m)*

Franklin's Gull

Leucophaeus pipixcan

Since its discovery, Franklin's Gull has been given many names, one of them being the Rosy Dove—"dove" alluding to its dainty appearance and "rosy" to the pink blush of its undersides. Its official name honors British Arctic explorer John Franklin, on whose first expedition the bird was discovered in 1823. Unlike other gulls, this species has two complete molts each year. As a result, its plumage rarely appears scruffy and usually looks fresh.

dark back of head

dark gray wings

gray back

short, straight bill

black wingtips bordered by white band

black head

dark gray back

broken white eye-ring

red bill

white in outer wing feathers

pink blush underneath

VOICE *Nasal weeh-a, weeh-a; shrill kuk kuk kuk kuk; extremely vocal on breeding colonies.*
NESTING *Floating mass of bulrushes or other plants, refreshed as nest sinks; 2–4 eggs; 1 brood; Apr–Jul.*
FEEDING *Earthworms, insects, and some seeds during breeding; opportunistic feeder during migration and winter.*
HABITAT *High prairies near water while breeding; agricultural areas during migration.*
LENGTH *12½–14in (32–36cm)*
WINGSPAN *33–37in (85–95cm)*

Ring-billed Gull

S

Larus delawarensis

One of the most common gulls in North America, the medium-sized Ring-billed Gull is distinguished by the black band on its yellow bill. From the mid-19th to the early 20th century, population numbers crashed due to egg and plumage hunting and habitat loss. Protection allowed the species to make a spectacular comeback, and in the 1990s, there were an estimated 3–4 million birds. It can often be seen scavenging in parking lots at malls and picnic sites.

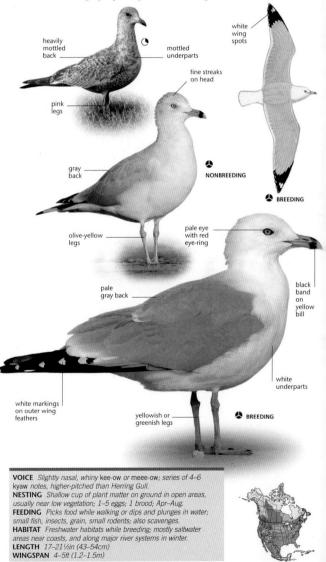

heavily mottled back

mottled underparts

fine streaks on head

pink legs

white wing spots

gray back

NONBREEDING

olive-yellow legs

BREEDING

pale eye with red eye-ring

pale gray back

black band on yellow bill

white markings on outer wing feathers

yellowish or greenish legs

white underparts

BREEDING

VOICE *Slightly nasal, whiny kee-ow or meee-ow; series of 4–6 kyaw notes, higher-pitched than Herring Gull.*
NESTING *Shallow cup of plant matter on ground in open areas, usually near low vegetation; 1–5 eggs; 1 brood; Apr–Aug.*
FEEDING *Picks food while walking or dips and plunges in water; small fish, insects, grain, small rodents; also scavenges.*
HABITAT *Freshwater habitats while breeding; mostly saltwater areas near coasts, and along major river systems in winter.*
LENGTH *17–21½in (43–54cm)*
WINGSPAN *4–5ft (1.2–1.5m)*

Herring Gull

S

Larus argentatus

The Herring Gull is the archetypal, large "white-headed" gull that nearly all other gulls are compared to. When people mention "seagulls" they are usually referring to this species; however, the Herring Gull, like most other gulls, does not commonly go far out to sea—it is a bird of near-shore waters, coasts, lakes, rivers, and inland waterways. Now very common, the Herring Gull was almost wiped out in the late 19th and early 20th centuries by plumage hunters and egg collectors.

streaked head and neck

🌓 NONBREEDING

white spots near wingtips

gray wings

🌓 BREEDING

mottled brown back

barred brown body

white head and neck

🌓 1ST ❄

gray back

large yellow bill with red spot

white underparts

black outer wing feathers

pink legs

🌓 BREEDING

VOICE *High-pitched, shrill, repeated heyaa…heyaa…heyaa…heyaa.*
NESTING *Shallow bowl on ground, lined with feathers, vegetation, detritus; 2–4 eggs; 1 brood; Apr–Aug.*
FEEDING *Fish, crustaceans, mollusks, worms; eggs and chicks of other seabirds; scavenges carrion, garbage; steals from other birds.*
HABITAT *Coasts, and inland on lakes, rivers, reservoirs, and garbage dumps.*
LENGTH *22–26in (56–66cm)*
WINGSPAN *4–5ft (1.2–1.5m)*

Iceland Gull

S

Larus glaucoides

Iceland Gulls of the subspecies *kumlieni* (seen in the images here) are the most familiar form of this species in North America. Young birds have a dark tail band and brown streaks on the wingtip, while adults vary from white wingtips to gray with white spots. A darker subspecies, *thayeri*, breeds on Arctic islands west of the *kumlieni*'s range, and has black-and-white wingtips and a darker eye. Thayer's Gull was considered to be a different species until 2017, when it was grouped with the Iceland Gull. The "Iceland" form of the gull, *L. g. glaucoides*, breeds in Greenland but is found farther eastward in winter, including in Iceland.

brown, barred plumage

gray wingtips

blackish bill

🌓 1ST ❄

🌓 ❄

short, pale yellow bill with red spot

markedly streaked head

gray back

🌓 ❄
(L. g. kumlieni)

wingtip white or marked with gray

white belly

pink legs

VOICE Clew, clew, clew or kak-kak-kak; *virtually silent on wintering grounds.*
NESTING *Loose nest of moss, vegetation, and feathers, usually on narrow rock ledge; 2–3 eggs; 1 brood; May–Aug.*
FEEDING *Small fish while in flight; crustaceans, mollusks, carrion, and garbage.*
HABITAT *Ledges on vertical sea cliffs while breeding; open water along coastline and occasionally Great Lakes in winter.*
LENGTH *20½–23½in (52–60cm)*
WINGSPAN *4½–5ft (1.4–1.5m)*

Lesser Black-backed Gull ⓢ

Larus fuscus

This bird has become an annual winter visitor to the East Coast of North America.
Nearly all the Lesser Black-backed Gulls found in North America are of the
Icelandic and western European subspecies *L. f. graellsii*, with a slate-gray back.
Another European subspecies, with a much darker back, has rarely
been reported in North America.

streaked head
and neck

black wingtips
with white spot

slate-
gray back

🅰 NONBREEDING

yellow
eye

white
underparts

🅰 NONBREEDING

dull
yellow legs

white
head

yellow bill
with red spot

🅰 BREEDING

bright
yellow legs

VOICE Kyow...yow...yow...yow, similar to
Herring Gull; also a deeper and throaty,
repeated gah-gah-gah-gah.
NESTING Scrape on ground lined with lichens,
grass, and feathers; 3 eggs; 1 brood; Apr–Sep.
FEEDING Mollusks, crustaceans, and various
insects; also scavenges carrion and garbage.
HABITAT Winter visitor to eastern coast, at
harbors and near fishing boats, and inland
at lakeshores and landfills.
LENGTH 20½–26in (52–67cm)
WINGSPAN 4¼–5ft (1.3–1.5m)

Glaucous Gull ⓢ

Larus hyperboreus

The Glaucous Gull is the largest of the "white-winged" gulls; it appears like a large
white specter among its smaller, darker cousins. In the Arctic, successful pairs of
Glaucous Gulls maintain pair bonds with their mates for years, often returning
to the same nest site year after year.

streaking
on head

yellow
bill with
distinct
red spot

white
head

pale gray
upperparts

white
underparts

white
wingtips

pink
legs

mottled pale
brown back

pale brown
underparts

🌓 1ST ❄

VOICE Similar to the Herring Gull, but slightly
harsher and deeper; hoarse, nasal ku-ku-ku.
NESTING Shallow cup, lined with vegetation
on ground, at edge of tundra pools, on cliffs
and islands; 1–3 eggs; 1 brood; May–Jul.
FEEDING Fish, crustaceans, mollusks; also
eggs and chicks of waterfowl, small seabirds,
and small mammals.
HABITAT High-Arctic coast while breeding;
coastlines and the Great Lakes in winter.
LENGTH 26–30in (65–75cm)
WINGSPAN 5–6ft (1.5–1.8m)

Great Black-backed Gull

Larus marinus

The largest gull in North America, the Great Black-backed Gull is an effective predator that also benefits from scavenging other seabirds and coastal prey. It is known for its aggressive disposition, often taking eider ducklings for food. In breeding colonies, it is especially defensive in the morning, early evening, and after the chicks hatch. Despite this gull's heavy, lumbering flight, the adults effectively dive at ground predators, striking with their feet.

whitish head

large white spot on wingtips

BREEDING

black bill

speckled back

1ST

red eye-ring

white head and neck

yellow bill with red spot

black upperparts

white tips to outer feathers

white underparts

BREEDING

pale pink legs and feet

VOICE *Often repeated, low-pitched heyaa…heyaa…heyaa…heyaa, similar to Herring Gull.*
NESTING *Bowl on ground, lined with vegetation, feathers, trash; 2–3 eggs; 1 brood; Apr–Aug.*
FEEDING *Fish, marine invertebrates, small mammals; eggs, nestlings and fledglings, adult seabirds, and waterfowl.*
HABITAT *Islands, barrier beaches, salt marshes, and sand dunes while breeding; coastlines, major rivers, and harbors in winter.*
LENGTH *28–31in (71–79cm)*
WINGSPAN *5–5¼ft (1.5–1.6m)*

Least Tern

Sternula antillarum

The Least Tern is the smallest North American tern. In summer, its distinctive black cap and white forehead distinguish it from other terns. This agile bird plunge-dives for prey without submerging; males offer fish to females during courtship. In the 1800s, Least Terns declined rapidly because their feathers were prized fashion accessories. Protected by law, their numbers grew, but they are still threatened by habitat loss and predators, such as foxes and skunks, that thrive near their coastal homes.

dark outer wing feathers

BREEDING

forked tail

streaked crown

patterned back

mostly dark bill

black cap with white forehead

yellow bill

pale gray back

two dark outer wing feathers

white underparts

yellow legs

BREEDING

VOICE Extremely vocal during breeding; a high-pitched ki-deek, ki-deek; also a rapid, almost nonstop chatter.
NESTING Shallow scrape on ground lined with dry vegetation, broken shells, and pebbles; 2–3 eggs; 1 brood; Apr–Sep.
FEEDING Fish and aquatic invertebrates, also insects.
HABITAT Favors sandy barrier islands, beaches, and sandbars; also breeds near rivers, lakes, and reservoirs.
LENGTH 8½–9in (21–23cm)
WINGSPAN 19–21in (48–53cm)

Gull-billed Tern

Ⓢ

Gelochelidon nilotica

Its heavy build, thick bill, long, pointed wings, and varied diet make this tern more gull-like than most terns. Gull-billed Terns often nest in colonies with other terns and skimmers, occasionally hunting their chicks and stealing prey. During the 1800s, they were hunted for their eggs and feathers. Gull-billed Tern numbers have since increased, but nesting site disturbances still threaten these birds.

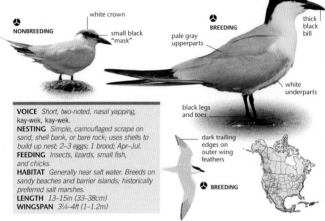

NONBREEDING — white crown, small black "mask"

BREEDING — black cap, thick black bill, pale gray upperparts, white underparts, black legs and toes, dark trailing edges on outer wing feathers

BREEDING

VOICE *Short, two-noted, nasal yapping, kay-wek, kay-wek.*
NESTING *Simple, camouflaged scrape on sand, shell bank, or bare rock; uses shells to build up nest; 2–3 eggs; 1 brood; Apr–Jul.*
FEEDING *Insects, lizards, small fish, and chicks.*
HABITAT *Generally near salt water. Breeds on sandy beaches and barrier islands; historically preferred salt marshes.*
LENGTH *13–15in (33–38cm)*
WINGSPAN *3¼–4ft (1–1.2m)*

Caspian Tern

Ⓢ

Hydroprogne caspia

The Caspian Tern is the world's largest tern. Unlike other "black-capped" terns, it never has a completely white forehead, even in winter. It steals prey from other seabirds, and also snatches eggs from, and hunts the nestlings of, other gulls and terns. It aggressively defends its nesting territory, giving hoarse alarm calls, and rhythmically opening and closing its beak in a threatening display.

short tail, dark-tipped outer wing feathers

BREEDING

thick red bill with dark tip, slightly crested black cap, light gray back, white underparts, streaked dark crown, black legs and feet

BREEDING

VOICE *Hoarse, deep kraaa, kraaa; also barks at intruders; male's wings vibrate loudly in courtship flight.*
NESTING *Shallow scrape on ground; 2–3 eggs; 1 brood; May–Aug.*
FEEDING *Plunges into water to snatch fish, barnacles, and snails.*
HABITAT *Interior lakes, salt marshes, and coastal barrier islands while breeding; wetlands during migration; coasts in winter.*
LENGTH *18½–21½in (47–54cm)*
WINGSPAN *4¼–5ft (1.3–1.5m)*

NONBREEDING

Black Tern

Chlidonias niger

This marsh-dwelling tern undergoes a remarkable change in appearance from summer to winter. The Black Tern's breeding plumage resembles the closely related White-winged Tern, an accidental visitor to North America. The Black Tern's nonbreeding plumage is much paler than its breeding plumage—the head turns white with irregular black streaks, and the neck, breast, and belly become whitish-gray.

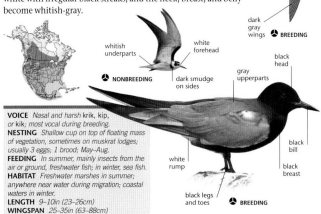

dark gray tail

dark gray wings **BREEDING**

whitish underparts

white forehead

NONBREEDING

dark smudge on sides

black head

gray upperparts

black bill

black breast

white rump

black legs and toes **BREEDING**

VOICE *Nasal and harsh krik, kip, or kik; most vocal during breeding.*
NESTING *Shallow cup on top of floating mass of vegetation, sometimes on muskrat lodges; usually 3 eggs; 1 brood; May–Aug.*
FEEDING *In summer, mainly insects from the air or ground, freshwater fish; in winter, sea fish.*
HABITAT *Freshwater marshes in summer; anywhere near water during migration; coastal waters in winter.*
LENGTH *9–10in (23–26cm)*
WINGSPAN *25–35in (63–88cm)*

Roseate Tern

Sterna dougallii

Mostly found nesting with the Common Tern, the Roseate Tern is paler and more slender. Its bill is black for a short time in the spring before turning at least half red during the nesting season. Pairs glide down from hundreds of feet in the air in courtship flights, swaying side to side with each other. Two females and a male may nest together, sharing egg incubation and rearing of young.

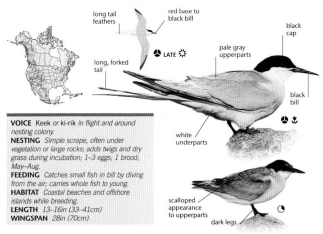

long tail feathers

red base to black bill

LATE ☼

long, forked tail

black cap

pale gray upperparts

black bill

white underparts

scalloped appearance to upperparts

dark legs

VOICE *Keek or ki-rik in flight and around nesting colony.*
NESTING *Simple scrape, often under vegetation or large rocks; adds twigs and dry grass during incubation; 1–3 eggs; 1 brood; May–Aug.*
FEEDING *Catches small fish in bill by diving from the air; carries whole fish to young.*
HABITAT *Coastal beaches and offshore islands while breeding.*
LENGTH *13–16in (33–41cm)*
WINGSPAN *28in (70cm)*

Common Tern

T

Sterna hirundo

One of North America's most widespread terns, the Common Tern was nearly wiped out in the late 19th century by hunters seeking its feathers. The 1918 Migratory Bird Treaty helped protect it, and numbers increased, but populations have declined again in recent decades due to human disturbance, habitat loss, and pollution.

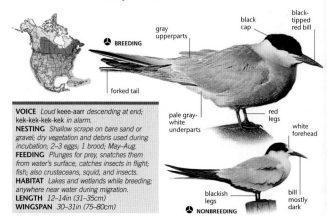

VOICE *Loud keee-aarr descending at end; kek-kek-kek-kek in alarm.*
NESTING *Shallow scrape on bare sand or gravel; dry vegetation and debris used during incubation; 2–3 eggs; 1 brood; May–Aug.*
FEEDING *Plunges for prey, snatches them from water's surface, catches insects in flight; fish; also crustaceans, squid, and insects.*
HABITAT *Lakes and wetlands while breeding; anywhere near water during migration.*
LENGTH *12–14in (31–35cm)*
WINGSPAN *30–31in (75–80cm)*

Arctic Tern

S

Sterna paradisaea

Most Arctic Terns breed in the Arctic, then migrate to the Antarctic seas for the Southern Hemisphere summer before returning north, a round trip of at least 25,000 miles (40,000km). Apart from during migration, it spends its life in areas of near-continuous daylight and rarely comes to land, except to nest. It can be distinguished from the Common Tern by its smaller bill, and shorter legs and neck.

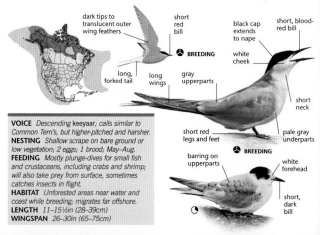

VOICE *Descending keeyaar; calls similar to Common Tern's, but higher-pitched and harsher.*
NESTING *Shallow scrape on bare ground or low vegetation; 2 eggs; 1 brood; May–Aug.*
FEEDING *Mostly plunge-dives for small fish and crustaceans, including crabs and shrimp; will also take prey from surface, sometimes catches insects in flight.*
HABITAT *Unforested areas near water and coast while breeding; migrates far offshore.*
LENGTH *11–15½in (28–39cm)*
WINGSPAN *26–30in (65–75cm)*

Forster's Tern

S

Sterna forsteri

This medium-sized tern can be differentiated from the Common Tern by its lighter outer wing feathers and longer tail. Early naturalists could not tell the two species apart until 1834, when English botanist Thomas Nuttall made the distinction. He named this tern after Johann Reinhold Forster, a naturalist who accompanied the English explorer Captain Cook on his second voyage (1772–75).

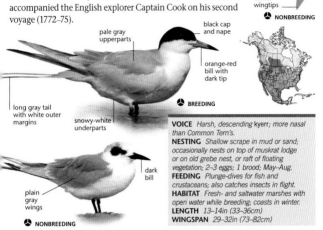

deeply forked tail

gray wings with slightly darker wingtips

NONBREEDING

pale gray upperparts

black cap and nape

orange-red bill with dark tip

long gray tail with white outer margins

snowy-white underparts

BREEDING

dark bill

plain gray wings

NONBREEDING

VOICE *Harsh, descending kyerr; more nasal than Common Tern's.*
NESTING *Shallow scrape in mud or sand; occasionally nests on top of muskrat lodge or on old grebe nest, or raft of floating vegetation; 2–3 eggs; 1 brood; May–Aug.*
FEEDING *Plunge-dives for fish and crustaceans; also catches insects in flight.*
HABITAT *Fresh- and saltwater marshes with open water while breeding; coasts in winter.*
LENGTH *13–14in (33–36cm)*
WINGSPAN *29–32in (73–82cm)*

Royal Tern

S

Thalasseus maximus

Royal Terns briefly sport a full black cap at the beginning of the breeding season; their foreheads are otherwise pure white. Their bill color is variable, ranging from yellowish-orange to red. Perhaps the red bills caused renowned ornithologist John James Audubon to confuse Royal Terns with the larger Caspian Terns. Unlike most other terns, Royal Tern pair bonds may not last from one year to the next.

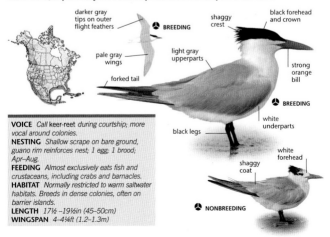

darker gray tips on outer flight feathers

BREEDING

pale gray wings

forked tail

shaggy crest

black forehead and crown

light gray upperparts

strong orange bill

BREEDING

white underparts

black legs

shaggy coat

white forehead

NONBREEDING

VOICE *Call keer-reet during courtship; more vocal around colonies.*
NESTING *Shallow scrape on bare ground, guano rim reinforces nest; 1 egg; 1 brood; Apr–Aug.*
FEEDING *Almost exclusively eats fish and crustaceans, including crabs and barnacles.*
HABITAT *Normally restricted to warm saltwater habitats. Breeds in dense colonies, often on barrier islands.*
LENGTH *17½–19½in (45–50cm)*
WINGSPAN *4–4¼ft (1.2–1.3m)*

Black Skimmer

Rynchops niger

The Black Skimmer's long, orange-red and black bill makes it easy to identify. The bill is compressed laterally into a knifelike shape, with the lower mandible about 1in (2.5cm) longer than the upper—perfect for skimming the sea surface and snapping shut on its prey. Although usually grouped with gulls and terns, the skimmer's unique bill and feeding behavior led some ornithologists to consider it a separate family. When disturbed, Black Skimmer chicks camouflage themselves by kicking sand over their backs.

long wing

short, forked tail

BREEDING

mottled brown upperparts

bill duller than adult

white forehead

orange-red and black bill

lower half of bill longer than upper

black upperparts

long, thick neck

BREEDING

white underparts

orange-red legs

VOICE *Calls given by both sexes, often at night; distinctive doglike yapping.*
NESTING *Shallow scrape or depression on sandy beach, dead saltmarsh vegetation, or gravel rooftops; 1–5 eggs; 1 brood; May–Aug.*
FEEDING *Catches small fish.*
HABITAT *Rarely far from salt water. Found on beaches; feeds in bays, estuaries, lagoons, and areas with relatively calm waters.*
LENGTH *15½–19½in (40–50cm)*
WINGSPAN *3½–4¼ft (1.1–1.3m)*

Pigeons and Doves

Pigeons and doves are all fairly heavy, plump birds with relatively small heads and short necks. They also possess slender bills, with their nostrils positioned in a bumpy mound at the base. Members of this family are powerful and agile fliers. When alarmed, they burst into flight with their wings emitting a distinctive clapping or swishing sound. Pigeons and doves produce a nutritious "crop-milk," which they secrete to feed their young. Despite human activity having severely affected members of this family in the past, the introduced Rock Pigeon has adapted and proliferated worldwide, as has the recently introduced Eurasian Collared-Dove. Among the species native to North America, only the elegant Mourning Dove is as widespread as the various species of introduced birds.

DOVE IN THE SUN
The Mourning Dove sunbathes each side of its body in turn, its wings and tail outspread.

Rock Pigeon

S

Columba livia

The Rock Pigeon was introduced to the Atlantic Coast of North America by 17th-century colonists. Now feral, this species is found all over the continent, especially around farms, cities, and towns. It comes in a wide variety of plumage colors and patterns, including bluish-gray, checkered, rusty-red, and nearly all-white. Its wings usually have two dark bars on them—unique among North American pigeons.

black wing bars

white underwings

white rump

two black wing bars

iridescence on neck

gray back

short bill

dark-tipped tail

ANCESTRAL FORM

variably colored body

no wing bars

FERAL

VOICE *Soft, gurgling* coo, roo-c'too-coo, *for courtship and threat.*
NESTING *Twig nest on flat, sheltered surface, such as caves, rocky outcrops, and buildings; 2 eggs; several broods; year-round.*
FEEDING *Seeds, fruit, and rarely insects; human foods, such as popcorn, bread, peanuts; various farm crops in rural areas.*
HABITAT *Nests in human structures of all sorts; urban areas, farmland, and rocky cliffs.*
LENGTH *11–14in (28–36cm)*
WINGSPAN *20–26in (51–67cm)*

White-crowned Pigeon

T

Patagioenas leucocephala

The large White-crowned Pigeon has a distinctive white crown and slate-gray back. In North America, this bird is only found in the Florida Keys and Everglades. Although more nervous around humans than Rock Pigeons, White-crowned Pigeons still feed around hotels and backyards. Since they subsist almost solely on fruit, fruit trees are key to their survival. Habitat loss and hunting pose threats to this species.

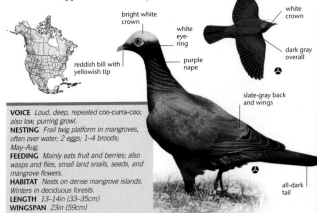

bright white crown

white eye-ring

reddish bill with yellowish tip

purple nape

white crown

dark gray overall

slate-gray back and wings

all-dark tail

VOICE *Loud, deep, repeated* coo-curra-coo; *also low, purring growl.*
NESTING *Frail twig platform in mangroves, often over water; 2 eggs; 1–4 broods; May–Aug.*
FEEDING *Mainly eats fruit and berries; also wasps and flies, small land snails, seeds, and mangrove flowers.*
HABITAT *Nests on dense mangrove islands. Winters in deciduous forests.*
LENGTH *13–14in (33–35cm)*
WINGSPAN *23in (59cm)*

Eurasian Collared-Dove ⓢ

Streptopelia decaocto

The Eurasian Collared-Dove is easily recognized by the black collar on the back of its neck and its square tail. Introduced in the Bahamas in the mid-1970s, this species is spreading rapidly across the continental mainland. It regularly nests and feeds in urban areas. Based on sightings from locations all over North America, the Eurasian Collared-Dove will soon be a common species.

black collar
on hind neck

pale
gray body

dark
bill

square
tail

gray undertail
wing feathers

gray
wing
feathers

dark outer
wing feathers

VOICE *Repeated four-note* coo-hoo-HOO-cook, *low pitched; harsh, nasal* krreeew *in flight.*
NESTING *Platform of twigs, stems, and grasses in trees or on buildings; 2 eggs; multiple broods; Mar–Nov.*
FEEDING *Seed and grain, plant stems and leaves, berries, and some invertebrates.*
HABITAT *Suburban and urban areas (although not large cities); agricultural areas with deciduous trees.*
LENGTH *11½–12in (29–30cm)*
WINGSPAN *14in (35cm)*

Mourning Dove ⓢ

Zenaida macroura

One of the most familiar of North American birds, the Mourning Dove has a grayish-tan body with a pale, rosy breast and black spots on folded wings, and is well known to those who live on farms and in suburbia. There are two subspecies—the larger, grayish-brown *Z. m. carolinensis* in the East, and the smaller, paler *Z. m. marginella* in the West.

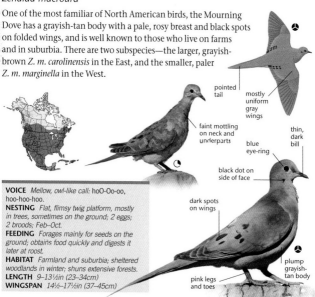

pointed
tail

mostly
uniform
gray wings

faint mottling
on neck and
underparts

thin,
dark
bill

blue
eye-ring

black dot on
side of face

dark spots
on wings

plump
grayish-
tan body

pink legs
and toes

VOICE *Mellow, owl-like call:* hoO-Oo-oo, hoo-hoo-hoo.
NESTING *Flat, flimsy twig platform, mostly in trees, sometimes on the ground; 2 eggs; 2 broods; Feb–Oct.*
FEEDING *Forages mainly for seeds on the ground; obtains food quickly and digests it later at roost.*
HABITAT *Farmland and suburbia; sheltered woodlands in winter; shuns extensive forests.*
LENGTH *9–13½in (23–34cm)*
WINGSPAN *14½–17½in (37–45cm)*

Common Ground Dove

Columbina passerina

Only slightly larger than a sparrow, the Common Ground Dove is the smallest North American dove. It is recognizable by prominent black wing spots, reddish wings, and a square, blackish tail. Unlike other doves, it retains its pair bond throughout the year and tends not to form flocks. Common Ground Doves blend in with the ground and can be overlooked as they quietly feed, mostly along the southernmost coastal regions of the continent.

rufous outer wing feathers

♂

short tail

pinkish or red base to bill

♀

scaly gray breast

scaly-looking head

black spots on wings

♂

square tail

scaly breast with pink tinge

VOICE Simple, ascending double-noted wah-up, repeated every 2–3 seconds.
NESTING Depression on ground lined with grass and palm fibers, or frail nest in trees; 2 eggs; several broods; Apr–Aug.
FEEDING Grass and weed seeds, grains, small berries, insects, and snails; also seeds from feeders.
HABITAT Prefers dry, sandy areas with short, open vegetation; other habitats include citrus groves and mesquite thickets.
LENGTH 6–7in (15–18cm)
WINGSPAN 11in (28cm)

Cuckoos

The family Cuculidae includes typical cuckoos, anis, and roadrunners. Cuckoos favor forested areas, while anis prefer more open bush country. Cuckoos have slender bodies and long tails, along with distinctive zygodactyl feet, with the two inner toes pointing forward and the two outer toes pointing backward. In flight, they are often mistaken for small birds of prey.

Cuckoos are notorious for laying eggs in other birds' nests, but of the three species in North America, one (Mangrove Cuckoo) never does this. The two others (Yellow-billed and Black-billed Cuckoos) build their own nest and raise their own offspring, but less often, parasitize those of other other species and, even, other nests of the same species.

Cuckoos are mainly insectivorous, specializing in caterpillars from the ground or gleaned from foliage. Anis have a more varied diet. They are sociable, blackish, heavy-billed birds, found only in Florida and along the Gulf Coast but they are more widespread in Central America.

TOUCH PREDATOR
Mangrove Cuckoo uses its thick bill to take larger prey like lizards as it skulks through coastal mangrove forests.

Black-billed Cuckoo

D

Coccyzus erythropthalmus

The Black-billed Cuckoo is usually difficult to spot because of its secretive nature and dense, leafy habitat. This species feeds mainly on spiny caterpillars, but the spines of these insects can become lodged in the cuckoo's stomach, obstructing digestion, so the bird periodically sheds its stomach lining to clear it. During the breeding season, the birds call throughout the night.

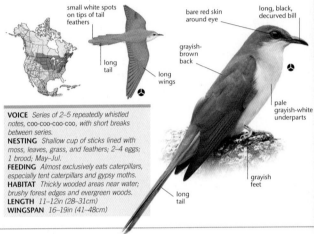

small white spots on tips of tail feathers

long tail

long wings

bare red skin around eye

long, black, decurved bill

grayish-brown back

pale grayish-white underparts

grayish feet

long tail

VOICE Series of 2–5 repeatedly whistled notes, coo-coo-coo-coo, with short breaks between series.
NESTING Shallow cup of sticks lined with moss, leaves, grass, and feathers; 2–4 eggs; 1 brood; May–Jul.
FEEDING Almost exclusively eats caterpillars, especially tent caterpillars and gypsy moths.
HABITAT Thickly wooded areas near water; brushy forest edges and evergreen woods.
LENGTH 11–12in (28–31cm)
WINGSPAN 16–19in (41–48cm)

Yellow-billed Cuckoo

D

Coccyzus americanus

The Yellow-billed Cuckoo is a shy, slow-moving bird with a habit of calling more often on cloudy days, earning it the nickname "rain crow." In addition to raising their young in their own nest, females occasionally lay eggs in the nests of other species, including the Black-billed Cuckoo. The host species may be chosen on the basis of how closely the color of its eggs matches those of its own.

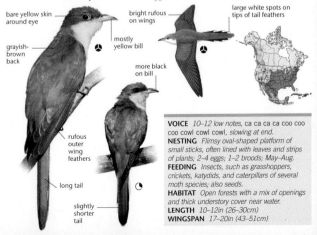

bare yellow skin around eye

grayish-brown back

mostly yellow bill

bright rufous on wings

large white spots on tips of tail feathers

more black on bill

rufous outer wing feathers

long tail

slightly shorter tail

VOICE 10–12 low notes, ca ca ca ca coo coo coo cowl cowl cowl, slowing at end.
NESTING Flimsy oval-shaped platform of small sticks, often lined with leaves and strips of plants; 2–4 eggs; 1–2 broods; May–Aug.
FEEDING Insects, such as grasshoppers, crickets, katydids, and caterpillars of several moth species; also seeds.
HABITAT Open forests with a mix of openings and thick understory cover near water.
LENGTH 10–12in (26–30cm)
WINGSPAN 17–20in (43–51cm)

Mangrove Cuckoo

(S)

Coccyzus minor

This bird's solitary, elusive behavior and preference for dense, nearly inaccessible mangrove forests make it one of the least-studied North American birds. This, combined with human development in Florida's mangrove areas, makes this cuckoo's future uncertain. Its black mask distinguishes it from North America's other two cuckoo species; its thick bill is useful for capturing larger prey, including lizards.

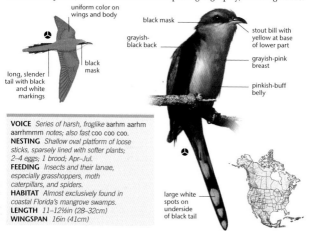

uniform color on wings and body

black mask

grayish-black back

black mask

long, slender tail with black and white markings

stout bill with yellow at base of lower part

grayish-pink breast

pinkish-buff belly

large white spots on underside of black tail

VOICE Series of harsh, froglike aarhm aarhm aarrhmmm notes; also fast coo coo coo.
NESTING Shallow oval platform of loose sticks, sparsely lined with softer plants; 2–4 eggs; 1 brood; Apr–Jul.
FEEDING Insects and their larvae, especially grasshoppers, moth caterpillars, and spiders.
HABITAT Almost exclusively found in coastal Florida's mangrove swamps.
LENGTH 11–12½in (28–32cm)
WINGSPAN 16in (41cm)

Smooth-billed Ani

(S) (D)

Crotophaga ani

In the US, the Smooth-billed Ani occurs only in southern Florida. The bird colonized Florida in the early 1930s, but for unknown reasons, declined in the early 1980s. Scrambling through grass and along low tree branches, Smooth-billed Anis capture insects and other prey flushed by grazing cattle and power mowers. This bird breeds communally, with multiple females laying eggs in the same nest.

upper mandible lacks grooves

dark back

long tail

quick wingbeats and choppy glide with wings held flat

very long tail

central tail feathers longest, rounded at edge

VOICE Main call a whiny, ascending yaahnee.
NESTING Open cup of twigs, lined with leaves, set in fork of dense, thorny shrub or tree.
FEEDING Arthropods, including insects; lizards, frogs, and some fruit.
HABITAT Occurs in shrubby areas, agricultural lands, and hedges; tropical savannas in the Caribbean and South America.
LENGTH 14½in (37cm)
WINGSPAN 18½in (47cm)

Owls

Most owls are active primarily at night and have developed adaptations for living in low-light environments. Their large eyes are sensitive enough to see in the dark and face forward to maximize binocular vision. Since the eyes are somewhat fixed in their sockets, a flexible neck allows the owls to turn their heads almost 270°. Ears are offset on each side of the head to help identify the source of a sound. Some species have "ear" tufts, which are used for camouflage and communication, not for hearing. Many owls have serrations on the forward edges of their flight feathers to cushion airflow, so their flight is silent while stalking prey. All North American owls are predatory to some degree, and they inhabit most areas of the continent. The Burrowing Owl is unique in that it hunts during the day and nests underground.

SHARP HEARING
The Great Gray Owl can hunt by sound alone, allowing it to locate and capture prey hidden even beneath a thick snow cover.

Barn Owl

Tyto alba

Aptly named, the Barn Owl inhabits old sheds, sheltered rafters, and empty buildings in rural fields. It is secretive and primarily nocturnal, flying undetected until its screeching call pierces the air. The Barn Owl has been affected by modern farming practices, which have cut prey populations and reduced the number of barns for nesting.

barring on wings and tail

head lacks "ear" tufts

long wings

rounded, heart-shaped facial disk

ruff surrounds facial disk

relatively small, dark eyes

pale buff upperparts

gray-and-black spots

white underparts

feathered legs

VOICE *Loud, raspy, screeching shriek, shkreee, often in flight; clicking sounds associated with courtship.*
NESTING *Unlined cavity in tree, cave, building, hay bale, or nest box; 5–7 eggs; 1–2 broods; Mar–Sep.*
FEEDING *Hunts on the wing for small rodents, such as mice.*
HABITAT *Open habitats, such as desert, grassland, and fields.*
LENGTH *12½–15½in (32–40cm)*
WINGSPAN *3¼ft (100cm)*

Eastern Screech-Owl

Megascops asio

This widespread little owl has adapted to suburban areas, and its distinctive call is a familiar sound across the eastern US at almost any time of the year. An entirely nocturnal species, it may be found roosting during the day in a birdhouse or tree cavity. With gray and red color morphs, this species shows considerably more plumage variation than the Western Screech-Owl.

dark gray bars on short, rounded wings

short tail

streaked underparts

"ear" tufts

yellow eyes

white spots on inner wing feathers

feathered legs

GRAY FORM

VOICE *Descending whinny, often used in movie soundtracks; also an even trill; occasional barks and screeches.*
NESTING *Lays eggs in tree cavity, woodpecker hole, nest box; 2–6 eggs; 1 brood; Mar–Aug.*
FEEDING *Insects, earthworms, rodents, songbirds, fish, frogs, snakes, lizards.*
HABITAT *Variety of different lowland wooded areas; suburban and urban parks; usually avoids mountain forests.*
LENGTH *6½–10in (16–25cm)*
WINGSPAN *19–24in (48–61cm)*

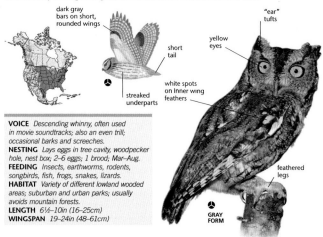

Snowy Owl

S

Bubo scandiacus

An icon of the far north, the Snowy Owl occasionally appears far to the south of its usual range. It is a bird of the open tundra, where it hunts from headlands or hummocks and nests on the ground. In such a harsh environment, the Snowy Owl largely depends on lemmings for prey. It is fiercely territorial, and will valiantly defend its young in the nest even against larger animals, such as the Arctic Fox.

white face

flecked gray-brown

dusky barring

variably barred underparts

large, round head

yellow eyes

variable barring on wings

nearly all-white breast

feathered legs

VOICE *Deep hoots, doubled or given in a short series, usually by male; also rattles, whistles, and hisses.*
NESTING *Scrape on a mound in short vegetation or dirt, with no lining; 3–12 eggs; 1 brood; May–Sep.*
FEEDING *Mostly hunts lemmings, but takes whatever small mammals and birds it can find, and even occasionally fish.*
HABITAT *Tundra while breeding; open, tree-less spaces, such as dunes, marshes, and airfields.*
LENGTH *20–27in (51–68cm)*
WINGSPAN *4¼–5¼ft (1.3–1.6m)*

Great Horned Owl

Bubo virginianus

The Great Horned Owl is perhaps the archetypal owl. Large and adaptable, it is resident from Alaska to Tierra del Fuego. With such a big range, geographical variation occurs; at least 13 subspecies have been described. The Great Horned Owl's deep hoots are easily recognized, and can often be heard in movie soundtracks. The bird is the top predator in its food chain, often killing and eating other owls, and even skunks. An early breeder and a fierce defender of its young, it starts hooting in the middle of winter, and often lays its eggs in January.

large "ear" tufts

yellow eyes

rusty facial disk

long, broad wing

dark arc on wing

heavy barring of underparts

white throat and chin

mottled, barred brownish and gray upperparts

barring on undertail

barred underparts

VOICE *Series of hoots whoo-hoo-oo-o; also screams, barks, and hisses; female higher-pitched.*
NESTING *Old stick nest in tree, exposed cavity, cliff, human structure, or on the ground; 1–5 eggs; 1 brood; Jan–Apr.*
FEEDING *Mammals, reptiles, amphibians, birds, and insects; mostly nocturnal.*
HABITAT *Prefers fragmented landscapes: desert, swamp, prairie, woodland, and urban areas.*
LENGTH *18–25in (46–63cm)*
WINGSPAN *3–5ft (0.9–1.6m)*

Barred Owl

Ⓢ

Strix varia

The Barred Owl is more adaptable and aggressive than its close relative in the West, the Spotted Owl. The former's recent range expansion has brought the two species into closer contact, which has led to Barred Owls displacing and even killing Spotted Owls, as well as occasional interbreeding. The Barred Owl is mostly nocturnal, but may also call or hunt during the day.

rounded wings

large, round head

brown upperparts

heavy white spotting

dark eyes

conspicuously yellowish bill

barred tail

barring on breast

streaking on belly

VOICE *Series of hoots in rhythm:* who-cooks-for-you, who-cooks-for-you-all; *also pair duetting, cawing, cackling, and guttural sounds.*
NESTING *No obvious nest; lays eggs in broken-off branches, cavities, old stick nests; 1–5 eggs; 1 brood; Jan–Sep.*
FEEDING *Perches then pounces; small mammals, birds, amphibians, reptiles, insects, and spiders.*
HABITAT *Variety of wooded habitats, such as conifer rainforest, mixed hardwoods, and cypress swamps.*
LENGTH *17–19½in (43–50cm)*
WINGSPAN *3½ft (1.1m)*

Great Gray Owl ⓢ

Strix nebulosa

With a thick layer of feathers that insulates it against cold northern winters, the Great Gray Owl is North America's tallest owl (although not its heaviest). Often able to detect prey by sound alone, it will even plunge through deep snow or into a burrow to snatch unseen prey. This somewhat nomadic bird, prone to occasional invasions in the south, may also hunt by daylight, usually at dawn or dusk.

long wings

white crescents between small yellow eyes

gray-and-white facial disks

black-and-white chin

mottled gray upperparts

thickset body

heavily streaked underparts

VOICE Slow series of deep hoots, evenly spaced; variety of hisses and chattering noises around nest site.
NESTING Reuses old eagle or hawk nests, broken-off trees; 2–5 eggs; 1 brood; Mar–Jul.
FEEDING Rodents and other small mammals; waits to pounce from perch or hunts in flight.
HABITAT Taiga and muskeg; fir, spruce, and pine forests, sometimes swampy.
LENGTH 24–33in (61–84cm)
WINGSPAN 4½ft (1.4m)

Northern Hawk Owl ⓢ

Surnia ulula

The Northern Hawk Owl is streamlined, a powerful flier, and an active daytime hunter. It is patchily distributed across northern North American forests, far from most human settlements, and thus is seldom seen on its breeding grounds. In winter, the bird is somewhat nomadic, and is occasionally seen south of its breeding range for a few days or weeks in southern Canada and the northern US.

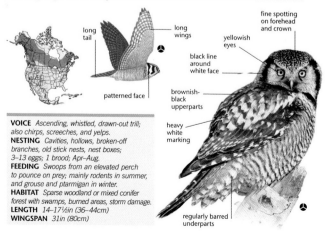

long tail

long wings

patterned face

fine spotting on forehead and crown

yellowish eyes

black line around white face

brownish-black upperparts

heavy white marking

regularly barred underparts

VOICE Ascending, whistled, drawn-out trill; also chirps, screeches, and yelps.
NESTING Cavities, hollows, broken-off branches, old stick nests, nest boxes; 3–13 eggs; 1 brood; Apr–Aug.
FEEDING Swoops from an elevated perch to pounce on prey; mainly rodents in summer, and grouse and ptarmigan in winter.
HABITAT Sparse woodland or mixed conifer forest with swamps, burned areas, storm damage.
LENGTH 14–17½in (36–44cm)
WINGSPAN 31in (80cm)

Burrowing Owl

Athene cunicularia

The Burrowing Owl is unique among North American owls in nesting underground. It mostly uses the abandoned burrows of prairie dogs, ground squirrels, armadillos, badgers, and other mammals, but will excavate its own burrow with its bill and feet. It usually nests in loose colonies, as well. Active by day or night, the Burrowing Owl hunts prey on foot or on the wing.

short, rounded wings

short tail

chest spotted with white

yellow eyes

white streaking

white contrasting with dark brown band below

white spots

brown upperparts with white spotting

brown streaks on lower belly

long, feathered legs

short tail

VOICE *Coo-cooo, or ha-haaa; nestlings imitate the rattling of a rattlesnake.*
NESTING *Cavity lined with grass, feathers, sometimes animal dung, at end of burrow; 8–10 eggs; 1 brood; Mar–Aug.*
FEEDING *Insects, and occasionally small mammals, birds, reptiles, and amphibians.*
HABITAT *Wide range of open habitats not prone to flooding: pastures, plains, deserts, grasslands, and steppes.*
LENGTH *7½–10in (19–25cm)*
WINGSPAN *21½in (55cm)*

Boreal Owl

Aegolius funereus

The female Boreal Owl is much bigger than the male. Males will mate with two or three females in years when voles and other small rodents are abundant. It is rarely seen, breeding at high elevations in isolated mountain ranges and hunting at night. White spotting on the crown, a grayish bill, and a black facial disk distinguish the Boreal Owl from the Northern Saw-whet Owl.

rounded wings

white-and-brown-streaked underparts

usually flat-topped head, with fine white spots

yellow eyes

pale bill

black border around face

short tail

VOICE *Series of whistles, usually increasing in volume and intensity; screeches and hisses.*
NESTING *Tree cavity, often woodpecker hole; nest boxes; 3–6 eggs; 1 brood; Mar–Jul.*
FEEDING *Small mammals; birds and insects; pounces from elevated perch; sometimes stores prey and uses its body to thaw it.*
HABITAT *Boreal forests of spruce, poplar, aspen, birch, and balsam fir; western populations in subalpine forests of fir, spruce.*
LENGTH *8½–11in (21–28cm)*
WINGSPAN *21½–24in (54–62cm)*

Northern Saw-whet Owl S T

Aegolius acadicus

One of the most secretive yet common and widespread owls in North America, the
Northern Saw-whet Owl is much more often heard than seen. Strictly nocturnal,
it is concealed as it sleeps by day in thick vegetation, usually in conifers, such as
cedars. Although a Saw-whet Owl may use the same site for months if undisturbed,
it is not an easy bird to locate. When it is discovered, it "freezes," and relies on its
camouflage rather than flying off. At night, it watches intently from a perch before
swooping down to snatch its prey.

thin white
streaks on
forehead
and crown

yellow
eyes

dark
bill

brown
streaks

rounded
wings

short
tail

white patch
between eyes

whitish
eyebrows

chestnut-brown
upperparts with
white spots

unmarked white
undertail feathers

VOICE *Long series of rapid whistling notes on a constant pitch similar
to the sharpening or "whetting" of a saw.*
NESTING *Unlined cavity in tree, usually old woodpecker hole or nest
box; 4–7 eggs; 1 brood; Mar–Jul.*
FEEDING *Hunts from elevated perch; small mammals, including
mice and voles; also insects and small birds.*
HABITAT *Coniferous, mixed deciduous, and swampy forests, wooded
wetlands, bogs; open woodlands, shrubby areas in winter.*
LENGTH *7–8½in (18–21cm)*
WINGSPAN *16½–19in (42–48cm)*

Long-eared Owl ⓢ

Asio otus

The widespread Long-eared Owl is seldom seen, being secretive and nocturnal. By day, it roosts, sometimes colonially, high up and out of sight in thick cover, flying out at nightfall to hunt small mammals on the wing over open areas. Its wing feathers have sound-suppressing structures that allow it to fly almost silently to hear the slightest rustle on the ground below and not alert its prey.

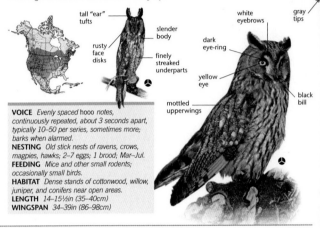

tan patch on outer wing

dark wrist patch

gray tips

tall "ear" tufts

slender body

rusty face disks

finely streaked underparts

white eyebrows

dark eye-ring

yellow eye

mottled upperwings

black bill

VOICE Evenly spaced hooo notes, continuously repeated, about 3 seconds apart, typically 10–50 per series, sometimes more; barks when alarmed.
NESTING Old stick nests of ravens, crows, magpies, hawks; 2–7 eggs; 1 brood; Mar–Jul.
FEEDING Mice and other small rodents; occasionally small birds.
HABITAT Dense stands of cottonwood, willow, juniper, and conifers near open areas.
LENGTH 14–15½in (35–40cm)
WINGSPAN 34–39in (86–98cm)

Short-eared Owl ⓓ

Asio flammeus

This owl is often seen on cloudy days or toward dusk, soaring back and forth low over open fields, sometimes with Northern Harriers. Although territorial in the breeding season, it sometimes winters in communal roosts of up to 200 birds, occasionally alongside Long-eared Owls. Unlike other North American owls, the Short-eared Owl builds its own nest.

black wingtips

row of pale spots along sides of back

dark wrist patch

orange-buff to yellowish outer wings

narrow, dark bar

whitish underwing

white belly

short "ear" tufts, usually not visible

blackish eye-ring

yellow eyes

pale face disks

large, round head

complex buff marbling on upperparts

fine, dark streaks

whitish-buff underparts

VOICE Usually silent; males: rapid hoo hoo hoo, often given during display flights; also barking, chee-oww.
NESTING Scrape lined with grass and feathers on ground; 4–7 eggs; 1–2 broods; Mar–Jun.
FEEDING Small mammals and some birds.
HABITAT Open areas: prairie, grasslands, tundra, fields, and marshes.
LENGTH 13½–16in (34–41cm)
WINGSPAN 2¾–3½ft (0.9–1.1m)

Nightjars

The nightjars are active mostly around dusk and dawn, and so are not well known to many people, although their remarkable songs and calls may be more familiar. Common Nighthawks are easily seen and may even be spotted over suburban areas, but most nightjars are elusive species. Some inhabit scrub and bushy slopes and plains, while others are found in woodlands. They are medium-sized birds with pointed wings and long tails. They have tiny legs and minute bills, but very wide mouths: they catch flying insects, such as moths, in the air, directly into the open gape. Their mouths are surrounded by bristles that help guide insects in when the birds are foraging.

SITTING PRETTY
Unusually for birds, members of the nightjar family, such as this Common Nighthawk, often perch lengthwise on branches.

Common Nighthawk

Chordeiles minor

Common Nighthawks are easy to spot as they swoop over parking lots, city streets, and athletic fields during the warm summer months. They are more active at dawn and dusk than at night, pursuing insect prey up to 250ft (76m) in the air. The species once took the name Booming Nighthawk, a reference to the males' remarkable flight display, during which they dive rapidly toward the ground, causing their feathers to vibrate and produce a characteristic "booming" sound.

narrow wings

♂

white bars on outer wing feathers

pointed wings

white wing patch

♂

white throat

very small bill

large, dark eye

delicate gray-black pattern overall

long wings

♀

barring on gray underparts

VOICE *Nasal peeent; also soft clucking noises from both sexes.*
NESTING *Nests on ground on rocks, wood, leaves, or sand; also on gravel-covered rooftops in urban areas; 2 eggs; 1 brood; May–Jul.*
FEEDING *Catches airborne insects, especially moths, mayflies, and beetles, also ants; predominantly active at dusk and dawn.*
HABITAT *Wide variety of open habitats, such as cleared forests, fields, grassland, beaches, sand dunes; also common in urban areas, including cities.*
LENGTH *9–10in (23–26cm)*
WINGSPAN *22–24in (56–61cm)*

Chuck-will's-widow

S

Antrostomus carolinensis

Chuck-will's-widows tolerate human development, often nesting in suburban and urban areas. Unlike other nightjars, they often feed by hawking—flying continuously and catching prey on the wing, occasionally capturing bats and small birds, and swallowing them whole. Chuck-will's-widows hunt at dawn and dusk, and during full moons. This nightjar sleeps by day, well camouflaged upon the forest floor.

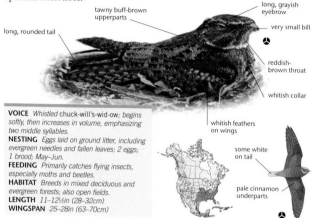

tawny buff-brown upperparts

long, grayish eyebrow

very small bill

long, rounded tail

reddish-brown throat

whitish collar

whitish feathers on wings

some white on tail

pale cinnamon underparts

VOICE *Whistled chuck-will's-wid-ow; begins softly, then increases in volume, emphasizing two middle syllables.*
NESTING *Eggs laid on ground litter, including evergreen needles and fallen leaves; 2 eggs; 1 brood; May–Jun.*
FEEDING *Primarily catches flying insects, especially moths and beetles.*
HABITAT *Breeds in mixed deciduous and evergreen forests; also open fields.*
LENGTH *11–12½in (28–32cm)*
WINGSPAN *25–28in (63–70cm)*

Eastern Whip-poor-will

T

Antrostomus vociferus

The Whip-poor-will is heard more often than seen. Its camouflage makes it difficult to spot on the forest floor, and it usually flies away only when an intruder is very close. While the male feeds the first brood until fledging, the female lays eggs for a second brood. The two eggs from each brood may hatch together, near a full moon, allowing the parents more light at night to forage for their young.

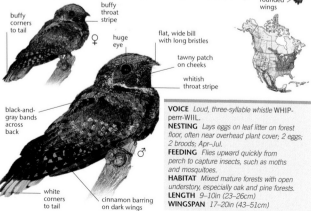

rounded wings

♂

buffy throat stripe

buffy corners to tail

huge eye

♀

flat, wide bill with long bristles

tawny patch on cheeks

whitish throat stripe

black-and-gray bands across back

white corners to tail

cinnamon barring on dark wings

♂

VOICE *Loud, three-syllable whistle WHIP-perrr-WIIL.*
NESTING *Lays eggs on leaf litter on forest floor, often near overhead plant cover; 2 eggs; 2 broods; Apr–Jul.*
FEEDING *Flies upward quickly from perch to capture insects, such as moths and mosquitoes.*
HABITAT *Mixed mature forests with open understory, especially oak and pine forests.*
LENGTH *9–10in (23–26cm)*
WINGSPAN *17–20in (43–51cm)*

Swifts

The most aerial birds in North America—if not the world— swifts eat, drink, court, mate, and even sleep on the wing. Unsurprisingly, swifts also are some of the fastest and most acrobatic flyers of the bird world. Several species have been clocked at over 100mph (160kmh). Looking like "flying cigars," they feed on insects caught in zooming, zigzagging, and dashing pursuits.

APTLY NAMED
Chimney Swifts will build their nest inside chimneys when they can get access.

Hummingbirds

Hummingbirds are sometimes referred to as the crown jewels of the bird world. Most North American male hummingbirds have a colorful throat patch called a gorget, but most females lack this attribute. Hummingbirds can fly backward, sideways, up, down, and hover due to their unique rapid, figure-eight wing strokes and reduced wing bone structure. Their long, thin bills allow them access to nectar in tubular flowers.

AGGRESSIVE MALES
This male Ruby-throated Hummingbird defends his territory from a perch.

Chimney Swift

Chaetura pelagica

The Chimney Swift is a familiar summer sight and sound, racing high through skies east of the Rockies while emitting rolling twitters. These birds do almost everything on the wing—feeding, drinking, and even bathing. Formerly tree-cavity nesters, Chimney Swifts now depend upon artificial structures for nesting, including real and even fake chimneys provided by humans. Although their range has expanded west and south, local populations have declined.

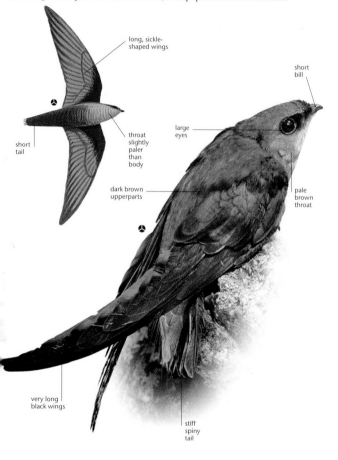

long, sickle-shaped wings

short bill

short tail

throat slightly paler than body

large eyes

dark brown upperparts

pale brown throat

very long black wings

stiff spiny tail

VOICE *High, rapid chips and twittering; notes from individuals in a flock run together into a rapid, descending chatter.*
NESTING *Shallow cup of twigs and saliva attached to inside of chimney or other artificial structure, rarely hollow tree; 4–5 eggs; 1 brood; Apr–Aug.*
FEEDING *Large variety of small aerial insects.*
HABITAT *Urban and suburban areas, small towns; hollow trees and caves while nesting.*
LENGTH *5in (13cm)*
WINGSPAN *14in (36cm)*

Ruby-throated Hummingbird ⓢ

Archilochus colubris

The Ruby-throated Hummingbird is easily identified in
most of its range, although more difficult to distinguish
in areas where other species are found, particularly during
migration. Before migration, these birds can add almost
¹⁄₁₆oz (2g) of fat to their weight to provide enough fuel for a
nonstop 800-mile (1,300-km) flight across the Gulf of Mexico.

♂

dark forked tail

white chin and throat

♀

rounded tail

white underparts with buff wash on sides and flanks

green crown

black face

straight black bill

glittering green upperparts

orange-red throat

white chest

greenish sides and flanks

grayish-white underparts

♂

VOICE *Soft, thick* chic, *sometimes doubled;
twittered notes; fast, slightly buzzy* tsi-tsi-tsi-
tsi-tsi-tsi-tsi-tsi *in chase.*
NESTING *Tiny cup of plant down, bound with
spider's silk, usually in deciduous trees; 2 eggs;
1–2 broods; Apr–Sep.*
FEEDING *Flower nectar; small insects and
spiders, caught aerially or gleaned from foliage;
sugar water from feeders.*
HABITAT *Variety of woodlands and gardens.*
LENGTH *3½in (9cm)*
WINGSPAN *4¼in (11cm)*

Rufous Hummingbird ⓢ

Selasphorus rufus

The Rufous Hummingbird is aggressive despite its small size; it often chases other
hummingbirds away from nectar sources. It also breeds farther north than
any other North American species of hummingbird and undertakes a lengthy
migration. Males are recognizable by their overall fiery orange-rufous color,
but females and immature birds are more difficult to distinguish.

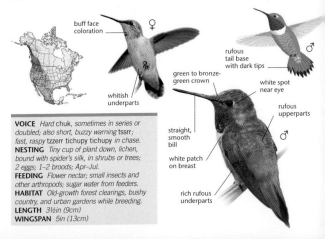

♀

buff face coloration

whitish underparts

green to bronze-green crown

straight, smooth bill

white patch on breast

rufous tail base with dark tips

♂

white spot near eye

rufous upperparts

♂

rich rufous underparts

VOICE *Hard* chuk, *sometimes in series or
doubled; also short, buzzy warning* tssr;
fast, raspy tzzerr tichupy tichupy *in chase.*
NESTING *Tiny cup of plant down, lichen,
bound with spider's silk, in shrubs or trees;
2 eggs; 1–2 broods; Apr–Jul.*
FEEDING *Flower nectar; small insects and
other arthropods; sugar water from feeders.*
HABITAT *Old-growth forest clearings, bushy
country, and urban gardens while breeding.*
LENGTH *3½in (9cm)*
WINGSPAN *5in (13cm)*

Kingfishers

Kingfishers are primarily a tropical family. Three species are found in North America, but only one, the Belted Kingfisher, is widespread. Although lacking the array of bright blues, greens, and reds associated with their tropical and European counterparts, Belted Kingfishers are striking birds, distinguished by shaggy head crests, breastbands, and white underparts. The females of the species are more brightly colored than the males, sporting chestnut-colored belly bands. Belted Kingfishers are primarily fish-eaters. They will perch along a waterway for hunting, or hover if no perch is available, and will plunge headfirst into the water to catch their prey. They routinely stun their prey by beating it against a perch before turning the fish around so that it can be swallowed headfirst.

FISH DINNER
A female Belted Kingfisher, distinguished by its rust-colored belly band, uses its large bill to catch and hold slippery prey.

Belted Kingfisher

Megaceryle alcyon

Its stocky body, double-pointed crest, large head, and contrasting white collar distinguish the Belted Kingfisher from other species in its range. This kingfisher's loud and far-carrying rattles are heard more often than the bird is seen. Interestingly, it is one of the few species in North America in which the female is more colorful than the male. The Belted Kingfisher can be found in a large variety of aquatic habitats, both coastal and inland, vigorously defending its territory all year round.

prominent crest

♀

chestnut band across belly

chestnut flanks

bluish-gray head with shaggy crest

barred tail

large head

single blue breastband

♂

long, thick, powerful bill

white collar

double crest

white collar

bluish-slate upperparts

white belly

♂

single dark breastband

♂

VOICE *Harsh mechanical rattle like an "angry chatter" in flight or from a perch; screams or trill-like warble during breeding.*
NESTING *Unlined chamber in subterranean burrow 3–6ft (1–2m) deep, in earthen bank usually over water; 6–7 eggs; 1 brood; Mar–Jul.*
FEEDING *Plunge-dives from perch to catch fish near the surface, including sticklebacks and trout; also crustaceans, such as crayfish.*
HABITAT *Clear, open waters of streams, rivers, lakes, and estuaries where perches are available.*
LENGTH *11–14in (28–35cm)*
WINGSPAN *19–23in (48–58cm)*

Woodpeckers

Woodpeckers are found throughout North America, except in the tundra. They grip upright tree trunks, using their tail as a support or prop. Most woodpeckers have two toes facing forward and two facing backward, giving an extra-strong grip. Unlike nuthatches, they do not perch upside-down but can cling to the underside of angled branches. They have striking plumage patterns of primarily black and white, with varying amounts of red or yellow. Many proclaim their territory by instrumental rather than vocal means, hammering the bill against a hard surface—even metal—to give a brief but rapid "drumroll." The bill is also used for chipping into bark and excavating deep nestholes. Sapsuckers make rows or rings of small holes on tree trunks, allowing sap to ooze freely: they feed on the sap and also on the insects that are attracted to it. Some species of woodpeckers, especially flickers, feed on the ground, probing inside ant nests and catching them with their long, sticky tongues.

RED ALERT
With its crimson head, the Red-headed Woodpecker is an instantly recognizable bird in North America.

Red-headed Woodpecker

Melanerpes erythrocephalus

The Red-headed Woodpecker is easy to identify with its completely red head. Unlike most other woodpecker species, it forages for food—both insects and nuts—and stores it for eating at a later time. It is one of the most skilled flycatchers in the woodpecker family. Its numbers have declined, largely because of the destruction of its habitat.

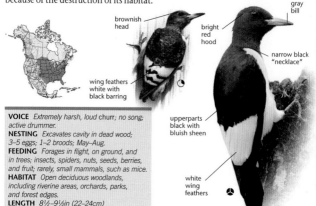

red head

white rump

bluish-gray bill

brownish head

bright red hood

narrow black "necklace"

upperparts black with bluish sheen

wing feathers white with black barring

white wing feathers

VOICE *Extremely harsh, loud churr; no song; active drummer.*
NESTING *Excavates cavity in dead wood; 3–5 eggs; 1–2 broods; May–Aug.*
FEEDING *Forages in flight, on ground, and in trees; insects, spiders, nuts, seeds, berries, and fruit; rarely, small mammals, such as mice.*
HABITAT *Open deciduous woodlands, including riverine areas, orchards, parks, and forest edges.*
LENGTH *8½–9½in (22–24cm)*
WINGSPAN *16–18in (41–46cm)*

Red-bellied Woodpecker

Melanerpes carolinus

Since the early 20th century, this woodpecker has expanded its range northward into Canada and westward. It does not actually possess a red belly; the male is distinguished by its red forehead, crown, and nape, while the female only has a red nape. Males excavate several holes in trees, one of which the female chooses for a nest.

white patches at base of outer wing

red nape

red crown

red nape

pale grayish-tan face

pale grayish-tan underparts

regular black-and-white barring

VOICE *Rather soft, clearly rolling, slightly quivering krrurrr call.*
NESTING *Cavity-nester; 4–5 eggs; 1–3 broods; May–Aug.*
FEEDING *Eats insects (but does not excavate trees to find them), fruit, seeds, acorns, and other nuts; in winter, eats mainly vegetable matter.*
HABITAT *Forests, swamps, suburban wooded areas, open woodlands, and parks.*
LENGTH *9–10½in (23–27cm)*
WINGSPAN *16in (41cm)*

Yellow-bellied Sapsucker

S

Sphyrapicus varius

The Yellow-bellied Sapsucker has a distinctive red, black, and white coloring and a soft yellow wash on its underparts. With its relatives, the Red-breasted Sapsucker and the Red-naped Sapsucker, it shares the habit of drilling holes in trees to drink sap. Sapsuckers are the only wholly migratory woodpeckers; female Yellow-bellied Sapsuckers move farther south than males.

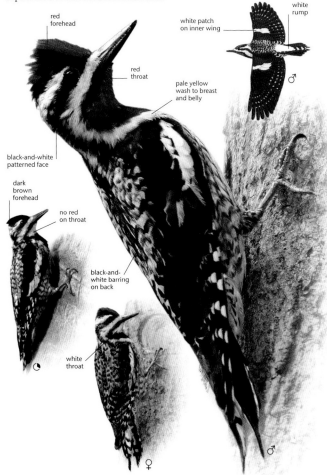

red forehead

white patch on inner wing

white rump

red throat

pale yellow wash to breast and belly

♂

black-and-white patterned face

dark brown forehead

no red on throat

black-and-white barring on back

white throat

♀

♂

VOICE *Primary call a mewing wheer-wheer-wheer.*
NESTING *Cavities in dead trees; 5–6 eggs; 1 brood; May–Jun.*
FEEDING *Drills holes in trees for sap; ants and other small insects; inner bark of trees, also a variety of fruit; occasionally suet feeders.*
HABITAT *Deciduous forests or mixed deciduous-coniferous forests while breeding; prefers young forests; open wooded areas in winter.*
LENGTH *8–9in (20–23cm)*
WINGSPAN *16–18in (41–46cm)*

Downy Woodpecker

S

Dryobates pubescens

The smallest North American woodpecker, the Downy Woodpecker is seen all year round from the Eastern Seaboard to California, north to Alaska, and in Canada from coast to coast. It is distinguished from the similar Hairy Woodpecker by its shorter bill and smaller size. After breeding, Downy Woodpeckers remain in the same area, but wander around in search of food in a variety of habitats, including suburbs and backyards.

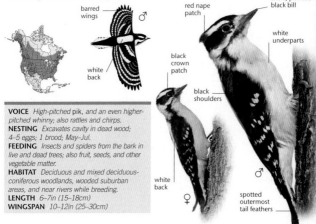

barred wings ♂

white back

red nape patch

black crown patch

black shoulders

short, pointed black bill

white underparts

white back ♀

♂

spotted outermost tail feathers

VOICE *High-pitched* pik, *and an even higher-pitched whinny; also rattles and chirps.*
NESTING *Excavates cavity in dead wood;
4–5 eggs; 1 brood; May–Jul.*
FEEDING *Insects and spiders from the bark in live and dead trees; also fruit, seeds, and other vegetable matter.*
HABITAT *Deciduous and mixed deciduous-coniferous woodlands, wooded suburban areas, and near rivers while breeding.*
LENGTH *6–7in (15–18cm)*
WINGSPAN *10–12in (25–30cm)*

Hairy Woodpecker

S

Dryobates villosus

Like the Downy Woodpecker, the Hairy Woodpecker is widespread in North America, breeding and wintering from coast to coast in the US and Canada. The two species look quite similar, but the Hairy Woodpecker has a larger, thicker bill and is noticeably larger than the Downy Woodpecker. It prefers forests, where it uses live tree trunks for nesting and foraging.

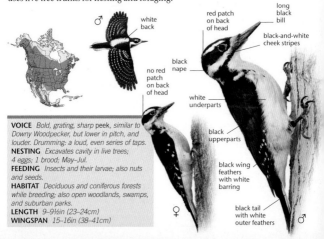

♂ white back

red patch on back of head

long black bill

black-and-white cheek stripes

no red patch on back of head

black nape

white underparts

black upperparts

black wing feathers with white barring

♀

black tail with white outer feathers ♂

VOICE *Bold, grating, sharp* peek, *similar to Downy Woodpecker, but lower in pitch, and louder. Drumming: a loud, even series of taps.*
NESTING *Excavates cavity in live trees;
4 eggs; 1 brood; May–Jul.*
FEEDING *Insects and their larvae; also nuts and seeds.*
HABITAT *Deciduous and coniferous forests while breeding; also open woodlands, swamps, and suburban parks.*
LENGTH *9–9½in (23–24cm)*
WINGSPAN *15–16in (38–41cm)*

Red-cockaded Woodpecker

Dryobates borealis

black rump
and upper tail

♂

white outer
tail feathers

Red-cockaded Woodpecker populations have been decimated by the clearing of old-growth pine forests for lumber and farmland in the southeastern US. This endangered bird breeds in small family groups, taking up to three years to drill its nest cavity in a living tree. During incubation, other clan members assist the parents. These birds drill for insects, working their way up and around tree trunks.

♀

no red
spot

small red spot
behind eye
(cockade)

white
eyebrow

♂

black
cheek
stripe

white
cheek

finely streaked
underparts

white spots and bars
on black wings

whitish
undertail feathers

VOICE *Very vocal; calls include a rolled shrit or shiff; also a kingfisherlike rattle.*
NESTING *Excavates cavity in live, mature longleaf and loblolly pines; 3–5 eggs; 1 brood; Apr–Jun.*
FEEDING *Insects, especially ants, and larvae; also pine seeds, grapes, and blueberries.*
HABITAT *Localized in southeastern US open pine forests.*
LENGTH 7½–8½in (19–22cm)
WINGSPAN 14–15in (36–38cm)

American Three-toed Woodpecker

Picoides dorsalis

This species breeds farther north than any other North American woodpecker, including the Black-backed Woodpecker. It resembles the Black-backed Woodpecker in terms of size and head markings, and they are the only two North American woodpeckers with three toes on each foot. These two species require mature forests with old or dead trees.

long,
straight
bill

black-and-white
barred back

large
yellow
patch

black
head

♂

black-and-white
streaked crown

white
breast

black bars
on flanks

♀

slightly forked
black tail with
white outer
tail feathers

VOICE *Queep, quip, or pik; generally quiet, likened to the Yellow-bellied Sapsucker.*
NESTING *Excavates cavity mainly in dead or dying wood, sometimes in live wood; 4 eggs; 1 brood; May–Jul.*
FEEDING *Flakes off bark and eats insects underneath, mainly larvae of bark beetles.*
HABITAT *Mature northern coniferous forests; largely nonmigratory; more open areas in winter.*
LENGTH 8–9in (20–23cm)
WINGSPAN 15in (38cm)

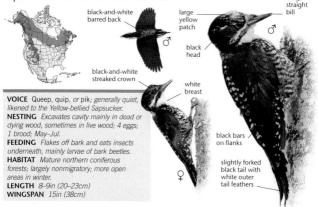

Black-backed Woodpecker

Picoides arcticus

Despite a widespread distribution, this bird is difficult to find. It often occurs in areas with burned forest, eating wood-boring beetles that occur after outbreaks of fire. This diet is very restrictive, and the species is negatively affected by the prevention of forest fires. Although its range overlaps with that of the American Three-toed Woodpecker, the two are rarely found together in the same locality.

black back

♀

white spots on outer wings

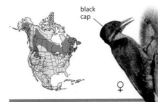

black cap

♀

yellow cap on black head

long black bill

white stripe on head

white underparts

black back and wings

♂

VOICE *Single pik.*
NESTING *Cavity excavated in tree; 3–4 eggs; 1 brood; May–Jul.*
FEEDING *Flakes off bark and eats beetles underneath, especially larvae of wood-boring beetles.*
HABITAT *Northerly, mountainous coniferous forests that require fire for renewal; moves from place to place, following outbreaks of wood-boring beetles.*
LENGTH *9–9½in (23–24cm)*
WINGSPAN *15–16in (38–41cm)*

Northern Flicker

Colaptes auratus

The Northern Flicker is a ground forager. The two subspecies groups—the Yellow-shafted Flicker in the East and the Red-shafted Flicker in the West—interbreed in a wide area in the Great Plains. They can be distinguished in flight by a white rump patch—depending on the subspecies, the yellow or red underwing feathers are apparent.

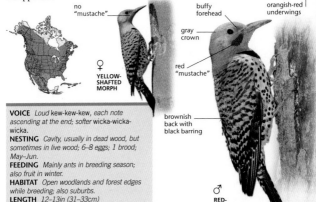

black crescent

♂

RED-SHAFTED MORPH

orangish-red underwings

no "mustache"

♀

YELLOW-SHAFTED MORPH

buffy forehead

gray crown

red "mustache"

brownish back with black barring

♂

RED-SHAFTED MORPH

VOICE *Loud kew-kew-kew, each note ascending at the end; softer wicka-wicka-wicka.*
NESTING *Cavity, usually in dead wood, but sometimes in live wood; 6–8 eggs; 1 brood; May–Jun.*
FEEDING *Mainly ants in breeding season; also fruit in winter.*
HABITAT *Open woodlands and forest edges while breeding; also suburbs.*
LENGTH *12–13in (31–33cm)*
WINGSPAN *19–21in (48–53cm)*

Pileated Woodpecker

S

Dryocopus pileatus

The largest woodpecker in North America, the Pileated Woodpecker is instantly recognizable by its spectacular large, tapering bright red crest. A mated pair of Pileated Woodpeckers defends their breeding territory all year. Indeed, a pair may live in the same dead tree every year, but will hammer out a new nest cavity with their powerful bills each season. Their abandoned squarish nest cavities are sometimes reused by other birds, and occasionally inhabited by mammals.

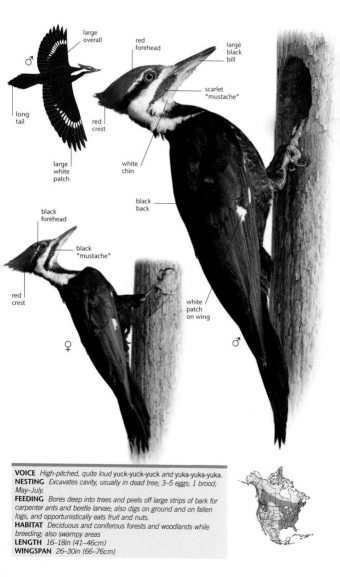

♂

large overall

long tail

large white patch

red forehead

red crest

white chin

large black bill

scarlet "mustache"

black back

black forehead

black "mustache"

red crest

♀

white patch on wing

♂

VOICE *High-pitched, quite loud yuck-yuck-yuck and yuka-yuka-yuka.*
NESTING *Excavates cavity, usually in dead tree; 3–5 eggs; 1 brood; May–July.*
FEEDING *Bores deep into trees and peels off large strips of bark for carpenter ants and beetle larvae; also digs on ground and on fallen logs, and opportunistically eats fruit and nuts.*
HABITAT *Deciduous and coniferous forests and woodlands while breeding; also swampy areas*
LENGTH *16–18in (41–46cm)*
WINGSPAN *26–30in (66–76cm)*

Falcons and Caracaras

Falcons include birds that catch insects on the wing, those that hover in one place searching for small prey below, and yet others that are dramatic aerial hunters. Some use high-speed "stoops" from above, seizing birds up to their own size, while larger species, such as the Gyrfalcon, can kill prey much heavier than themselves. They are distinguished from bird-eating hawks in the genus *Accipiter* by their dark eyes and their hunting styles: both use their feet to catch prey, but while falcons kill primarily with their bills, hawks kill with their feet. Falcons' bills are equipped with a notch or "tooth" on the upper mandible. Unlike hawks and eagles, falcons do not build nests, but some use old nests of other birds. Caracaras are broader-winged, longer-legged birds. They have a stripe of brightly colored, bare skin on the face and often forage by walking on the ground.

PRECISION LANDING
A Peregrine Falcon swoops down to settle on the branch, thrusting out its feet to absorb the shock of landing.

Crested Caracara ⓉⓈ

Caracara plancus

The hawklike Crested Caracara, a member of the falcon family, is found in Arizona, Texas, and Florida. These monogamous, long-lived, highly territorial birds raid nests for eggs, patrol roads for carrion, and feast on carcasses, regularly foraging in groups, together with vultures.

slightly bent wings

white patch on wing

yellowish cheek

barred tail

streaked breast

black tail band

pale legs

black crown and crest

white cheek

thin dark bars on white breast and nape

thick, pale blue bill

black back

VOICE *Adults disturbed at the nest emit cackles, hollow rattles, and high-pitched screams.*
NESTING *Large nest of vines, stems, twigs, in tall trees; 2–4 eggs; 1–2 broods; Jan–May.*
FEEDING *Eats live and dead mammals, birds, reptiles, and insects.*
HABITAT *Breeds and winters in open deserts and grasslands; also agricultural land, dumps, and slaughterhouses.*
LENGTH 19–23in (48–58cm)
WINGSPAN 4ft (1.2m)

cream or whitish undertail feathers

long yellow to orange legs

American Kestrel Ⓢ

Falco sparverius

The smallest of the North American falcons, the American Kestrel features typically pointed wings, a "tooth and notch" bill structure, and the dark brown eyes typical of falcons, but shorter toes. They often dive into long grass to capture insects and small mammals. Male and female American Kestrels show striking differences in plumage, the latter also being larger.

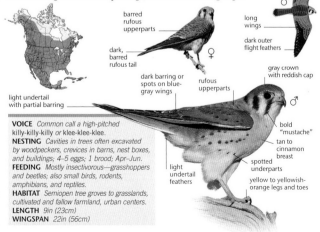

barred rufous upperparts

long wings

dark, barred rufous tail

dark outer flight performance feathers

♀

gray crown with reddish cap

dark barring or spots on blue-gray wings

rufous upperparts

♂

light undertail with partial barring

bold "mustache"

tan to cinnamon breast

spotted underparts

VOICE *Common call a high-pitched killy-killy-killy or klee-klee-klee.*
NESTING *Cavities in trees often excavated by woodpeckers, crevices in barns, nest boxes, and buildings; 4–5 eggs; 1 brood; Apr–Jun.*
FEEDING *Mostly insectivorous—grasshoppers and beetles; also small birds, rodents, amphibians, and reptiles.*
HABITAT *Semiopen tree groves to grasslands, cultivated and fallow farmland, urban centers.*
LENGTH 9in (23cm)
WINGSPAN 22in (56cm)

light undertail feathers

yellow to yellowish-orange legs and toes

Merlin

Ⓢ

Falco columbarius

Merlins are small, fast-flying falcons that can overtake and capture a wide variety
of prey. They can turn on a dime and use their long, thin toes, typical of falcons,
to pluck small birds from the air. Males are smaller than females, and different
in color. Both males and females show geographical color variations.

♀
brown upperparts

blue-gray or gray barring on square tail
white band at the tail tip
small, fairly square head
♂

blue-gray or gray upperparts
dark head
dark brown eye
indistinct "mustache"

dark brown tail with less bold buff barring

♂
brown streaking on underparts

buff undertail feathers
yellow legs and feet

dark tail with horizontal barring

VOICE *Males: high-pitched ki-ki-ki-ki;
females: low-pitched kek-ek-ek-ek-ek.*
NESTING *Small scrapes on ground in open
country, or abandoned nests of other species,
such as crows, in both forested and urban
areas; 4–6 eggs; 1 brood; Apr–Jun.*
FEEDING *Small birds in midair, from sparrows
to doves; dragonflies, rodents, and bats.*
HABITAT *Coastlines, marshlands, open fields,
and desert areas.*
LENGTH *10in (25cm)*
WINGSPAN *24in (61cm)*

Gyrfalcon

Ⓢ

Falco rusticolus

The Arctic-breeding Gyrfalcon is used to harsh environments. It is the largest
of all the falcons and is known by falconers for its power, beauty, and gentle
nature. It uses its speed to pursue prey in a "tail chase," sometimes striking its
quarry on the ground, but also in flight. Three forms are known, ranging from
almost pure-white to gray and dark.

pointed tips
dark brown to black all over
darker wing linings
paler flight feathers

🦅 DARK MORPH

yellow patch of skin near bill
dark brown iris

blue bill with dark tip

gray, barred upperparts

long barred tail

lighter underparts with spots

yellow toes and legs

🦅 GRAY MORPH

VOICE *Loud, harsh KYHa-KYHa-KYHa.*
NESTING *Scrape on cliff or old raven nests;
2–7 eggs; 1 brood; Apr–Jul.*
FEEDING *Large birds, such as ptarmigans,
grouse, and ducks; may also hunt mammals,
such as lemmings and hares.*
HABITAT *Barren regions of tundra, high
mountains and tundra foothills, Arctic and
sub-Arctic evergreen forests and woodlands;
not common outside breeding range.*
LENGTH *22in (56cm)*
WINGSPAN *4ft (1.2m)*

Peregrine Falcon

S

Falco peregrinus

Peregrine Falcons are distributed worldwide and are long-distance travelers—
"peregrine" means "wanderer." It can dive from great heights at speeds of
up to 200mph (320kmh)—a technique known as "stooping." Like all true
falcons, this species has a pointed "tooth" on its upper beak and a "notch"
on the lower one, apparently used to sever the neck
vertebrae of captured prey to kill it. Its breeding ability
was drastically reduced from the 1950s to the 1980s due
to insecticide poisoning, but with conservation efforts,
the population has rebounded.

long, pointed wings

short tail

dark "hood" on head

yellow eye-ring

dark spots on light buff breast

bluish-gray upperparts

light underparts with horizontal barring

brown upperparts

streaked underparts

light yellow or bluish-gray legs and toes

yellow toes and legs

VOICE *Sharp cack-cack-cack when alarmed.*
NESTING *Shallow scrape on cliff or building (nest sites are used year after year); 2–5 eggs; 1 brood; Mar–Jun.*
FEEDING *Dives on birds from jays to ducks in flight; feeds on pigeons and migratory birds in cities, and occasionally mammals.*
HABITAT *Cliffs along coasts, inland mountain ranges, scrubland and salt marshes, cities with tall buildings.*
LENGTH *16in (41cm)*
WINGSPAN *3¼–3½ft (1–1.1m)*

New World Flycatchers

The North American species of flycatchers are all members of a New World family—the Tyrant Flycatchers. They are uniform in appearance; most are drab-colored, olive-green or gray birds, sometimes with yellow on the underparts. The members of the genus *Empidonax* include some of the most difficult birds to identify in North America; they are best distinguished by their songs. Typical flycatcher feeding behavior is to sit on a branch or exposed perch and sally forth to catch flying insects. Most are found in wooded habitats, though the kingbirds prefer woodland edges and deserts. Nearly all flycatchers are long-distance migrants and spend the winter in Central and South America.

CATCHY TUNE
The Eastern Wood-pewee would be difficult to spot if not for its distinctive pee-ah-wee *song.*

Olive-sided Flycatcher

T

Contopus cooperi

The Olive-sided Flycatcher is identified by its distinctive song, relatively large size, and contrasting belly and flank colors, which make its underside appear like a vest with the buttons undone. Breeding pairs are known to defend their territory aggressively. This flycatcher undertakes a long journey from northern parts of North America to winter in Panama and the Andes.

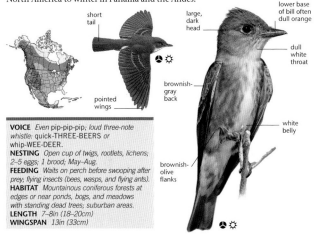

short tail

large, dark head

lower base of bill often dull orange

dull white throat

pointed wings

brownish-gray back

white belly

brownish-olive flanks

VOICE *Even pip-pip-pip; loud three-note whistle; quick-THREE-BEERS or whip-WEE-DEER.*
NESTING *Open cup of twigs, rootlets, lichens; 2–5 eggs; 1 brood; May–Aug.*
FEEDING *Waits on perch before swooping after prey; flying insects (bees, wasps, and flying ants).*
HABITAT *Mountainous coniferous forests at edges or near ponds, bogs, and meadows with standing dead trees; suburban areas.*
LENGTH *7–8in (18–20cm)*
WINGSPAN *13in (33cm)*

Eastern Wood-Pewee

D

Contopus virens

The Eastern Wood-Pewee is found in many types of woodlands in the eastern US and southeastern Canada. The male is slightly larger than the female, but their plumage is practically identical. Recent population declines have been attributed to loss of breeding habitat due to heavy browsing by white-tailed deer. This has been compounded by its susceptibility to brood parasitism by Brown-headed Cowbirds.

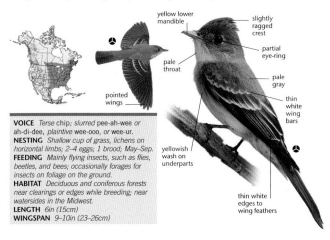

yellow lower mandible

slightly ragged crest

partial eye-ring

pale gray

pale throat

thin white wing bars

pointed wings

yellowish wash on underparts

thin white edges to wing feathers

VOICE *Terse chip; slurred pee-ah-wee or ah-di-dee, plaintive wee-ooo, or wee-ur.*
NESTING *Shallow cup of grass, lichens on horizontal limbs; 2–4 eggs; 1 brood; May–Sep.*
FEEDING *Mainly flying insects, such as flies, beetles, and bees; occasionally forages for insects on foliage on the ground.*
HABITAT *Deciduous and coniferous forests near clearings or edges while breeding; near watersides in the Midwest.*
LENGTH *6in (15cm)*
WINGSPAN *9–10in (23–26cm)*

Yellow-bellied Flycatcher

Empidonax flaviventris

The Yellow-bellied Flycatcher is characteristic of northern coniferous forests and sphagnum-moss peatlands. It is not well known because of its remote habitats and its secretive habits; it is much more often heard than seen. It remains on its breeding grounds for only about two months, then migrates to its winter quarters in southern Mexico and Central America to Panama.

bright wing bars

green back and head

rounded crown

broad base of bill

dark breastband

yellowish belly

big head

rounded wings

conspicuous yellow eye-ring

yellow-olive throat

white wing bars

short, narrow, square tail

VOICE *Chu-wee and abrupt brrrrt; abrupt killink, che-lek, or che-bunk, with variations.*
NESTING *Cup of moss, twigs, and needles on or near ground, often in a bog; 3–5 eggs; 1 brood; Jun–Jul.*
FEEDING *Insects in the air or mosquitoes, midges, and flies from foliage; sometimes berries and seeds.*
HABITAT *Boreal forests and bogs with spruce trees while breeding.*
LENGTH *5½in (14cm)*
WINGSPAN *8in (20cm)*

Acadian Flycatcher

Empidonax virescens

Its often drooped wings and minimal wing- and tail-flicking give the Acadian Flycatcher an outwardly calm appearance compared to other flycatchers. It bathes by diving into water, then preens on a perch. It suffers more parasitism from Brown-headed Cowbirds in small wood lots than in large forests. Where Cowbirds lay their eggs in the flycatcher's nest, they displace the flycatcher's young.

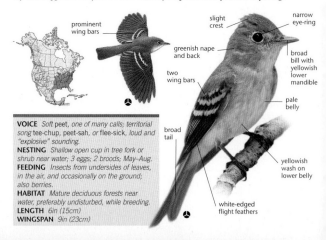

prominent wing bars

slight crest

narrow eye-ring

greenish nape and back

two wing bars

broad bill with yellowish lower mandible

pale belly

broad tail

yellowish wash on lower belly

white-edged flight feathers

VOICE *Soft peet, one of many calls; territorial song tee-chup, peet-sah, or flee-sick, loud and "explosive" sounding.*
NESTING *Shallow open cup in tree fork or shrub near water; 3 eggs; 2 broods; May–Aug.*
FEEDING *Insects from undersides of leaves, in the air, and occasionally on the ground; also berries.*
HABITAT *Mature deciduous forests near water, preferably undisturbed, while breeding.*
LENGTH *6in (15cm)*
WINGSPAN *9in (23cm)*

Alder Flycatcher

S

Empidonax alnorum

Until 1973, the Alder Flycatcher and the Willow Flycatcher were considered to be one species, called Traill's Flycatcher. The two species cannot be reliably identified by sight, but they do have distinctive songs. The Alder Flycatcher also breeds farther north than the Willow Flycatcher, arriving late in spring and leaving early in fall. Its nests are extremely hard to locate.

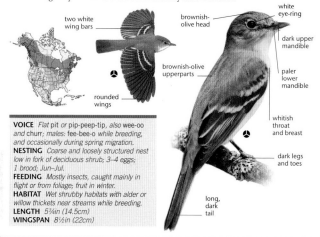

two white wing bars

brownish-olive head

white eye-ring

dark upper mandible

paler lower mandible

brownish-olive upperparts

rounded wings

whitish throat and breast

dark legs and toes

long, dark tail

VOICE *Flat* pit *or* pip-peep-tip, *also* wee-oo *and* churr; *males:* fee-bee-o *while breeding, and occasionally during spring migration.*
NESTING *Coarse and loosely structured nest low in fork of deciduous shrub; 3–4 eggs; 1 brood; Jun–Jul.*
FEEDING *Mostly insects, caught mainly in flight or from foliage; fruit in winter.*
HABITAT *Wet shrubby habitats with alder or willow thickets near streams while breeding.*
LENGTH 5¾in (14.5cm)
WINGSPAN 8½in (22cm)

Willow Flycatcher

S

Empidonax traillii

The Willow Flycatcher is only distinguished from the nearly identical Alder Flycatcher by its song. A territorial bird, it spreads its tail and flicks it upward during aggressive encounters. It is, however, frequently parasitized by the Brown-headed Cowbird, which lays its eggs in the flycatcher's nest and removes its host's eggs.

two buff to yellow wing bars

brown eye

thin eye-ring

dark upper mandible

paler lower mandible

grayish-green upperparts

square tail

yellow-tinged flanks

whitish belly

dark legs and toes

dark tail

VOICE *Soft, dry* whit *and several buzzy notes; sharp* fitz-bew *with accent on the first syllable; also* creet.
NESTING *Rather loose, untidy cup in base of shrub near water; 3–4 eggs; 1 brood; May–Aug.*
FEEDING *Insects, mostly caught in flight; fruit in winter.*
HABITAT *Willow thickets and other moist, shrubby areas along watercourses while breeding.*
LENGTH 5–6¾in (13–17cm)
WINGSPAN 7½–9½in (19–24cm)

Least Flycatcher

Ⓢ

Empidonax minimus

The Least Flycatcher is a solitary bird and is very aggressive toward intruders encroaching upon its breeding territory. This combative behavior reduces the likelihood of brood parasitism by the Brown-headed Cowbird. The Least Flycatcher is very active, and frequently flicks its wings and tail upward. Common in the eastern US in mixed and deciduous woodlands, especially at the edges, it spends a short time—up to only two months—on its northern breeding grounds before migrating south. Adults molt in winter, while the young molt before and during fall migration.

short, broad-based bill

large head

short, narrow tail

two wing bars

pale throat

buffy wing bars

marked white eye-ring

greenish-brown back

short wings

pale yellow belly

VOICE *Soft, short* whit; *frequent, persistent, characteristic* tchebeck, *sings during spring migration and breeding season.*
NESTING *Compact cup of tightly woven bark strips and plant fibers in fork of deciduous tree; 3–5 eggs; 1 brood; May–Jul.*
FEEDING *Insects, such as flies, midges, beetles, ants, butterflies, and larvae; occasionally berries and seeds.*
HABITAT *Coniferous and mixed deciduous forests while breeding; conifer groves or wooded wetlands.*
LENGTH *5¼in (13.5cm)*
WINGSPAN *7¾in (19.5cm)*

Eastern Phoebe

(S)

Sayornis phoebe

The Eastern Phoebe is an early spring migrant that tends to nest under bridges, culverts, and on buildings, in addition to rocky outcroppings. Not shy, it is also familiar because of its *fee-bee* vocalization and constant tail wagging. By tying a thread on the leg of several Eastern Phoebes, ornithologist John James Audubon established that individuals return from the south to a previously used nest site. Although difficult to tell apart, males tend to be slightly larger and darker than females.

rounded wings with two faint wing bars

brownish-gray upperparts

white throat

white throat

pale edges to wing feathers

♂

round, dark-capped head

yellowish tint on lower belly

dark eye

olive tint to sides and breast

long, dark tail

🦋 BREEDING

VOICE *Common call a clear, weak chip; song an emphatic* fee-bee *or* fee-b-be-bee.
NESTING *Open cup of mud, moss, and leaves, almost exclusively on artificial structures; 3–5 eggs; 2 broods; Apr–Jul.*
FEEDING *Flying insects, such as wasps, flies, moths, and dragonflies; also small fruit from fall through winter.*
HABITAT *Open woodland and along deciduous or mixed forest edges, gardens, and parks near water.*
LENGTH *5½–7in (14–17cm)*
WINGSPAN *10½in (27cm)*

Eastern Kingbird

S

Tyrannus tyrannus

The Eastern Kingbird is a tame yet highly territorial species and is known for its aggressive behavior toward potential predators, particularly crows and hawks. It is able to identify and remove the eggs of the Brown-headed Cowbird when they are laid in its nest. The Eastern Kingbird is generally monogamous and pairs will return to the same territory in subsequent years.

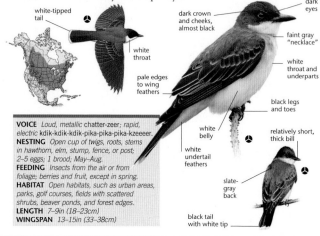

white-tipped tail

white throat

pale edges to wing feathers

dark crown and cheeks, almost black

dark eyes

faint gray "necklace"

white throat and underparts

black legs and toes

white belly

white undertail feathers

relatively short, thick bill

slate-gray back

black tail with white tip

VOICE *Loud, metallic chatter-zeer; rapid, electric kdik-kdik-kdik-pika-pika-pika-kzeeeer.*
NESTING *Open cup of twigs, roots, stems in hawthorn, elm, stump, fence, or post; 2–5 eggs; 1 brood; May–Aug.*
FEEDING *Insects from the air or from foliage; berries and fruit, except in spring.*
HABITAT *Open habitats, such as urban areas, parks, golf courses, fields with scattered shrubs, beaver ponds, and forest edges.*
LENGTH *7–9in (18–23cm)*
WINGSPAN *13–15in (33–38cm)*

Gray Kingbird

T

Tyrannus dominicensis

Large, conspicuous, and noisy, Gray Kingbirds are tolerant of humans, but aggressive around their nests, attacking mammals and birds of prey. The Shiny Cowbird lays its eggs in Gray Kingbird nests, but the flycatcher is adept at ejecting this brood parasite's eggs. Gray Kingbirds often frequent exposed perches, from which they fly off to catch large flying insects, including beetles and dragonflies.

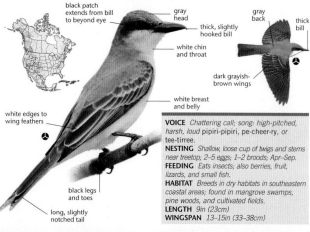

black patch extends from bill to beyond eye

gray head

thick, slightly hooked bill

white chin and throat

white breast and belly

white edges to wing feathers

black legs and toes

long, slightly notched tail

gray back

thick bill

dark grayish-brown wings

VOICE *Chattering call; song: high-pitched, harsh, loud pipiri-pipiri, pe-cheer-ry, or tee-tirree.*
NESTING *Shallow, loose cup of twigs and stems near treetop; 2–5 eggs; 1–2 broods; Apr–Sep.*
FEEDING *Eats insects; also berries, fruit, lizards, and small fish.*
HABITAT *Breeds in dry habitats in southeastern coastal areas; found in mangrove swamps, pine woods, and cultivated fields.*
LENGTH *9in (23cm)*
WINGSPAN *13–15in (33–38cm)*

Great Crested Flycatcher

Myiarchus crinitus

The Great Crested Flycatcher is locally common and geographically quite widespread in summer from Alberta and the Maritimes to Florida and Texas, but is often overlooked because it remains in the forest canopy, although it visits the ground for food and nest material. Its presence is usually given away by its loud, sharp, double-syllabled notes. It lines its nest with shed snakeskins (or similar materials like cellophane) like other *Myiarchus* flycatchers.

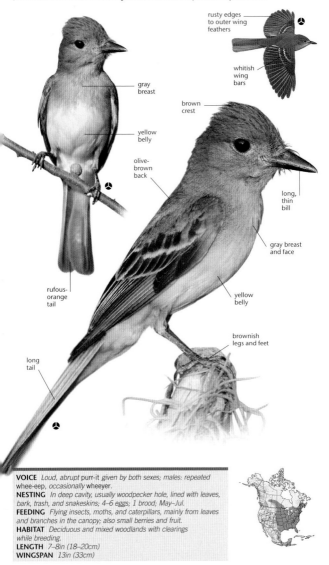

rusty edges to outer wing feathers

whitish wing bars

gray breast

yellow belly

brown crest

olive-brown back

long, thin bill

gray breast and face

rufous-orange tail

yellow belly

brownish legs and feet

long tail

VOICE Loud, abrupt purr-it *given by both sexes; males: repeated* whee-eep, *occasionally* wheeyer.
NESTING *In deep cavity, usually woodpecker hole, lined with leaves, bark, trash, and snakeskins; 4–6 eggs; 1 brood; May–Jul.*
FEEDING *Flying insects, moths, and caterpillars, mainly from leaves and branches in the canopy; also small berries and fruit.*
HABITAT *Deciduous and mixed woodlands with clearings while breeding.*
LENGTH *7–8in (18–20cm)*
WINGSPAN *13in (33cm)*

Vireos

Recent studies suggest that vireos are related to crows rather than the similar-looking warblers. Vireos are drab birds, often grayish or greenish above and whitish below, augmented by eye-rings, eye-stripes, and wing bars. Most vireos prefer broad-leaved trees, where they forage for prey. Because they mainly eat large insects, most migrate to warmer climates in wintertime. Vireos are often detected by the male's loud, clear, persistent territorial song.

SEPARATE SPECIES
The Blue-headed Vireo is one of three species that were formerly considered just one, the Solitary Vireo.

Jays and Crows

Jays and crows are highly social, opportunistic birds that use their strong bills, toes, and brains to obtain a varied, omnivorous diet. Ravens, magpies, and crows are highly intelligent, and exhibit self-awareness, counting, toolmaking, and problem-solving skills. Crows and jays were significantly affected by the spread of the West Nile virus in the early 2000s, but most populations have since recovered.

BRAINY BIRD
Common Ravens are one of the smartest birds, known for their problem-solving skills.

Loggerhead Shrike

D E

Lanius ludovicianus

Although a songbird, the Loggerhead Shrike behaves like a small bird of prey and has a hooked bill and strong, sharp, curved claws. It sits atop posts or tall trees, swooping down to catch prey on the ground. It has the unusual habit of impaling its prey on thorns, barbed wire, or sharp twigs, which is the reason for the nickname "butcher bird."

white flash in wings

white edges to tail

black wings

gray crown

hooked bill

black mask

pale undertail feathers

unstreaked gray underparts

rounded tail

VOICE Quiet warbles, trills, and harsh notes singly or in series: chaa chaa chaa.
NESTING Open cup of vegetation, placed in thorny tree; 5 eggs; 1 brood; Mar–Jun.
FEEDING Kills large insects and small vertebrates—rodents, birds, reptiles—with powerful bill.
HABITAT Semiopen country with grazed short grass and scattered perches in generally remote regions; distribution is erratic.
LENGTH 9in (23cm)
WINGSPAN 12in (31cm)

Northern Shrike

S

Lanius borealis

This northern relative of the familiar Loggerhead Shrike is an uncommon winter visitor to the northern US and southern Canada. The Northern Shrike is paler, larger-bodied, and larger-billed than the Loggerhead Shrike, which enables it to attack and subdue larger prey. Mostly, this bold, eye-catching shrike looks like an obvious whitish "spot" on top of an isolated tree or bush, but at times it can be remarkably elusive, perching lower down among foliage.

conspicuous white wing bar

pale gray upperparts

delicately barred breast

brownish underparts

strongly hooked bill

large head

narrow black mask

pale gray upperparts

long tail

black wings

black tail with white outer tail feathers

gray-white underparts

VOICE Short warbles, trills, and harsh notes; generally silent on wintering grounds.
NESTING Open, bulky cup in low tree or large shrub, lined with feathers and hair; 4–6 eggs; 1 brood; May–Jun.
FEEDING Rodents, small birds, and insects, which it impales on thorns or pointed branches.
HABITAT Sub-Arctic coniferous forests while breeding; open country with sufficient perches in winter.
LENGTH 10in (25cm)
WINGSPAN 14in (35cm)

White-eyed Vireo

Vireo griseus

The White-eyed Vireo is a vocal inhabitant of dense thickets, where it forages actively. It is heard more often than it is seen, singing persistently into the heat of the day and late into the year, long after most birds have become silent. It is parasitized by the Brown-headed Cowbird, and as many as half of the White-eyed Vireo's nestlings do not survive.

bright yellow "spectacles"

white eye

gray nape

whitish throat

two prominent wing bars

short tail

two wing bars

yellow flanks

yellow-and-black wing markings

VOICE *Raspy, angry scold; males: highly variable repertoire of over a dozen distinct songs.*
NESTING *Deep cup in dense vegetation, lined with fine fibers, often near water, suspended from twigs by the rim; 3–5 eggs; 2 broods; Mar–Jul.*
FEEDING *Bees, flies, beetles, and bugs, plucked from leaves or from the air; fruit in winter.*
HABITAT *Dense brush, scrub while breeding.*
LENGTH *5in (13cm)*
WINGSPAN *7½in (19cm)*

Yellow-throated Vireo

Vireo flavifrons

This large vireo of eastern US woodlands is usually found foraging and singing high in the canopy. It is distinctly patterned, with a bright yellow throat, breast, and "spectacles," and a white belly and flanks. The fragmentation of forests, spraying of insecticides, and parasitism by Brown-headed Cowbirds have led to regional declines in Yellow-throated Vireo populations, but the bird's range as a whole has expanded.

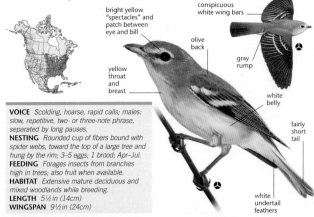

bright yellow "spectacles" and patch between eye and bill

conspicuous white wing bars

olive back

gray rump

yellow throat and breast

white belly

fairly short tail

white undertail feathers

VOICE *Scolding, hoarse, rapid calls; males: slow, repetitive, two- or three-note phrase, separated by long pauses.*
NESTING *Rounded cup of fibers bound with spider webs, toward the top of a large tree and hung by the rim; 3–5 eggs; 1 brood; Apr–Jul.*
FEEDING *Forages insects from branches high in trees; also fruit when available.*
HABITAT *Extensive mature deciduous and mixed woodlands while breeding.*
LENGTH *5½in (14cm)*
WINGSPAN *9½in (24cm)*

Blue-headed Vireo

(S)

Vireo solitarius

The Blue-headed Vireo has a blue-gray helmeted head, adorned with striking white "spectacles" around its dark eyes, which helps distinguish it from other vireos in its range. This stocky and slow-moving bird is heard more often than it is seen in its forest breeding habitat. During migration, it can be more conspicuous and is the first vireo to return in spring.

two wing bars

greenish back

blue-gray head

looks "big-headed"

conspicuous white "spectacles"

contrasting white throat

white belly

bright greenish flanks

relatively short tail

VOICE Harsh, scolding chatter; males: sweet, high phrases of two to six slurred notes.
NESTING Shallow, rounded cup loosely constructed of animal and plant fibers, suspended from twigs by the rim; 3–5 eggs; 2 broods; May–Jul.
FEEDING Insects from high in shrubs and trees; often makes short sallies after prey.
HABITAT Undisturbed coniferous and mixed forests with rich understory while breeding.
LENGTH 5½in (14cm)
WINGSPAN 9½in (24cm)

Warbling Vireo

(S)

Vireo gilvus

This vireo has a cheerful warbling song and a somewhat warblerlike appearance. Eastern and Western Warbling Vireos are quite different and may, in fact, be separate species. Eastern birds are heavier and have a larger bill. Of all the vireos, the Warbling Vireo is most likely to breed in human developments, such as city parks and suburbs.

grayish-green upperparts

blackish bill

grayish overall

white eyebrow

grayish behind eye

pale patch between eye and bill

yellowish flanks

pale brownish crown contrasts with darker back

VOICE Harsh, raspy scold call; males: high, rapid, and highly variable warble.
NESTING Rough cup placed high in a deciduous tree, hung from the rim between forked twigs; 3–5 eggs; 2 broods; Mar–Jul.
FEEDING Insects, including grasshoppers, aphids, and beetles from leaves; eats fruit in winter.
HABITAT Deciduous and mixed forests near water while breeding.
LENGTH 5½in (14cm)
WINGSPAN 8½in (21cm)

Philadelphia Vireo

Vireo philadelphicus

Despite being widespread, the Philadelphia Vireo remains relatively poorly studied. It shares its breeding habitat with the similar-looking, but larger and more numerous, Red-eyed Vireo, and, interestingly, modifies its behavior to avoid competition. It is the most northerly breeding vireo, with its southernmost breeding range barely reaching the US. This vireo derives its scientific and English names from the fact that the bird was first discovered near Philadelphia in the mid-1800s. However, it is an uncommon migrant to Philadelphia, and does not nest there.

gray cap

slightly hooked black bill

dark line through eye

white eyebrow

greenish upperparts

yellow throat

yellowish underparts

VOICE *Series of two- and four-note phrases, similar to the song of the Red-eyed Vireo.*
NESTING *Rounded cup of plant fibers bound by spiderwebs, hanging between forked twigs that narrows at the rim; 3–5 eggs; 1–2 broods; Jun–Aug.*
FEEDING *Caterpillars, bees, flies, and bugs from leaves, high in trees.*
HABITAT *Deciduous and mixed woodlands, and woodland edges while breeding.*
LENGTH *5¼in (13.5cm)*
WINGSPAN *8in (20cm)*

Red-eyed Vireo

Vireo olivaceus

Probably the most common songbird of northern and eastern North America, the Red-eyed Vireo is perhaps the quintessential North American vireo, although it is heard more often than it is seen. It sings persistently and monotonously all day long and late into the season, long after other species have stopped singing. It generally stays high in the canopy of the deciduous and mixed woodlands where it breeds. The entire population migrates in the fall to central South America in winter.

brown eyes

head held at downward angle

generally olive above

whitish breast and belly

gray crown

heavy eye-line

long bill

white eye-stripe with black upper border

deep red eye

bird appears long and slender

whitish underparts

bluish legs and toes

VOICE *Nasal mewing call; males: slurred three-note phrases, ending in either an upturn or downturn.*
NESTING *Open cup nest of plant fibers bound with spider's web hanging on horizontal fork of tree branch; exterior is sometimes decorated with lichen; 3–5 eggs; 1 brood; May–Jul.*
FEEDING *Insects from leaves, in the canopy and subcanopy of deciduous trees; primarily fruit during fall and winter.*
HABITAT *Canopy of deciduous forests and pine hardwood forests.*
LENGTH *6in (15cm)*
WINGSPAN *10in (25cm)*

Canada Jay

Ⓢ

Perisoreus canadensis

The fearless, cunning Canada Jay is well known to campers for its inquisitive behavior. It is adept at stealing food and shiny metal objects, which has earned it the nickname "Camp Robber." These jays often gather in small, noisy groups to investigate intruders encroaching upon their territory. Canada Jays store food for later use by sticking it to trees with their viscous saliva—a good technique for surviving long northern winters.

long tail with white corners

dark gray upperparts

gray overall, darker upperparts

**P. c. canadensis
NORTHERN**

dark crown

brownish back with white streaks

short bill

white collar

**P. c. obscurus
NORTHWESTERN**

black legs and toes

dark smoky-gray tail and wings

VOICE *Mostly silent; odd clucks and screeches; sometimes Blue Jay-like* jay! *and eerie whistles, including bi-syllabic* whee-oo *or* ew.
NESTING *Bulky platform of sticks with cocoons on south side of coniferous tree; 2–5 eggs; 1 brood; Feb–May.*
FEEDING *Insects and berries; also raids birds' nests; raisins, peanuts, bread.*
HABITAT *Coniferous forests, especially lichen-festooned areas with firs and spruces.*
LENGTH *10–11½in (25–29cm)*
WINGSPAN *18in (46cm)*

Blue Jay

Cyanocitta cristata

The Blue Jay is common in rural and suburban backyards across Canada and the eastern US. Beautiful as it is, the Blue Jay has a darker side: it often raids the nests of smaller birds for eggs and nestlings. Although usually thought of as a nonmigratory species, some Blue Jays undertake impressive migrations, with loose flocks sometimes numbering in the hundreds visible overhead in spring and fall. They are true omnivores, eating almost anything they can find.

long tail with white corners

white streak in blue wings

white patches on wing

white trailing edge to feathers

black legs and feet

black patch between eye and bill

blue crest

black collar

plain blue mantle

black bill

long black bill

whitish throat

blue wings and tail

grayish underparts

black bars on tail

VOICE *Harsh, screaming* jay! jay!*; odd, ethereal, chortling* queedle-ee-dee*; soft clucks when feeding; can mimic hawk calls.*
NESTING *Cup of strong twigs at variable height in trees or shrubs; 3–6 eggs; 1 brood; Mar–Jul.*
FEEDING *Insects, acorns; small vertebrates, such as lizards, rodents; bird eggs, birds, tree frogs; fruit and seeds.*
HABITAT *Deciduous, coniferous, and mixed woodlands; suburban vegetation and backyards.*
LENGTH *9½–12in (24–30cm)*
WINGSPAN *16in (41cm)*

American Crow

Corvus brachyrhynchos

S

The American Crow is common in almost all habitats—from wilderness to urban centers. Like most birds with large ranges, there is substantial geographical variation in this species. Birds are black across the whole continent, but size and bill shape vary from region to region. The birds of the coastal Pacific Northwest (*C. b. hesperis*), are on average smaller and have a lower-pitched voice.

black overall

dull black overall

shorter bill

black overall, with greenish sheen

long black bill

strong legs and feet

VOICE Loud, familiar caw!; juveniles' call higher-pitched.
NESTING Stick base with finer inner cup; 3–7 eggs; 1 brood; Apr–Jun.
FEEDING Omnivorous; fruit, carrion, garbage, insects, spiders; raids nests.
HABITAT Prefers open areas with widely spaced, large trees; urban areas, including lawns, parking lots, roadsides, and garbage dumps; partial migrant.
LENGTH 15½–19½in (39–49cm)
WINGSPAN 3¼ft (1m)

Fish Crow

Corvus ossifragus

S

Fish Crows are often found alongside the nearly identical, but slightly larger, American Crow. This highly social species breeds in small colonies. Fish Crows are numerous along coastlines and riverbanks, where they eat virtually anything edible; they are notorious nest-raiders. When a good source of food is found, they may cache the surplus for later, or to feed nestlings.

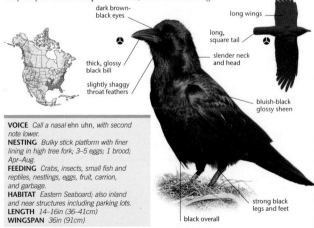

dark brown-black eyes

long wings

long, square tail

slender neck and head

thick, glossy black bill

slightly shaggy throat feathers

bluish-black glossy sheen

VOICE Call a nasal ehn uhn, with second note lower.
NESTING Bulky stick platform with finer lining in high tree fork; 3–5 eggs; 1 brood; Apr–Aug.
FEEDING Crabs, insects, small fish and reptiles, nestlings, eggs, fruit, carrion, and garbage.
HABITAT Eastern Seaboard; also inland and near structures including parking lots.
LENGTH 14–16in (36–41cm)
WINGSPAN 36in (91cm)

strong black legs and feet

black overall

Common Raven

S

Corvus corax

The Common Raven, twice the size of the American Crow, is a bird of legend, literature, and scientific wonder. Its Latin name, *Corvus corax*, means "crow of crows." Ravens are among the most intelligent of all birds: they learn quickly, adapt to new circumstances with remarkable agility, and are master problem-solvers. They communicate with each other via an array of vocal and body behaviors, sometimes even using ingenious methods to trick one another.

flared outer wing feathers

large, protruding head

wedge-shaped tail

long black wings

dark gray neck and underparts

thick, long bill with pronounced curvature

black upperparts with purplish gloss

shaggy throat

long black legs and feet

VOICE *Hoarse, rolling krruuk, twangy peals, guttural clicks, and resonant bonks.*
NESTING *Platform of sticks with fine inner material on trees, cliffs, or artificial structure; 4–5 eggs; 1 brood; Mar–Jun.*
FEEDING *Carrion, small crustaceans, fish, rodents, fruit, grain, and garbage; raids nests.*
HABITAT *Tundra, mountainous areas, forests, woodlands, prairies, arid regions, coasts, and near human settlements.*
LENGTH 23½–27in (60–69cm)
WINGSPAN 4½ft (1.4m)

Swallows

Swallows are nearly everywhere, except in the polar regions and some of the largest deserts. Most species have relatively short, notched tails but some have elongated outer tail feathers. All North American swallows are migratory, and most of them winter in Central and South America. They are all superb fliers, and skilled at aerial pursuit and the capture of flying insects.

SURFACE SKIMMER
This Tree Swallow flies low over freshwater to catch insects as they emerge into the air.

Chickadees and Titmice

Some chickadees are frequent visitors to backyards and are readily identified by their smooth-looking dark caps and black bibs. The name "chickadee" is derived from the common calls of several species. Highly social outside the breeding season and generally tolerant of people, they form sociable flocks in winter. Titmice are distinguished from chickadees by their crests; most also have plain throats. Like chickadees, titmice are highly territorial and insectivorous during the breeding season, and then become gregarious seedeaters afterward.

TAME BIRDS
Black-capped Chickadees have distinctive black-and-white markings and are often very tame.

Horned Lark

S E

Eremophila alpestris

The Horned Lark favors open country, especially places with extensive bare ground. It is characteristic of arid, alpine, and Arctic regions; in these areas, it flourishes in the bleakest of habitats, from sun-scorched, arid lakes in the Great Basin to windswept tundra above the timberline. In some places, the only breeding bird species are the Horned Lark and the Common Raven.

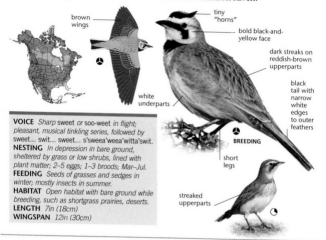

brown wings

tiny "horns"

bold black-and-yellow face

dark streaks on reddish-brown upperparts

black tail with narrow white edges to outer feathers

white underparts

BREEDING

short legs

streaked upperparts

VOICE *Sharp* sweet *or* soo-weet *in flight; pleasant, musical tinkling series, followed by* sweet... swit... sweet... s'sweea'weea'witta'swit.
NESTING *In depression in bare ground, sheltered by grass or low shrubs, lined with plant matter; 2–5 eggs; 1–3 broods; Mar–Jul.*
FEEDING *Seeds of grasses and sedges in winter; mostly insects in summer.*
HABITAT *Open habitat with bare ground while breeding, such as shortgrass prairies, deserts.*
LENGTH *7in (18cm)*
WINGSPAN *12in (30cm)*

Purple Martin

S

Progne subis

The Purple Martin is the largest of all North American swallows. In the eastern half of the continent, the Purple Martin depends almost entirely on specially built "apartment-style" birdhouses for nest sites. In the west, this glossy blue swallow is a more localized bird, although common in some areas. There, it nests principally in old woodpecker holes.

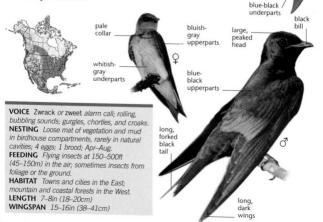

♂

blue-black underparts

black bill

pale collar

bluish-gray upperparts

large, peaked head

whitish-gray underparts

♀

blue-black upperparts

long, forked black tail

♂

long, dark wings

VOICE *Zwrack or* zweet *alarm call; rolling, bubbling sounds; gurgles, chortles, and croaks.*
NESTING *Loose mat of vegetation and mud in birdhouse compartments, rarely in natural cavities; 4 eggs; 1 brood; Apr–Aug.*
FEEDING *Flying insects at 150–500ft (45–150m) in the air; sometimes insects from foliage or the ground.*
HABITAT *Towns and cities in the East; mountain and coastal forests in the West.*
LENGTH *7–8in (18–20cm)*
WINGSPAN *15–16in (38–41cm)*

Tree Swallow

Tachycineta bicolor

One of the most common North American swallows, the Tree Swallow is
found from coast to coast in the northern half of the continent all the way
up to Alaska. It has iridescent bluish-green upperparts and white underparts.
Juveniles can be confused with the smaller Bank Swallow, which has a more
complete breastband. The Tree Swallow lives in a variety of habitats, but its
hole-nesting habit makes it completely dependent on abandoned woodpecker
cavities in dead trees and on nest boxes.

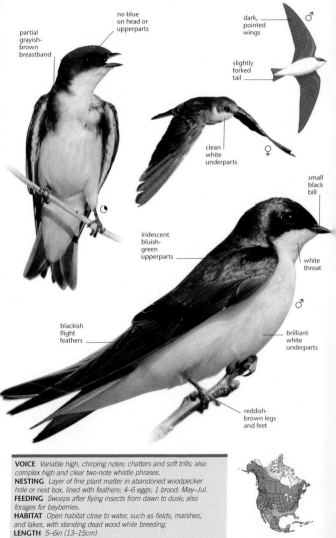

no blue
on head or
upperparts

partial
grayish-
brown
breastband

dark,
pointed
wings ♂

slightly
forked
tail

clean
white
underparts ♀

small
black
bill

iridescent
bluish-
green
upperparts

white
throat

♂

blackish
flight
feathers

brilliant
white
underparts

reddish-
brown legs
and feet

VOICE *Variable high, chirping notes; chatters and soft trills; also
complex high and clear two-note whistle phrases.*
NESTING *Layer of fine plant matter in abandoned woodpecker
hole or nest box, lined with feathers; 4–6 eggs; 1 brood; May–Jul.*
FEEDING *Swoops after flying insects from dawn to dusk; also
forages for bayberries.*
HABITAT *Open habitat close to water, such as fields, marshes,
and lakes, with standing dead wood while breeding.*
LENGTH *5–6in (13–15cm)*
WINGSPAN *12–14in (30–35cm)*

Northern Rough-winged Swallow

Stelgidopteryx serripennis

The Northern Rough-winged Swallow is found across southern Canada and throughout the US. It can be spotted hunting insects over water. In size and habit, it shares many similarities with the Bank Swallow, including breeding habits and color, but the latter's notched tail and smaller size make it easy to tell them apart.

dark face

dark brown overall

black eye

pale underparts

tan-buffy wing bars

brown head

light crescent from cheek to crown

long brown wings

pale brown breast

pale, grayish-brown belly

square tail

VOICE *Repeated, short* brrrt, *inflected upward; buzzy* jee-jee-jee *or high-pitched* brzzzzzt.
NESTING *Loose cup of twigs and straw in a cavity or burrow in a bank; 4–7 eggs; 1 brood; May–Jul.*
FEEDING *Flying insects (flies, wasps, bees, damselflies, beetles); more likely to feed over water and at lower altitudes than other swallows.*
HABITAT *Gorges, shale banks, and gravel pits while breeding; forages along watercourses.*
LENGTH *4¾–6in (12–15cm)*
WINGSPAN *11–12in (28–30cm)*

Bank Swallow

Riparia riparia

The Bank Swallow is the smallest of the North American swallows. It nests in the banks and bluffs of rivers, streams, and lakes, and favors sand and gravel quarries in the East. It breeds from south of the tundra–taiga line down to the central US. The nesting colonies, which can range from 10 to 2,000 pairs, are noisy when all the birds are calling.

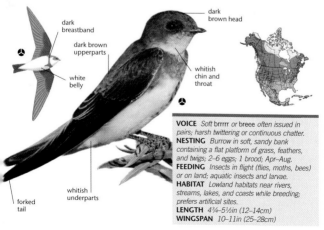

dark breastband

dark brown upperparts

white belly

dark brown head

whitish chin and throat

forked tail

whitish underparts

VOICE *Soft* brrrr *or* breee *often issued in pairs; harsh twittering or continuous chatter.*
NESTING *Burrow in soft, sandy bank containing a flat platform of grass, feathers, and twigs; 2–6 eggs; 1 brood; Apr–Aug.*
FEEDING *Insects in flight (flies, moths, bees) or on land; aquatic insects and larvae.*
HABITAT *Lowland habitats near rivers, streams, lakes, and coasts while breeding; prefers artificial sites.*
LENGTH *4¾–5½in (12–14cm)*
WINGSPAN *10–11in (25–28cm)*

Cliff Swallow

Petrochelidon pyrrhonota

The Cliff Swallow is one of North America's most social land birds, sometimes nesting in colonies of over 3,500 pairs. Its square tail and orange rump distinguish it from other North American swallows. The Cliff Swallow resembles the closely related Cave Swallow in color and pattern, and in its habit of affixing its mud nests to highway culverts, bridges, and buildings. This ability has enabled the Cliff Swallow to expand its range considerably.

long, roundish wings

rusty cheek patch

mottled throat

brown-tinged black back

bluish-black cap

whitish forehead

rusty-brown cheeks

pale hind neck collar

dark throat

bluish-black back

pale underparts

pale reddish rump

slight notch in squared tail

VOICE Purr and churr alarm calls; low, squeaky twitter given in flight and near nests.
NESTING Domed nests of mud pellets on cave walls, buildings, culverts, bridges, and dams; 3–5 eggs; 1–2 broods; Apr–Aug.
FEEDING Flying insects (often swarming varieties); sometimes forages on the ground; ingests grit to aid digestion.
HABITAT Most habitats except deserts, tundra, and unbroken forests.
LENGTH 5in (13cm)
WINGSPAN 11–12in (28–30cm)

Barn Swallow

Hirundo rustica

The Barn Swallow is found just about everywhere in North America south of the Arctic timberline. Originally a cave-nester, it now mostly nests under the eaves of houses, under bridges, and inside buildings, such as barns. Steely-blue upperparts, reddish underparts, and a deeply forked tail readily identify this bird. While still a fairly common sight, populations of Barn Swallows are in decline across the northern part of its range, likely due to loss of nesting sites and foraging habitats.

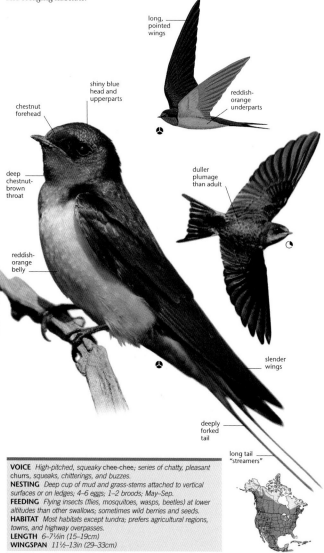

long, pointed wings

reddish-orange underparts

shiny blue head and upperparts

chestnut forehead

deep chestnut-brown throat

duller plumage than adult

reddish-orange belly

slender wings

deeply forked tail

long tail "streamers"

VOICE High-pitched, squeaky chee-chee; series of chatty, pleasant churrs, squeaks, chitterings, and buzzes.
NESTING Deep cup of mud and grass-stems attached to vertical surfaces or on ledges; 4–6 eggs; 1–2 broods; May–Sep.
FEEDING Flying insects (flies, mosquitoes, wasps, beetles) at lower altitudes than other swallows; sometimes wild berries and seeds.
HABITAT Most habitats except tundra; prefers agricultural regions, towns, and highway overpasses.
LENGTH 6–7½in (15–19cm)
WINGSPAN 11½–13in (29–33cm)

Carolina Chickadee

S

Poecile carolinensis

The Carolina Chickadee is the only chickadee found in the southeastern US, and was first described and named by John James Audubon in 1834, when he was in South Carolina. Its northern range limit locally overlaps the Black-capped Chickadee's southern limit in a narrow band from Kansas to New Jersey, where the two species interbreed regularly, creating hybrids with mixed plumage that are hard to identify. The Carolina Chickadee hides food in caches under branches or even within curled dead leaves, returning for it within a few days. It has a strong preference for sunflower seeds, and can be seen at bird feeders along with the Black-capped Chickadee, where the Carolina's characteristic call is the easiest way to distinguish the two species.

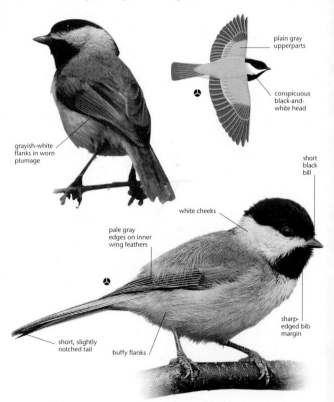

plain gray upperparts

conspicuous black-and-white head

grayish-white flanks in worn plumage

short black bill

white cheeks

pale gray edges on inner wing feathers

sharp-edged bib margin

short, slightly notched tail

buffy flanks

VOICE Fast dee-dee-dee call; song: clear, whistled, four-note sequence wee-bee wee-bay, second note lower in pitch.
NESTING Cavity lined with moss, fur, hair, plant down in soft, rotting tree; 5–8 eggs; 1–2 broods; Apr–May.
FEEDING Forages for insects and spiders; visits bird feeders in winter.
HABITAT Year-round dweller in southeastern deciduous, mixed, and pine woodlands, urban parks, and suburbs.
LENGTH 4¾in (12cm)
WINGSPAN 7½in (19cm)

Black-capped Chickadee

Poecile atricapillus

The Black-capped Chickadee is the most widespread chickadee in North America, equally at home in the cold far north and in warm valleys in the south. To cope with the harsh northern winters, this species can decrease its body temperature, entering a state of controlled hypothermia to conserve energy. Appearance varies according to location, with northern birds being slightly larger and having brighter white wing edgings than southern birds. Although it is a nonmigratory species, in winter flocks occasionally travel south of their traditional range in large numbers.

black bib with faded lower margin

white on wings and tail

black-and-white head

grayish-brown upperparts

buff flanks fading to white on belly

bright white cheeks

short black bill

white edges on wing feathers

white edges on outer tail feathers

black cap and bib

faded buff flanks

VOICE *Raspy* tsick-a-dee-dee-dee; *loud, clear whistle* bee-bee *or* bee-bee-be, *first note higher in pitch.*
NESTING *Cavity in rotting tree stump, lined with hair, fur, feathers, plant fibers; 6–8 eggs; 1 brood; Apr.–Jun.*
FEEDING *Insects and their eggs, and spiders in trees and bushes; mainly seeds in winter; may take seeds from an outstretched hand.*
HABITAT *Wooded habitats including forests, woodlands, parks, and suburbs.*
LENGTH 5¼in (13.5cm)
WINGSPAN 8½in (22cm)

Boreal Chickadee ⓢ

Poecile hudsonicus

The Boreal Chickadee was previously known by other names, including Hudsonian Chickadee and Brown-capped Chickadee. In the past, this species journeyed south of its usual range during winters of food shortage, but this pattern has not occurred in recent decades. Its back color shows geographic variation—grayish in the West and brown in the central and eastern portions of its range.

gray tail

gray cheeks

grayish-brown back

gray wings

brown cap

black bib

rich brown flanks and belly

VOICE Low-pitched, buzzy, lazy tsee-day-day; also high-pitched trill, dididididididi.
NESTING Cavity lined with fur, hair, plant down; in natural, excavated, or old woodpecker hole; 4–9 eggs; 1 brood; May–Jun.
FEEDING Insects, conifer seeds; hoards larvae and seeds in bark crevices in fall in preparation for winter.
HABITAT Spruce-fir forests.
LENGTH 5½in (14cm)
WINGSPAN 8½in (21cm)

Tufted Titmouse ⓢ

Baeolophus bicolor

The Tufted Titmouse is the most widespread of the North American titmice, and one of the two largest and most fearless; it has adapted very well to human habitations. In the last century, its range has expanded significantly northward into southern Canada, probably due to the increased numbers of bird feeders, which allow it to survive the cold northern winters.

crest may be flattened

tufted dark gray head

black forehead

conspicuous black eye in whitish face

gray wings

prominent orange flanks

gray tail

gray underparts

VOICE Loud, harsh pshurr, pshurr, pshurr; ringing, far-carrying peto peto peto, or peer peer peer.
NESTING Tree cavities, old woodpecker holes, and nest boxes lined with damp leaves, moss, grass, hair; 5–6 eggs; 1 brood; Mar–May.
FEEDING Insects, spiders, and their eggs; in winter, corn kernels, seeds, and small fruit.
HABITAT Deciduous and coniferous woodlands; parks and gardens.
LENGTH 6½in (16cm)
WINGSPAN 10in (25cm)

Nuthatches

Nuthatches are plump-bodied, large-headed birds, often located by their loud, squeaky calls. Their strong toes and arched claws provide them with a secure grip as they hop around on tree trunks feeding on spiders, insects, and larvae, frequently hanging upside-down. They also eat seeds and nuts, which they may wedge into a crevice and break open with noisy taps of the bill—hence the name "nuthatch."

ACROBATIC POSE
Downward-facing nuthatches, such as this one, often lift their heads in a characteristic pose.

Wrens

Wrens are often best located by their calls; these small birds have disproportionately loud voices. They are intricately patterned, most with dark bars and streaks, and pale spots on buff-and-rusty backgrounds. The short- to medium-length tails are frequently cocked upward. The family name, Troglodytidae ("cave dweller"), fits Winter and Pacific Wrens, which forage inside thick plant cover or in dense growth inside ditches.

COCKED TAIL
As they sing, Winter Wrens often hold their tails upward in a near-vertical position.

Red-breasted Nuthatch

S

Sitta canadensis

This inquisitive nuthatch, with its distinctive black eye-stripe, breeds in conifer forests across North America. The bird inhabits mountains in the West; in the East, it is found in lowlands and hills. However, sometimes it breeds in conifer groves away from its core range. Each fall, birds move from their main breeding grounds, but the extent of this exodus varies from year to year, depending on population cycles and food availability.

dark blue-gray crown and eye-stripe

rounded wings

slightly muted head pattern

white bands on tail

♀

pale orange underparts

bold black-and-white head pattern

pointed chisel-like bill

black eye-stripe

blue-gray upperparts

white cheeks

♂

rusty underparts

short blue-gray tail, with black side feathers

compact body shape

VOICE *One-note tooting sound, often repeated, with nasal yet musical quality: aaank, enk, ink, like a horn.*
NESTING *Excavates cavity in pine tree; nest of grass lined with feathers, with sticky pine resin applied to entrance to thwart predators; 5–7 eggs, 1 brood; May–Jul.*
FEEDING *Beetle grubs from bark; also insect larvae found on conifer needles; seeds in winter.*
HABITAT *Coniferous and mixed hardwood forests.*
LENGTH *4¼ in (11cm)*
WINGSPAN *8½ in (22cm)*

White-breasted Nuthatch

S

Sitta carolinensis

The amiable White-breasted Nuthatch inhabits woodlands across the US and southern Canada, but often visits bird feeders in winter. The largest of our nuthatches, it spends more time probing on trunks and boughs than other nuthatches do, walking forward, backward, upside-down, or horizontally. Five subspecies occur in Canada and in the US. They differ in call notes, and to a lesser extent, in plumage.

white flashes on tail

♂

rounded wings

narrower black band on nape

dull gray upperparts

gray crown

♀

whitish underparts

black crown and nape

conspicuous black eye

white face

white throat

long, pointed, chisel-like bill

blue-gray upperparts

short tail

whitish-gray underparts

chestnut undertail and lower belly

long strong claws

♂

VOICE *Eastern birds: nasal* yank yank*; interior birds: stuttering* st't't't't'*; Pacific slope birds: tremulous* yiiiirk*; all populations: mellow* tu tu tu tu*, like a flicker, but softer.*
NESTING *Old woodpecker hole lined with grass and hair, adds mud to cavity opening; 5–9 eggs, 1 brood; Apr–Jun.*
FEEDING *Insects (beetle larvae) from bark.*
HABITAT *Coniferous forests, and broadleaf deciduous or mixed forests.*
LENGTH *5¾in (14.5cm)*
WINGSPAN *11in (28cm)*

Brown-headed Nuthatch

D

Sitta pusilla

This pine-loving species is the southeastern counterpart of the western Pygmy Nuthatch. These two nuthatches play similar ecological roles in their respective ecosystems. The Brown-headed Nuthatch is a busy bird that travels in noisy packs, foraging upside-down along branches, and headfirst down tree trunks. Young are raised by both parents and one or more non-parent relatives.

white spot on nape

gray overall

rounded wings

white cheek and throat with pale yellow wash

warm brown nape and crown

pointed, chisel-like, dark bill

pale lower bill

blue-gray upperparts

short tail with white on uppertail feathers

sturdy legs and toes

long claws

VOICE *Call: a short* bek*; foraging flocks:* bwee! tutututu*, emphatic first note.*
NESTING *Excavates cavity in pine tree; lines nest with fur and feathers; 4–6 eggs; 1–2 broods; Mar–May.*
FEEDING *Gleans tree trunks for beetles, bugs, spiders; pine seeds in winter.*
HABITAT *Breeds in southeastern pine forests and oak-pine woods.*
LENGTH *4¼in (11cm)*
WINGSPAN *8in (20cm)*

Brown Creeper

S

Certhia americana

Although widespread and fairly common, the Brown Creeper's soft vocalizations and cryptic plumage make it one of the most understated forest birds. As it forages, it hops up a tree trunk, then flies down to another tree, and starts up again from near the ground. Although these birds' numbers have increased in regenerating forests, populations in the Midwest and Southwest have declined because deforestation has reduced their breeding habitat.

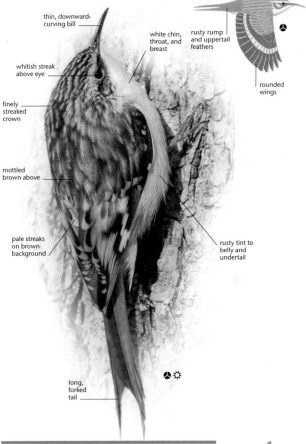

buff wing bars

rusty rump and uppertail feathers

rounded wings

thin, downward-curving bill

white chin, throat, and breast

whitish streak above eye

finely streaked crown

mottled brown above

pale streaks on brown background

rusty tint to belly and undertail

long, forked tail

VOICE *High-pitched and easily overlooked, buzzy* zwisss; *abrupt* tswit *in flight; wheezy jumble of thin whistles and short buzzes.*
NESTING *Hammock-shaped nest, behind peeling bark; 5–6 eggs, 1 brood; May–Jul.*
FEEDING *Probes bark for insects, especially larvae, eggs, pupae, and aphids.*
HABITAT *Fairly moist coniferous or mixed hardwood forests while breeding; small groves without coniferous trees and suburbs in winter.*
LENGTH *5¼in (13.5cm)*
WINGSPAN *8in (20cm)*

House Wren

S

Troglodytes aedon

Of all the North American wrens, the House Wren is the plainest, yet one of the most familiar and endearing. However, it can be a fairly aggressive species, driving away nearby nesting birds of its own species and others by destroying nests, puncturing eggs, and even killing young. In the 1920s, distraught bird-lovers campaigned to eradicate the House Wren, although the campaign did not last long because most were fortunately in favor of letting nature take its course.

plain brown crown

browner upperparts

faintly barred wings

pale buffy throat

EASTERN

T. a. aedon
EASTERN

thin, indistinct eyebrow

narrow, pale eye-ring

grayish-brown back

thin, slightly curved bill

narrow black barring on tail

pale gray-brown underparts

T. a. parkmanii
WESTERN

VOICE Sharp chep or cherr; several short notes followed by a bubbly explosion of spluttering notes.
NESTING Cup lined with soft material on stick platform in natural or constructed cavities, such as nest boxes; 5–8 eggs; 2–3 broods; Apr–Jul.
FEEDING Insects and spiders from trees and shrubs, gardens, and yards.
HABITAT Cities, towns, parks, farms, yards, gardens, and woodland edges while breeding.
LENGTH 4½ in (11.5cm)
WINGSPAN 6in (15cm)

Winter Wren

S

Troglodytes hiemalis

The Winter Wren has one of the loudest songs of any small
North American species. Once considered more widespread,
it has recently been split from the Pacific Wren, which
occupies much of the western fringe of the continent. It
frequently appears in full view, gives a few harsh, scolding
calls, then dives back out of sight into low cover.

short, barred tail

barred, rounded wings

stubby tail, usually cocked straight up

dark brown, barred back

distinct tan eyebrow

small, thin bill

VOICE *Double chek-chek or chimp-chimp;
complex series of warbles, trills, single notes.*
NESTING *Messy mound lined with feathers in
well-hidden cavity near ground with dead wood
and crevices; 4–7 eggs; 1–2 broods; Apr–Jul.*
FEEDING *Insects from low, dense
undergrowth, often along streams; sometimes
thrusts its head into water to capture prey.*
HABITAT *Prefers evergreen trees with dense
understory and stream banks while breeding.*
LENGTH *4in (10cm)*
WINGSPAN *5½in (14cm)*

flanks strongly barred

Sedge Wren

S

Cistothorus stellaris

A shy bird, the Sedge Wren stays out of sight except when singing atop a sedge
stalk or shrub. If discovered, it flies a short distance, drops, and runs to hide in
vegetation. The Sedge Wren breeds from May to June in the north-central region
of its range, and July to September in the southern and eastern regions. The male
will build up to 8–10 unlined "dummy" nests before the female builds the
better-concealed, real nest.

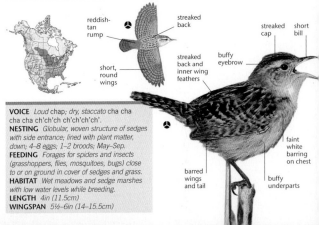

reddish-tan rump

streaked back

streaked cap

short bill

streaked back and inner wing feathers

buffy eyebrow

short, round wings

faint white barring on chest

VOICE *Loud chap; dry, staccato cha cha
cha cha cha ch'ch'ch ch'ch'ch'ch'.*
NESTING *Globular, woven structure of sedges
with side entrance; lined with plant matter,
down; 4–8 eggs; 1–2 broods; May–Sep.*
FEEDING *Forages for spiders and insects
(grasshoppers, flies, mosquitoes, bugs) close
to or on ground in cover of sedges and grass.*
HABITAT *Wet meadows and sedge marshes
with low water levels while breeding.*
LENGTH *4in (11.5cm)*
WINGSPAN *5½–6in (14–15.5cm)*

barred wings and tail

buffy underparts

Marsh Wren ⓢ

Cistothorus palustris

The Marsh Wren, a common resident of saltwater and freshwater marshes, is known for singing loudly through both day and night. The males perform aerial courtship flights while singing, and mate with two or more females. The male builds several "dummy" nests before his mate constructs one herself. Eastern and Western Marsh Wrens differ in voice and behavior, and are thought by some to be separate species.

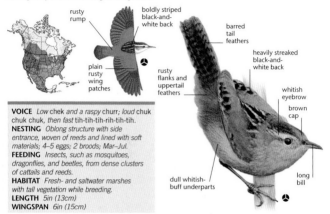

rusty rump

boldly striped black-and-white back

barred tail feathers

heavily streaked black-and-white back

plain rusty wing patches

rusty flanks and uppertail feathers

whitish eyebrow

brown cap

dull whitish-buff underparts

long bill

VOICE Low chek and a raspy churr; loud chuk chuk chuk, then fast tih-tih-tih-rih-tih-tih.
NESTING Oblong structure with side entrance, woven of reeds and lined with soft materials; 4–5 eggs; 2 broods; Mar–Jul.
FEEDING Insects, such as mosquitoes, dragonflies, and beetles, from dense clusters of cattails and reeds.
HABITAT Fresh- and saltwater marshes with tall vegetation while breeding.
LENGTH 5in (13cm)
WINGSPAN 6in (15cm)

Carolina Wren ⓢ

Thryothorus ludovicianus

The Carolina Wren is rarely still, often flicking its tail and looking around nervously. Extremely harsh winters at the northernmost fringe of the Carolina Wren's range in New England, to where it has expanded, can cause a sudden decline in numbers because food resources are covered for long periods by ice and heavy snow. At such times, survival may depend on human help for food and shelter.

thin black barring on tail

white wing spots

huge head

white eyebrow bordered by black above

powerful-looking bluish bill

duller overall

tiny tail

FLEDGLING

white spots on wing

rufous upperparts

VOICE Sharp chlip or long, harsh chatter; loud, long, fast whee'dle-dee whee'dle-dee whee'dle-dee.
NESTING Cup of weeds, twigs, leaves in natural or artificial cavity; 4–8 eggs; 2–3 broods; Apr–Jul.
FEEDING Insects in shrubs and on ground; in winter, prefers peanut butter or suet at a feeder.
HABITAT Bushy woodland habitats, such as thickets, parks, and gardens while breeding.
LENGTH 5¼in (13.5cm)
WINGSPAN 7½in (19cm)

pinkish legs and toes

buffy underparts

Blue-gray Gnatcatcher

(S)

Polioptila caerulea

The Blue-gray Gnatcatcher spends much of its time foraging high in tall trees, giving its continual wheezy call; in winter, it is generally silent. This species is the most northerly of the North American gnatcatchers and is also the only one to migrate. It can exhibit aggressive behavior and is capable of driving off considerably larger birds than itself.

white outer tail feathers

♂

pale gray overall

blue-gray upperparts

blue-gray nape

black line above eye; lacks it in winter

white eye-ring

white throat

white bar on tail

pale gray underparts

♂

black central tail feathers

pale patch on wing

lacks black line

paler upperparts

♀

VOICE *Soft, irregular zhee, zhee while foraging; soft, short notes and nasal wheezes.*
NESTING *Cup of plant fibers, spiderwebs, mosses; usually high on branch; lined with soft plant material; 4–5 eggs; 1–2 broods; Apr–Jun.*
FEEDING *Small insects and spiders; acrobatically flits from twig to twig while twitching long tail.*
HABITAT *Deciduous or pine woodlands in the East while breeding.*
LENGTH *4¼in (11cm)*
WINGSPAN *6in (15cm)*

Golden-crowned Kinglet

(S)

Regulus satrapa

This hardy little bird, barely more than a ball of feathers, breeds in northern and mountainous coniferous forests in North America. Other unconnected populations are residents of high-elevation forests in Mexico and Guatemala. Planting of spruce trees in parts of the US Midwest has allowed this species to increase its breeding range in recent years.

♂

whitish wing bars

orange-and-yellow patch on crown with black border

broad whitish stripe above eye

olive-green upperparts

♂

short, straight bill

white wing bar

notched tail

pale buff to whitish underparts

yellow crown patch with black border

♀

VOICE *High-pitched tsee or see see; tsee-tsee-tsee-tsee-teet-teetle, followed by brief trill.*
NESTING *Cup-shaped nest made of moss and bark; 8–9 eggs; 1–2 broods; May–Aug.*
FEEDING *Flies, beetles, mites, spiders, and their eggs from tips of branches, under bark, conifer needles; seeds and persimmon fruit.*
HABITAT *Spruce or fir forests, mixed coniferous–deciduous forests, single-species stands while breeding.*
LENGTH *3¼–4¼in (8–11cm)*
WINGSPAN *5½–7in (14–18cm)*

Ruby-crowned Kinglet

Corthylio calendula

The Ruby-crowned Kinglet is recognizable because of its very small size, white eye-ring, white wing bars, and habit of incessantly flicking its wings while foraging. This bird is renowned for its loud, complex song and for laying up to 12 eggs in a clutch—among the highest of any North American songbird. Despite local declines resulting from logging and forest fires, the Ruby-crowned Kinglet is common across the continent.

patch on crown often concealed

notched tail

white wing bars

no red patch on crown

♀

red patch on crown

incomplete white eye-ring

♂

olive-green upperparts

olive underparts

VOICE *Husky* jidit; *2–3 clear* tee *or* zee, *5–6 lower* tu *or* turr, *and repeated* tee-da-leet.
NESTING *Globular nest with enclosed or open cup, made of mosses, feathers, spider's silk, bark, fur; 5–12 eggs; 1 brood; May–Oct.*
FEEDING *Insects, spiders, and their eggs from leaves; fruit and seeds.*
HABITAT *Near water in black spruce and tamarack forests, muskegs, mixed conifer, and hardwood forests while breeding.*
LENGTH *3½1½–4¼in (9–11cm)*
WINGSPAN *6–7in (15–18cm)*

Thrushes

Thrushes and chats frequent forests, primarily feeding on the ground. Many are brownish, with spotting underneath. Except for the Varied Thrush, American Robin, and bluebirds, thrushes often lack vivid colors. Others compensate with exquisite patterning and beautiful songs.

GROUND BIRDS
Although they perch to sing, thrushes, including this Gray-cheeked Thrush, spend a lot of their time on or near the ground.

Thrashers

Thrashers, mockingbirds, and catbirds are known for their ability to mimic the songs of other species. Thrashers are more elongated than thrushes and have longer, more decurved bills, and longer legs and tails. While mockingbirds are bold and conspicuous, thrashers are more reclusive.

GROUND BIRDS
Though they perch to sing, thrushes, including this Gray-cheeked Thrush, spend a lot of their time on or near the ground.

Pipits

Pipits inhabit open, treeless country, walking rather than hopping on the ground. They are more likely to be seen in their widespread wintering areas, in their brown nonbreeding plumage, than in their remote breeding range.

COUNTRY-LOVERS
Pipits, such as this American Pipit, live in open country, including beaches, dunes, and tundra.

Northern Wheatear

S

Oenanthe oenanthe

Although widely distributed in Eurasia, the Middle East, and Africa, the Northern Wheatear is present in North America only during its brief breeding season in Alaska and northeastern Canada. Two subspecies breed in North America—the larger *O. o. leucorhoa* in the Northeast and *O. o. oenanthe* in the Northwest. The Northern Wheatear can be recognized by its black-and-white tail, which bobs when the bird walks.

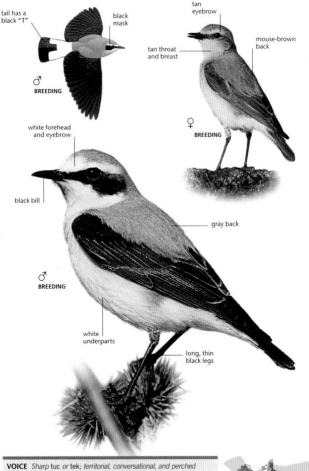

tail has a black "T"

black mask

♂ BREEDING

tan eyebrow

tan throat and breast

mouse-brown back

♀ BREEDING

white forehead and eyebrow

black bill

gray back

♂ BREEDING

white underparts

long, thin black legs

VOICE Sharp tuc or tek; territorial, conversational, and perched song, consisting of sweet and harsh notes; imitates other species.
NESTING Under rocks or in abandoned burrows; nests have coarse outer foundation lined with finer material; 5–6 eggs; 1 brood; Jun–Jul.
FEEDING Insects; also berries; diet in North America not well known.
HABITAT Rocky tundra while breeding.
LENGTH 5½–6in (14–15cm)
WINGSPAN 10¾in (27cm)

Eastern Bluebird

S

Sialia sialis

The Eastern Bluebird's vibrant blue-and-chestnut body is a beloved sight in eastern North America, especially after the remarkable comeback of the species in the past 30 years. After much of the bird's habitat was eliminated by agriculture in the mid-20th century, nest boxes were designed and constructed for the bluebirds to provide alternatives for their traditional nesting sites in tree cavities. The Eastern Bluebird's mating system can entail males breeding with multiple partners.

gray-brown upperparts

spotted throat and breast

♂

bluish-gray underwings

white belly

rufous breast and throat

pale chestnut throat

♀

gray upperparts

blue wings, rump, and tail

bright blue upperparts

♂

chestnut-brown chin, throat, breast, and flanks

white belly

white undertail

VOICE *Melodious series of soft, whistled notes; churr-wi or churr-li.*
NESTING *Cavity-nester, in trees or artificial boxes; nest lined with grass, weeds, and twigs; uses old nests of other species; 3–7 eggs; 2 broods; Feb–Sep.*
FEEDING *Insects in breeding season, such as grasshoppers and caterpillars; also fruit and plants in winter.*
HABITAT *Clearings and woodland edges; open habitats in rural, urban, and suburban areas.*
LENGTH 6–8in (15–20cm)
WINGSPAN 10–13in (25–33cm)

Veery

D

Catharus fuscescens

The Veery is medium-sized, like the other *Catharus* thrushes, but browner overall and less spotted. Its plumage shows geographic variation, and four subspecies have been described to reflect this. Eastern birds (*C. f. fuscescens*) are ruddier than their western relatives (*C. f. salicicola*). The Veery migrates to spend the northern winter months in central Brazil.

pale reddish-brown upperparts

brownish-tan upperparts

creamy-pink at base of bill

less distinct spotting on breast

C. f. fuscescens EASTERN

inconspicuous pale eye-ring

black upper bill

white underparts

poorly marked brown spots on buff breast and throat

tan wash on flanks

creamy-pink legs and feet

C. f. salicicola WESTERN

VOICE Series of descending *da-vee-ur, vee-ur, veer, veer,* somewhat bitonal, sounding like the name Veery; rather soft *veer.*
NESTING Cup of dead leaves, bark, weed stems, and moss on or near ground; 4 eggs; 1–2 broods; May–Jul.
FEEDING Insects, spiders, snails from ground; fruit and berries after breeding.
HABITAT Canopy in damp deciduous forests or habitat near rivers in summer.
LENGTH 7in (18cm)
WINGSPAN 11–11½in (28–29cm)

Gray-cheeked Thrush

S

Catharus minimus

The Gray-cheeked Thrush is the least known of the five North American *Catharus* thrushes because it breeds in remote areas of northern Canada and Alaska. During migration, the Gray-cheeked Thrush is more likely to be heard in flight at night than seen on the ground by birders.

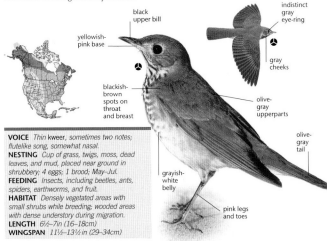

black upper bill

indistinct gray eye-ring

yellowish-pink base

gray cheeks

blackish-brown spots on throat and breast

olive-gray upperparts

olive-gray tail

grayish-white belly

pink legs and toes

VOICE Thin *kweer,* sometimes two notes; flutelike song, somewhat nasal.
NESTING Cup of grass, twigs, moss, dead leaves, and mud, placed near ground in shrubbery; 4 eggs; 1 brood; May–Jul.
FEEDING Insects, including beetles, ants, spiders, earthworms, and fruit.
HABITAT Densely vegetated areas with small shrubs while breeding; wooded areas with dense understory during migration.
LENGTH 6½–7in (16–18cm)
WINGSPAN 11½–13½in (29–34cm)

Bicknell's Thrush

Catharus bicknelli

Previously considered a subspecies of the Gray-cheeked Thrush, Bicknell's Thrush is best distinguished by its song, which is less full and lower in pitch than the Gray-cheeked Thrush's. It breeds only in dwarf conifer forests on mountaintops in the northeastern US and adjacent Canada, usually above 3,000ft (1,000m). They mate with multiple partners in a single season, and males may care for the young in multiple nests.

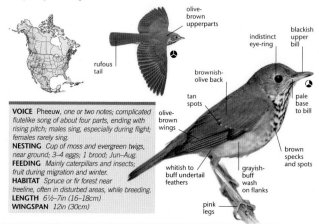

olive-brown upperparts

rufous tail

indistinct eye-ring

blackish upper bill

brownish-olive back

tan spots

olive-brown wings

pale base to bill

brown specks and spots

whitish to buff undertail feathers

grayish-buff wash on flanks

pink legs

VOICE *Pheeuw, one or two notes; complicated flutelike song of about four parts, ending with rising pitch; males sing, especially during flight; females rarely sing.*
NESTING *Cup of moss and evergreen twigs, near ground; 3–4 eggs; 1 brood; Jun–Aug.*
FEEDING *Mainly caterpillars and insects; fruit during migration and winter.*
HABITAT *Spruce or fir forest near treeline, often in disturbed areas, while breeding.*
LENGTH *6½–7in (16–18cm)*
WINGSPAN *12in (30cm)*

Swainson's Thrush

Catharus ustulatus

Swainson's Thrush can be distinguished from other spotted thrushes by its buffy face and the rising pitch of its flutelike, melodious song. It also feeds higher in the understory than most of its close relatives. There are six subspecies; the western ones are russet-backed and migrate to Central America, and the others, both northern and eastern, are olive-backed and winter in South America.

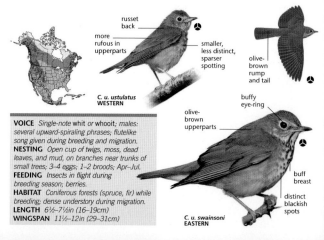

russet back

more rufous in upperparts

smaller, less distinct, sparser spotting

olive-brown rump and tail

C. u. ustulatus
WESTERN

buffy eye-ring

olive-brown upperparts

buff breast

distinct blackish spots

C. u. swainsoni
EASTERN

VOICE *Single-note whit or whooit; males: several upward-spiraling phrases; flutelike song given during breeding and migration.*
NESTING *Open cup of twigs, moss, dead leaves, and mud, on branches near trunks of small trees; 3–4 eggs; 1–2 broods; Apr–Jul.*
FEEDING *Insects in flight during breeding season; berries.*
HABITAT *Coniferous forests (spruce, fir) while breeding; dense understory during migration.*
LENGTH *6½–7½in (16–19cm)*
WINGSPAN *11½–12in (29–31cm)*

Hermit Thrush Ⓢ

Catharus guttatus

This bird's song is the signature sound of northern and mountain forests in the West—fluted, almost bitonal, far-carrying, and ending up with almost a question mark. The Hermit Thrush has a solitary lifestyle, especially in winter, when birds maintain inter-individual territories. Geographical variation within the vast range of the species has led to the recognition of nine subspecies (two are shown here). It winters in the southern US, Mexico, Guatemala, and El Salvador.

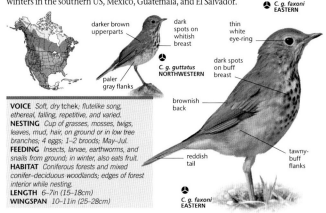

gray-brown upperparts

C. g. faxoni
EASTERN

darker brown upperparts

dark spots on whitish breast

thin white eye-ring

C. g. guttatus
NORTHWESTERN

paler gray flanks

dark spots on buff breast

brownish back

reddish tail

tawny-buff flanks

C. g. faxoni
EASTERN

VOICE *Soft, dry tchek; flutelike song, ethereal, falling, repetitive, and varied.*
NESTING *Cup of grasses, mosses, twigs, leaves, mud, hair, on ground or in low tree branches; 4 eggs; 1–2 broods; May–Jul.*
FEEDING *Insects, larvae, earthworms, and snails from ground; in winter, also eats fruit.*
HABITAT *Coniferous forests and mixed conifer–deciduous woodlands; edges of forest interior while nesting.*
LENGTH *6–7in (15–18cm)*
WINGSPAN *10–11in (25–28cm)*

Wood Thrush Ⓣ

Hylocichla mustelina

The Wood Thrush has distinctive black spots that cover its underparts and a rufous head and back. In the breeding season, its flutelike song echoes through the northeastern hardwood forests and suburban forested areas. Wood Thrush populations have fallen over the past 30 years due to habitat destruction and its susceptibility to brood parasitism by the Brown-headed Cowbird.

roundish brown wings

rusty-orange head and back

white eye-ring

black bill with pink base

rusty-orange head

reddish-brown lower back and rump

short reddish-brown tail

creamy-pink legs and toes

large black triangular spots on breast, sides, and flanks

VOICE *Rapid pip-pippipip or rhuu-rhuu; a three-part flutelike song, ending with a trill.*
NESTING *Cup-shaped nest made with dried grass and weeds in trees or shrubs; 3–4 eggs; 1–2 broods; May–Jul.*
FEEDING *Worms, beetles, moths, caterpillars from leaf litter; fruit after breeding season.*
HABITAT *Interior and edges of deciduous and mixed forests while breeding; dense understory, shrubbery, and moist soil.*
LENGTH *7½–8½in (19–21cm)*
WINGSPAN *12–13½in (30–34cm)*

American Robin

S

Turdus migratorius

The American Robin is the largest and most abundant of the North American thrushes. It is probably the most familiar bird on the continent, and its presence on suburban lawns and in urban parks is an early sign of spring. It has adapted and prospered in human-altered habitats, breeding across Canada and the US and migrating out of most of Canada in the fall. Migration is largely governed by changes in the availability of food, and thus, it is possible to observe some robins living off berries in suburban areas in midwinter.

more complete white eye-ring

gray back

♀

orangish-red breast

white rump

dark head

♂

broken white eye-ring

yellow bill

dark streaks on chin

♂

mottled gray back

spotted breast

dark gray back

fairly long, dark tail

brick-red underparts

VOICE *High-pitched* tjip *and multi-note, throaty* tjuj-tjuk; *melodious* cheer-up, cheer-up, cheer-wee; *sings from early morning to late evening.*
NESTING *Substantial cup of grass, weeds, and trash in tree forks or on branches, shelves, and porch lights; 4 eggs; 2–3 broods; Apr.–Jul.*
FEEDING *Earthworms and small insects from leaf litter; fruit in winter.*
HABITAT *Forest, woodland, suburban gardens, parks, and farms while breeding; woodlands with berry-bearing trees.*
LENGTH *8–11in (20–28cm)*
WINGSPAN *12–16in (30–41cm)*

Gray Catbird

S

Dumetella carolinensis

In addition to its felinelike, mewing calls, the Gray Catbird can also sing two notes simultaneously. It has been reported to imitate the vocalizations of over 40 bird species, at least one frog species, and several sounds produced by machines and electronic devices. Despite their shy, retiring nature, Gray Catbirds tolerate human presence and will nest in shrubs in suburban and urban lots.

long black tail

gray overall

straight blackish bill

gray upperparts

dark gray to black head

large black eye

bright brick-red undertail feathers

gray underparts

VOICE *Mew call, like a young kitten; long, complex series of unhurried notes, sometimes interspersed with whistles and squeaks.*
NESTING *Large, untidy cup of woven twigs, grass, and hair lined with finer material; 3–4 eggs; 1–2 broods; May–Aug.*
FEEDING *Wide variety of berries and insects, whatever is most abundant in season.*
HABITAT *Mixed young to mid-aged forests with abundant undergrowth while breeding.*
LENGTH *8–9½in (20–24cm)*
WINGSPAN *10–12in (25–30cm)*

Brown Thrasher

S

Toxostoma rufum

The Brown Thrasher, another well-known mimic, usually keeps to dense underbrush and prefers running or hopping to flying. When nesting, it can recognize and remove the eggs of brood parasites like the Brown-headed Cowbird. The Brown Thrasher is an energetic singer and has one of the largest repertoires of any songbird in North America.

rufous wings and upperparts

fairly straight dark bill

bright yellow eye

grayish cheeks

reddish-brown upperparts

long tail with pale outer tips

indistinct "mustache"

two pale wing bars

dark streaking on pale underparts

long tail, paler than back

VOICE *Rasping sounds; long series of musical notes, often imitating other species; repeats phrase twice before moving on to the next one.*
NESTING *Bulky cup of twigs close to ground, lined with leaves, grass, bark; 3–5 eggs; 1 brood; Apr–Jul.*
FEEDING *Mainly beetles and worms from leaf litter; cultivated grains, nuts, berries, and fruit.*
HABITAT *Densely wooded habitats with thick undergrowth; woodland edges, riverside trees.*
LENGTH *10–12in (25–30cm)*
WINGSPAN *11–14in (28–36cm)*

Northern Mockingbird

Mimus polyglottos

An impressive mimic, the Northern Mockingbird can incorporate more than 100 different phrases of as many different birds in its songs. Its range has expanded in the last few decades, partly due to its high tolerance for human habitats. It frequently gives a "wing-flash" display, showing its white outer wing feathers by raising its wings while foraging on the ground, ostensibly to scare insects into the open.

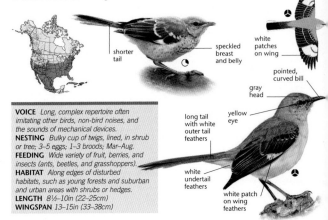

shorter tail

speckled breast and belly

white patches on wing

pointed, curved bill

gray head

long tail with white outer tail feathers

yellow eye

white undertail feathers

white patch on wing feathers

VOICE *Long, complex repertoire often imitating other birds, non-bird noises, and the sounds of mechanical devices.*
NESTING *Bulky cup of twigs, lined, in shrub or tree; 3–5 eggs; 1–3 broods; Mar–Aug.*
FEEDING *Wide variety of fruit, berries, and insects (ants, beetles, and grasshoppers).*
HABITAT *Along edges of disturbed habitats, such as young forests and suburban and urban areas with shrubs or hedges.*
LENGTH *8½–10in (22–25cm)*
WINGSPAN *13–15in (33–38cm)*

European Starling

Sturnus vulgaris

This nonnative species is perhaps the most successful bird in North America—and probably the most maligned. In the 1890s, 100 European Starlings were released in New York City's Central Park; these were the ancestors of the millions of birds that now live across Canada and the US. These birds compete with native species like Kestrels for nesting cavities, and usually win.

BREEDING

short, square tail

pointed, triangular wings

body feathers tipped whitish or buff

wing feathers edged bright orange-buff

large spots on undertail

NONBREEDING

black face with hints of shiny, glossy purple

blue-based, sharp yellow bill; pink-based on female

glossy black body with mostly green sheen

dark, glossy blue-black belly

long pinkish-brown legs and strong toes

♂ BREEDING

VOICE *Whooshing sssssheer; whistled wheeeooo; elaborate pulsing series with slurred whistles and clicking notes; imitates other species' vocalizations and nonnatural sounds.*
NESTING *Natural or artificial cavity of any sort; 4–6 eggs; 1–2 broods; Mar–Jul.*
FEEDING *Omnivorous; insects, berries; visits bird feeders and trash cans; grubs in lawns.*
HABITAT *Cities, towns, and farmlands; also relatively "wild" settings far from people.*
LENGTH *8½in (21cm)*
WINGSPAN *16in (41cm)*

American Pipit

Anthus rubescens

In its nonbreeding plumage, the American Pipit is a drab-looking bird that forages for insects along water and shores, or in cultivated fields. In the breeding season, molting transforms it into a beauty, with gray upperparts and reddish underparts. American Pipits are known for pumping their tails up and down. Breeding males display by rising into the air, then flying down with wings open and singing.

white outer tail feathers

gray cheek with buffy eye-stripes

buffy eye-stripe

no streaking on grayish back

thin, dark bill

dark "mustache"

wing bars

pale edges to wing feathers

light reddish-buffy chest and flanks

white outer tail feathers

BREEDING

long hind claw

dark legs and toes

pale eyebrow

thin "mustache"

whitish, with streaking on chest and flanks

faint streaking on gray upperparts

NONBREEDING

VOICE Tzeeep *in alarm; repeated* tzwee-tzooo *from the air.*
NESTING *Cup in shallow depression on ground, outer frame of grass, lined with fine grass and hair; 4–6 eggs; 1 brood; Jun–Jul.*
FEEDING *Picks insects; also seeds during migration.*
HABITAT *Arctic and alpine tundra and treeless mountaintops while breeding; open coastal areas in winter.*
LENGTH *6–8in (15–20cm)*
WINGSPAN *10–11in (25–28cm)*

Bohemian Waxwing

Bombycilla garrulus

The Bohemian Waxwing is the wilder and rarer of the two waxwing species in North America. It breeds mainly in Alaska and western Canada. The species is migratory, but the extent of its wintertime movement is notoriously variable, depending on the availability of wild fruit. They are slightly larger than Cedar Waxwings, with distinctive rusty undertail feathers.

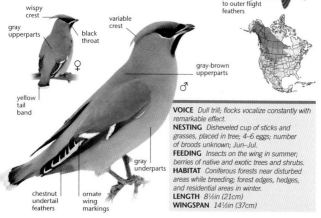

yellow edges to outer flight feathers

wispy crest

gray upperparts

black throat

variable crest

♀

yellow tail band

gray-brown upperparts

♂

gray underparts

chestnut undertail feathers

ornate wing markings

VOICE *Dull trill; flocks vocalize constantly with remarkable effect.*
NESTING *Disheveled cup of sticks and grasses, placed in tree; 4–6 eggs; number of broods unknown; Jun–Jul.*
FEEDING *Insects on the wing in summer; berries of native and exotic trees and shrubs.*
HABITAT *Coniferous forests near disturbed areas while breeding; forest edges, hedges, and residential areas in winter.*
LENGTH *8½in (21cm)*
WINGSPAN *14½in (37cm)*

Cedar Waxwing

S

Bombycilla cedrorum

Flocks of nomadic Cedar Waxwings wander around North America looking for sugary fruits, their favorite food. Common in a specific location one year, they may disappear the next and occur elsewhere. Northern breeders tend to be more migratory than southern ones. In winter, they may travel as far south as South America. They can often be heard and identified by their calls, long before the flock settles to feed.

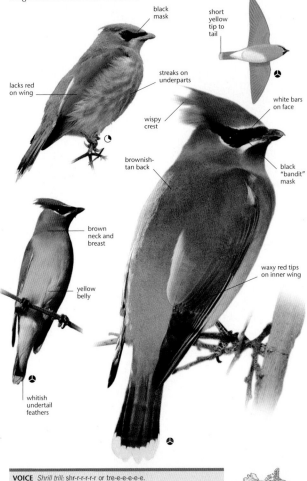

black mask

short yellow tip to tail

streaks on underparts

lacks red on wing

white bars on face

wispy crest

brownish-tan back

black "bandit" mask

brown neck and breast

yellow belly

waxy red tips on inner wing

whitish undertail feathers

VOICE *Shrill trill: shr-r-r-r-r-r or tree-e-e-e-e-e.*
NESTING *Open cup placed in fork of tree, often lined with grasses, plant fibers; 3–5 eggs; 1–2 broods; Jun–Aug.*
FEEDING *Eats in flocks at trees and shrubs with ripe berries throughout the year; also flying insects in summer.*
HABITAT *Woodlands near streams and clearings while breeding; habitats with trees, shrubs, and fruit in winter; spends a lot of time in treetops, but may come down to shrub level.*
LENGTH *7½in (19cm)*
WINGSPAN *12in (30cm)*

Longspurs and Snow Buntings

Longspurs and Snow Buntings are small birds of open country that forage on bare or open ground, from tundra and mountaintops to open prairies, often in flocks. They have recently been designated a separate family, distinct from the Old World buntings and New World sparrows with which they had been linked previously.

Snow Buntings have distinctive white bands on their wings. Mostly Arctic tundra breeders, they are gregarious, eye-catching birds, especially when they rise in a blizzard of white wings.

Longspurs derive their name from their long, curved hindclaws. Their short, blackish legs help give them a long, low shape on the ground. Their calls provide useful clues for identification as they fly. Lapland Longspurs form immense flocks, sometimes millions strong.

CHANGING COLORS
Snow Buntings are well camouflaged against exposed rocks and snow throughout the year. Brown edges on the feathers in winter wear off, so they become pristine black and white in spring.

Lapland Longspur

S

Calcarius lapponicus

One of the most numerous breeding birds of the Arctic tundra, Lapland Longspurs migrate south of the deepest snows during winter to frequent open habitats, such as American farm fields, in the winter. They are especially visible on gravel roads and in barren countryside immediately following heavy snowfalls. The longspurs and the Snow Bunting were formerly part of the Emberizidae family but are now placed in a distinct family of their own. They consume mostly weed seeds in the winter, which can be in scarce supply in farm fields treated with herbicides.

rich buffy hood

black face

♂ **BREEDING**

thin white edge to tail

NONBREEDING

thick streaking on flanks

thick yellowish bill

white eye-line

bright rufous nape

rusty wing panel

black flanks

white underparts

♂ **BREEDING**

VOICE *Flight call a dry rattle, tyew, unlike other longspurs; song a series of thin tinklings and whistles, often in flight.*
NESTING *Cup of grass and sedges placed in depression on ground next to a clump of vegetation; 4–6 eggs; 1 brood; May–Jul.*
FEEDING *Insects while breeding; seeds in winter.*
HABITAT *Tundra while breeding; open grasslands, fields, beaches in winter.*
LENGTH *6½in (16cm)*
WINGSPAN *10½–11½in (27–29cm)*

Snow Bunting

S

Plectrophenax nivalis

The bold white wing patches of the Snow Bunting make it recognizable in a winter flock of dark-winged longspurs and larks. To secure the best territories, some male Snow Buntings arrive as early as April in their barren high-Arctic breeding grounds. The species is very similar in appearance to the rare and localized McKay's Bunting, which generally has less black on the back, wings, and tail, and the two species can be difficult to distinguish.

less white in wings

white outer tail feathers

♀ NONBREEDING

♂ NONBREEDING

yellow bill

large white patches on black wings

gray body

white eye-ring

dark brown eyes

rusty-orange cheek patch

black peeks through buffy feather edgings

rusty-orange breast patch

♂ NONBREEDING

white underparts

VOICE *Musical, liquid rattle in flight, also* **tyew** *notes and short buzz; pleasant series of squeaky and whistled notes.*
NESTING *Bulky cup of grass and moss, lined with feathers, in sheltered rock crevice; 3–6 eggs; 1 brood; Jun–Aug.*
FEEDING *Seeds (sedge in the Arctic), flies and other insects, and buds on migration.*
HABITAT *Rocky areas, usually near sparsely vegetated tundra, while breeding; open areas and shores in winter.*
LENGTH *6½–7in (16–18cm)*
WINGSPAN *12½–14in (32–35cm)*

Wood Warblers

Wood warblers are remarkable for their diversity in plumage, song, feeding, breeding biology, and sexual dimorphism. In general, though, wood warblers share similar shapes: all are smallish birds with longish, thin bills used mostly for snapping up invertebrates. Their varied colors and patterns make the lively, busy, mixed groups seen on migration especially appealing and fascinating to watch. Ground-dwelling warblers tend to be larger and clad in olives, browns, and yellows, while many arboreal species are small and sport bright oranges, cool blues, and even ruby-reds. The color, location, and presence or absence of paler wing bars and tail spots is often a good identification aid.

STATIC PLUMAGE
Some warblers, such as this male Golden-winged Warbler, keep their stunning plumage year-round.

Ovenbird

Seiurus aurocapilla

The Ovenbird is named for the domed, ovenlike nests it builds on the ground in mixed and deciduous forests. Males flit around boisterously, often at night, incorporating portions of their main song into a jumble of spluttering notes. In the forest, one male singing loudly to declare his territory can set off a whole chain of responses from his neighbors.

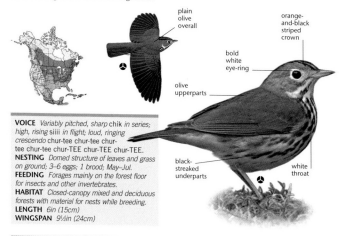

plain olive overall

orange-and-black striped crown

bold white eye-ring

olive upperparts

black-streaked underparts

white throat

VOICE *Variably pitched, sharp* chik *in series; high, rising* siiii *in flight; loud, ringing crescendo* chur-tee chur-tee chur-tee chur-tee chur-TEE chur-TEE chur-TEE.
NESTING *Domed structure of leaves and grass on ground; 3–6 eggs; 1 brood; May–Jul.*
FEEDING *Forages mainly on the forest floor for insects and other invertebrates.*
HABITAT *Closed-canopy mixed and deciduous forests with material for nests while breeding.*
LENGTH *6in (15cm)*
WINGSPAN *9½in (24cm)*

Worm-eating Warbler

Helmitheros vermivorum

The only member of its genus, the Worm-eating Warbler actually consumes caterpillars rather than worms. It often hangs upside-down, prying into a mass of dead curled leaves for unsuspecting caterpillars. The bird then levers the curl open with its bill to claim its prize. This bird blends in with the forest leaf litter and forages fairly low, but singing males perch in treetops.

dull olive overall

short tail

boldly striped buff-and-black crown

blurry pattern on undertail feathers

large, pinkish bill

tawny wash on breast

VOICE *Thick* chip *call; flight call a thin, rolling* ziiit *series; thin, dry trilling song.*
NESTING *Concealed leaf litter cup at sapling or shrub base, often on hillside; 3–6 eggs; 1 brood; May–Jul.*
FEEDING *Forages for caterpillars; also insects and spiders.*
HABITAT *Breeds in expansive hilly, mature deciduous forests with abundant leaf litter and dense undergrowth.*
LENGTH *5in (13cm)*
WINGSPAN *8½in (21cm)*

Louisiana Waterthrush

(T)

Parkesia motacilla

The Louisiana Waterthrush is one of the earliest warblers to return north in the spring; as early as March, eastern ravines are filled with its cascading song. Both the stream-loving Louisiana Waterthrush and its still-water cousin, the Northern Waterthrush, bob their tails as they walk, but the Louisiana Waterthrush arcs its entire body at the same time.

short tail

dull brown overall

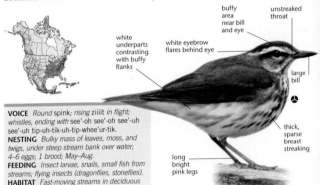

buffy area near bill and eye

unstreaked throat

white underparts contrasting with buffy flanks

white eyebrow flares behind eye

large bill

thick, sparse breast streaking

long bright pink legs

VOICE Round spink; rising ziiiit in flight; whistles, ending with see'-oh see'-oh see'-uh see'-uh tip-uh-tik-uh-tip-whee'ur-tik.
NESTING Bulky mass of leaves, moss, and twigs, under steep stream bank over water; 4–6 eggs; 1 brood; May–Aug.
FEEDING Insect larvae, snails, small fish from streams; flying insects (dragonflies, stoneflies).
HABITAT Fast-moving streams in deciduous forests while breeding.
LENGTH 6in (15cm)
WINGSPAN 10in (25cm)

Northern Waterthrush

(S)

Parkesia noveboracensis

The tail-bobbing Northern Waterthrush is often heard giving a *spink!* call as it swiftly flees from observers. Although this species may be mistaken for the closely related Louisiana Waterthrush, the Northern Waterthrush can be distinguished by its song and its preference for still over running water.

pale eyebrow

streaking on white or yellowish flanks

dull brown upperparts

pale eyebrow narrows behind eye

small, short bill

short tail

dull, fleshy-colored legs and toes

fine, dense breast streaking

VOICE Sharp, rising, ringing spink!; rising, buzzy ziiiit in flight; loud, accelerating, staccato notes teet, teet, toh-toh toh-toh tyew-tyew!
NESTING Hair-lined, mossy cup, in tree roots or riverbank; 4–5 eggs; 1 brood; May–Aug.
FEEDING Insects, such as ants, mosquitoes, moths, and beetles; slugs and snails; small crustaceans and tiny fish when migrating.
HABITAT Still-water swamps and bogs while breeding; also still edges of rivers and lakes.
LENGTH 6in (15cm)
WINGSPAN 9½in (24cm)

Golden-winged Warbler

Vermivora chrysoptera

This species is unfortunately being genetically swamped by the Blue-winged Warbler. The Golden-winged interbreeds with the Blue-winged, resulting in two more frequently seen hybrid forms: Brewster's Warbler, which is similar to the Golden-winged Warbler; and Lawrence's Warbler, which looks like a Blue-winged Warbler with the mask and black throat of a Golden-winged.

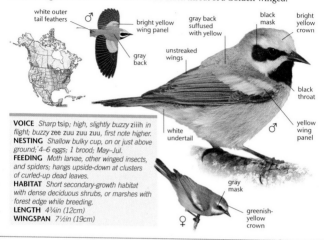

white outer tail feathers ♂

bright yellow wing panel

gray back

gray back suffused with yellow

unstreaked wings

black mask

bright yellow crown

black throat

white undertail

♂

yellow wing panel

gray mask

greenish-yellow crown

♀

VOICE Sharp tsip; high, slightly buzzy ziiih in flight; buzzy zee zuu zuu zuu, first note higher.
NESTING Shallow bulky cup, on or just above ground; 4–6 eggs; 1 brood; May–Jul.
FEEDING Moth larvae, other winged insects, and spiders; hangs upside-down at clusters of curled-up dead leaves.
HABITAT Short secondary-growth habitat with dense deciduous shrubs, or marshes with forest edge while breeding.
LENGTH 4¾in (12cm)
WINGSPAN 7½in (19cm)

Blue-winged Warbler

Vermivora cyanoptera

The Blue-winged Warbler breeds along forest edges and in second-growth forests. It interbreeds freely with Golden-winged Warblers, producing a variety of fertile combinations. The most frequently produced hybrid, Brewster's Warbler, is similar to the Golden-winged Warbler (yellowish breast, two yellow wing bars), but has the Blue-winged's facial pattern, without the black mask and throat.

white in outer tail

♂

fine white wing bars

blue-gray wings

black eye-line

yellow head

black mask

♂

yellow breast and belly

white undertail feathers

two wing bars

spiky bill

yellow underparts

♀

VOICE Tsip call; high, slightly buzzy ziiih in flight; low, harsh, buzzy beee-burrrrr, second note very low in pitch and rattling.
NESTING Deep, bulky cup of vegetation, just off the ground in grasses; 4–5 eggs; 1 brood; May–Jun.
FEEDING Moth larvae and small insects; hangs upside-down at clusters of dead leaves.
HABITAT Second-growth forest while breeding; will use older and taller stands.
LENGTH 4¾in (12cm)
WINGSPAN 7½in (19cm)

Black-and-white Warbler

Mniotilta varia

The Black-and-white Warbler is best known for its creeperlike habit of feeding in vertical and upside-down positions as it pries into bark crevices, where its relatively long bill allows it to reach into tiny nooks and crannies. It is a long-distance migrant, with some birds wintering in parts of northern South America.

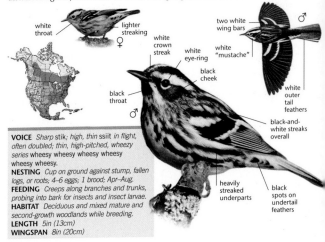

white throat

lighter streaking

♀

white crown streak

white eye-ring

black cheek

two white wing bars

white "mustache"

♂

black throat

♂

white outer tail feathers

black-and-white streaks overall

black spots on undertail feathers

heavily streaked underparts

VOICE *Sharp* stik; *high, thin* ssiit *in flight, often doubled; thin, high-pitched,* wheezy *series* wheesy wheesy wheesy wheesy wheesy wheesy.
NESTING *Cup on ground against stump, fallen logs, or roots; 4–6 eggs; 1 brood; Apr–Aug.*
FEEDING *Creeps along branches and trunks, probing into bark for insects and insect larvae.*
HABITAT *Deciduous and mixed mature and second-growth woodlands while breeding.*
LENGTH *5in (13cm)*
WINGSPAN *8in (20cm)*

Prothonotary Warbler

Protonotaria citrea

The ringing song of the Prothonotary Warbler echoes through the swampy forests of southern Ontario and the southeastern US every summer. This is one of the few cavity-nesting warbler species; it will use human-made birdhouses placed close to still water. Prothonotary Warblers also tend to stay fairly low over the water, making them easy to spot.

duller colored head

large bill

♀

blue wings and tail

yellowish breast and head

white in tail

bluish rump

♂

black eye

glowing gold head

large bill

bluish wings and tail

olive back

♂

bright yellow underparts

VOICE *Loud* chip; *loud, high* sviit *in flight; penetrating and internally rising notes* tsveet tsveet tsveet tsveet tsveet tsveet tsveet.
NESTING *Over or near still water; woodpecker holes often used; 3–8 eggs; 1–2 broods; Apr–Jul.*
FEEDING *Mostly insects and small mollusks; also seeds, fruit, and nectar.*
HABITAT *Wooded areas near still water while breeding, especially swampy deciduous forest.*
LENGTH *5½in (14cm)*
WINGSPAN *9in (23cm)*

Tennessee Warbler ⓢ

Leiothlypis peregrina

The Tennessee Warbler was named after its place of
discovery, but this bird would have been on migration,
because it breeds almost entirely in Canada and winters
in Central America. These warblers inhabit fairly remote
areas, and their nests are difficult to find. The population
of Tennessee Warblers tends to increase in years when
budworms are abundant.

VOICE *Sharp* tzit; *thin* seet *in flight;
three-part staccato chip-chip-chip.*
NESTING *Nest woven of fine plant matter,
in ground depression; 4–7 eggs; 1 brood; Jun.*
FEEDING *Caterpillars, bees, wasps, beetles,
and spiders from tree branches; fruit in winter;
drinks nectar by piercing the base of flowers.*
HABITAT *Woodlands with dense understory
and thickets of willows and alders while
breeding; parks and gardens while migrating.*
LENGTH 4¾in (12cm)
WINGSPAN 7¾in (19.5cm)

Orange-crowned Warbler ⓢ

Leiothlypis celata

Common and relatively brightly colored in the West but uncommon and
duller in the East, the Orange-crowned Warbler has a large breeding range. The
19th-century American naturalist Thomas Say described this species based on
specimens collected in Nebraska. Because its tiny orange cap is concealed in
the plumage of the crown, he named it *celata*, which is Latin for "hidden."

VOICE *Clean, sharp* tsik; *high, short* seet
in flight; loose, lazy trill.
NESTING *Cup of grasses, fibers, and down,
usually on the ground under a bush; 4–5 eggs;
1 brood; Mar–Jul.*
FEEDING *Arthropods, such as beetles, ants,
spiders, and their larvae; also fruit; drinks
nectar by piercing the base of a flower.*
HABITAT *Varied habitats while breeding;
prefers stream-side thickets.*
LENGTH 5in (13cm)
WINGSPAN 7¼in (18.5cm)

Nashville Warbler ⓢ

Leiothlypis ruficapilla

Although often confused with the ground-walking Connecticut Warbler, the
Nashville Warbler is smaller, hops around in trees, and has a yellow throat.
There are two subspecies: *L. r. ruficapilla* in the East and *L. r. ridgwayi* in the West.
Differences in voice, habitat, behavior, and plumage hint that they may be separate
species. *L. r. ridgwayi* has more white on its belly and a grayish-green back.

rufous
crown
patch

conspicuous
white eye-ring

blue-gray
helmet

grayish-
green back

♂ *L. r. ruficapilla*
EASTERN

olive-green
upperparts

olive
wings

rounded
wings

♂ *L. r. ridgwayi*
WESTERN

yellow
undertail
feathers

white
patch
on belly

duller olive
back

♀ *L. r. ruficapilla*
EASTERN

less contrast
between gray
and yellow

VOICE *Sharp* tik; *high, thin* siit *in flight;
eastern song: first lazy, then faster trill* tee-tsee
tee-tsee tee-tsee tee-tsee titititititi; *western song:
slightly lower with a seldom trilled* tee-tsee
tee-tsee tee-tsee weesay weesay way.
NESTING *Cup hidden on ground in dense
cover; 3–6 eggs; 1 brood; May–Jul.*
FEEDING *Insects and spiders from trees.*
HABITAT *Wet habitats in East and brushy
montane areas in West while breeding.*
LENGTH *4¾in (12cm)*
WINGSPAN *7½in (19cm)*

Connecticut Warbler ⓢ

Oporornis agilis

Despite its name, the Connecticut Warbler does not breed in
Connecticut—it breeds in remote, boggy habitats in Canada.
Seldom heard and hard to spot during migration, it is the only
warbler that walks along the ground, gleaning insects from
under leaves in a bouncy manner, with its tail bobbing up and
down. The yellow undertail feathers nearly reach the tail tip.

olive
flanks

♂

very
long yellow
undertail feathers

gray hood

♂

olive upperparts

short tail

conspicuous
white eye-
ring

dark gray
bib

pale sunshine-
yellow
underparts

pink legs
and feet

olive upperparts

grayish-
green
hood

♀

VOICE *Call a nasal* champ; *buzzy* ziiiit *flight
call; loud accelerating* chuh WHIP-uh chee-uh-
WHIP-uh chee-uh-WAY *song.*
NESTING *Concealed cup of grass or leaves,
lined with plants and hair; on the ground
in damp moss or grass clump; 3–5 eggs;
1 brood; Jun–Jul.*
FEEDING *Gleans insects, larvae, and spiders;
also small fruit.*
HABITAT *Breeds in bogs and pine forests.*
LENGTH *6in (15cm)*
WINGSPAN *9in (23cm)*

Mourning Warbler

Ⓢ

Geothlypis philadelphia

The Mourning Warbler's song is often used in movies as a background sound of idyllic suburban settings. However, this warbler is unlikely to be found in a backyard—it prefers dense, herbaceous tangles for breeding and during migration. These birds are late spring migrants and the leaves are fully out when they arrive in the East, making them difficult to see.

"hooded" look

♂ **BREEDING**

yellow undertail feathers

pale gray hood

lacks speckled markings on throat

olive upperparts

♀

gray head

black mask

black bib and speckled throat

yellow underparts

pink toes and legs

♂ **BREEDING**

VOICE *Flat* tchik; *high, thin, clear* svit *in flight; burry notes with low-pitched ending:* churrr-ee churrr-ee churrr-ee churr-ee churrr-ee-oh.
NESTING *Well-concealed cup of leaves, lined with grass, on or near ground in dense tangle; 2–5 eggs; 1 brood; Jun–Aug.*
FEEDING *Insects and spiders from low foliage; some plant material in winter.*
HABITAT *Dense thickets of disturbed woodlands while breeding.*
LENGTH *5in (13cm)*
WINGSPAN *7½in (19cm)*

Kentucky Warbler

Ⓓ

Geothlypis formosa

The loud, cheery song of the Kentucky Warbler is a characteristic sound of dense eastern US forests. This warbler breeds in Kentucky, its namesake state. It is a rather secretive species. It forages near the ground in the underbrush for insects that inhabit the forest floor. This bird is rarely out in the open.

short tail

black-and-yellow facial pattern

black crown with gray spots

yellow streak above eyes

black cheek

dark olive upperparts

yellow chin and throat

bright yellow underparts

pale pinkish legs and feet

less black on face

♀

pale olive upperparts

VOICE *Low, hollow* chup *call, buzzy* dziiip *in flight; song a loud rolling* chur-ee' chur-ee' chur-ee' churee' chur-ee' *series.*
NESTING *Concealed bulky leaf and grass cup on or near ground; 4–5 eggs; 1–2 broods; May–Aug.*
FEEDING *Gleans beetles and spiders in low vegetation.*
HABITAT *Breeds in moist deciduous eastern forests with dense understory.*
LENGTH *5in (13cm)*
WINGSPAN *8½in (21cm)*

Common Yellowthroat

S

Geothlypis trichas

This common warbler is noticeable partly because of its loud, simple song. This species varies in voice and plumage across its range, and 14 subspecies have been described. Western populations have yellower underparts, brighter white head stripes, and louder, simpler songs than the eastern birds. The male often flies upward rapidly, delivering a more complex version of its song.

black mask

♂

plain olive-green overall

black mask including forehead

pale stripe over mask, varies from gray to white or yellowish

yellow throat

pale eye-ring

olive upperparts

yellow throat

♀

yellow throat

olive-green upperparts

♂

greenish-gray underparts

olive-green tail

VOICE Harsh, buzzy *tchak*, repeated into chatter when agitated; low, flat, buzzy *dzzzit* in flight; rich (often three-note) phrases: WITCH-uh-tee WITCH-uh-tee WHICH.
NESTING Concealed bulky cup of grasses just above ground; 3–5 eggs; 1 brood; May–Aug.
FEEDING Insects and spiders from low vegetation; also seeds.
HABITAT Dense herbaceous understory in marshes, grasslands, forests, hedges.
LENGTH 5in (13cm)
WINGSPAN 6¾in (17cm)

Hooded Warbler

S

Setophaga citrina

The Hooded Warbler is a strikingly patterned and loud warbler. Both males and females frequently flash the white markings hidden on the inner webs of their tails. The extent of the black hood varies in female Hooded Warblers; it ranges from none in first fall birds to almost as extensive as males in some adult females.

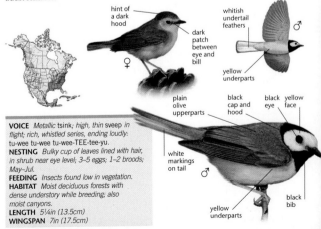

hint of a dark hood

♀

dark patch between eye and bill

whitish undertail feathers

♂

yellow underparts

plain olive upperparts

black cap and hood

black eye

yellow face

white markings on tail

♂

black bib

yellow underparts

VOICE Metallic *tsink*; high, thin *sveep* in flight; rich, whistled series, ending loudly: tu-wee tu-wee tu-wee-TEE-tee-yu.
NESTING Bulky cup of leaves lined with hair, in shrub near eye level; 3–5 eggs; 1–2 broods; May–Jul.
FEEDING Insects found low in vegetation.
HABITAT Moist deciduous forests with dense understory while breeding; also moist canyons.
LENGTH 5¼in (13.5cm)
WINGSPAN 7in (17.5cm)

American Redstart

Setophaga ruticilla

The American Redstart is a vividly colored, energetic, and acrobatic warbler with a fairly broad range across North America. One of its behavioral quirks is to fan its tail and wings while foraging, supposedly using the flashes of bold color to scare insects into moving, making them easy prey. It possesses well-developed rictal bristles: hairlike feathers extending from the corners of the mouth, which help it "feel" insects.

yellow tail base

olive back

grayish head

♀

conspicuous orange wing bar

yellowish flanks

whitish underparts

black inverted "T" on tail

♂

yellow tail base

♂

irregular dark patches

yellow flanks

black head and back

long black tail with orange on sides

blackish smudge on undertail

♂

orange flank patch with black border

white belly

VOICE Harsh tsiip; high, thin sveep in flight; song variable, high, thin, penetrating series of notes; burry, emphatic, and downslurred see-a see-a see-a see-a ZEE-urrrr.
NESTING Cup of grasses and rootlets, lined with feathers, placed low in deciduous tree; 2–5 eggs; 1–2 broods; May–Jul.
FEEDING Insects and spiders from leaves at midlevels in trees; also moths, flies in flight; fruit.
HABITAT Moist deciduous and mixed woodlands while breeding.
LENGTH 5in (13cm)
WINGSPAN 8in (20cm)

Cape May Warbler

Setophaga tigrina

The Cape May Warbler is a spruce-budworm specialist; its population increases during outbreaks of that insect. These birds often chase away other birds aggressively from flowering trees, where they use their thin, pointed bills and semitubular tongues to suck the nectar from blossoms. It also uses its bill to feed on insects by plucking them from clumps of conifer needles.

white patches on wings ♂

pale yellow nape

black cap

gray back

yellow nape

thin, pointed bill

rufous cheeks

yellow underparts, heavily streaked with black

♀

white patches on flanks and breast

♂

white marks on outer tail feathers

VOICE High, even-pitched series of whistles see see see see.
NESTING Cup placed near trunk, high in spruce or fir; 4–9 eggs; 1 brood; Jun–Jul.
FEEDING Arthropods, especially spruce budworms; flies, moths, and beetles from midhigh levels in canopy; fruit and nectar during the nonbreeding season.
HABITAT Mature spruce–fir forests while breeding; varied habitats during migration.
LENGTH 5in (13cm)
WINGSPAN 8in (20cm)

Cerulean Warbler

Setophaga cerulea

This unusually colored species is difficult to spot because it spends the majority of its time foraging in the canopy of deciduous forests. It was once common across the Midwest and the Ohio River Valley, but its habitat is being cleared for agriculture and development. In winter, this bird lives high in the canopy of the Andean foothills, a habitat threatened by coffee cultivation.

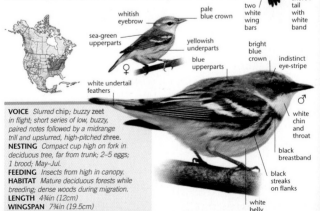

♂

two white wing bars

short tail with white band

whitish eyebrow

pale blue crown

sea-green upperparts

yellowish underparts

blue upperparts

bright blue crown

indistinct eye-stripe

♀

white undertail feathers

♂

white chin and throat

black breastband

black streaks on flanks

white belly

VOICE Slurred chip; buzzy zeet in flight; short series of low, buzzy, trailed notes followed by a midrange trill and upslurred, high-pitched zhree.
NESTING Compact cup high on fork in deciduous tree, far from trunk; 2–5 eggs; 1 brood; May–Jul.
FEEDING Insects from high in canopy.
HABITAT Mature deciduous forests while breeding; dense woods during migration.
LENGTH 4¾in (12cm)
WINGSPAN 7¾in (19.5cm)

Northern Parula

Ⓢ

Setophaga americana

Northern Parulas have an active foraging habitat, similar to chickadees. They depend on very specific nesting materials—*Usnea* lichens ("old man's beard") in the North, and *Tillandsia* (Spanish moss) in the South. The presence of these "air plants" limits the geographical range of Northern Parulas, but they find leaf mulch as an alternative in some midwestern forests. Northern Parulas interbreed with Tropical Parulas in southern Texas where their ranges overlap, producing hybrids.

♂

two white
wing bars

♀

yellow chest
lacks chestnut
streaks

dark patch
between eye
and bill

interrupted
white eye-ring

♂

blue-gray
neck and head

yellow
throat

olive
back

chestnut
streaks
on chest

gray
rump and
uppertail

delicate
pale gray
belly

white patches
on outer
tail feathers

dark
legs

pinkish-
yellow
feet

VOICE *Very sharp* tsip; *thin, weak, descending* tsiif *in flight; buzzy upslurred trill, ending high, then dropping off in an emphatic* zip.
NESTING *Hanging pouch in clump of lichens; 4–5 eggs; 1 brood; Apr–Aug (north).*
FEEDING *Caterpillars, flies, moths, beetles, wasps, ants, spiders; also berries, nectar, some seeds.*
HABITAT *Wooded areas with preferred nesting material while breeding.*
LENGTH *4¼in (11cm)*
WINGSPAN *7in (18cm)*

Magnolia Warbler

Ⓢ

Setophaga magnolia

The bold, flashy, and common Magnolia Warbler is hard to miss as it flits around at eye level, fanning its uniquely marked tail. This species nests in young forests and winters in almost any habitat, so its numbers have not suffered in recent decades, unlike some of its relatives. Although it really has no preference for its namesake plant, the 19th-century ornithologist Alexander Wilson discovered one feeding in a magnolia tree during migration, which is how it got its name.

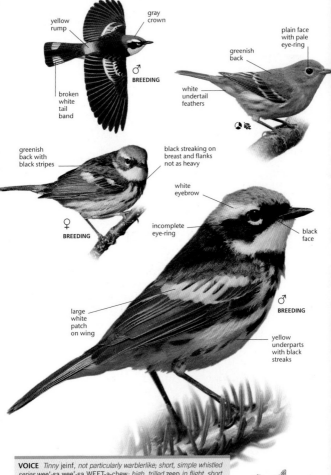

yellow rump

gray crown

BREEDING ♂

broken white tail band

plain face with pale eye-ring

greenish back

white undertail feathers

greenish back with black stripes

♀ **BREEDING**

black streaking on breast and flanks not as heavy

white eyebrow

incomplete eye-ring

black face

♂ **BREEDING**

large white patch on wing

yellow underparts with black streaks

VOICE Tinny *jeinf, not particularly warblerlike; short, simple whistled series* wee'-sa wee'-sa WEET-a-chew; *high, trilled* zeep *in flight, short and distinctive.*
NESTING *Flimsy cup of black rootlets placed low in dense conifer against trunk; 3–5 eggs; 1 brood; Jun–Aug.*
FEEDING *Mostly caterpillars, beetles, and spiders from the underside of conifer needles and broadleaf foliage.*
HABITAT *Dense, young mixed and coniferous forests while breeding.*
LENGTH *5in (13cm)*
WINGSPAN *7½in (19cm)*

Bay-breasted Warbler (S)

Setophaga castanea

Male Bay-breasted Warblers in breeding plumage are striking birds, but fall females are very different, with their dull greenish plumage. The species depends largely on outbreaks of spruce budworms (a major food source), so its numbers rise and fall according to those outbreaks. Overall, the Bay-breasted Warbler population has decreased because of the increased use of pesticide sprays.

chestnut crown, streaked black

two white wing bars

white tips on outer tail feathers

buffy wash on flanks and undertail

dusky ear patch

bold buffy neck patch

♂ BREEDING

♀ BREEDING

gray upperparts with black streaks

chestnut-brown crown

chestnut-brown chin and flanks

two white wing bars

buff undertail

yellowish-buff belly

black face

♂ BREEDING

VOICE *Upslurred* tsip; *high, buzzy* tzzzt; *high, thin* wee-si wee-si wee-si wee, *ending on lower pitch.*
NESTING *Fragile-looking cup of grass and lichens on horizontal branch at midlevel in forest; 4–5 eggs; 1 brood; May–Jul.*
FEEDING *Moths, smaller insects, worms, spiders, caterpillars while breeding; fruit in winter.*
HABITAT *Mature spruce-fir forest while breeding; varied habitats during migration.*
LENGTH *5½in (14cm)*
WINGSPAN *9in (23cm)*

Blackburnian Warbler (S)

Setophaga fusca

The Blackburnian Warbler's orange throat is unique among the North American warblers. It coexists with many other *Setophaga* warblers in the coniferous and mixed woods of the North and East, but is able to do so by exploiting a slightly different niche for foraging—in this case, the treetops. It also seeks the highest trees for nesting.

more subdued facial pattern

white wing bars

white edges on outer tail feathers

black streaks on flanks

orange throat and breast

bold white wing patches

♂

♀

pale orange line in center of crown

brilliant orange throat

complex black-and-orange face pattern

white streaks on black back

white belly

black streaks on breast and belly

white patch on wing

♂

VOICE *Husky* chik; *high, thin* zzee *in flight; series of lisps ending in quiet trill.*
NESTING *Fine cup in conifer on horizontal branch away from trunk, usually high in tree; 4–5 eggs; 1 brood; May–Jul.*
FEEDING *Arthropods, such as spiders, worms, and beetles; also fruit.*
HABITAT *Coniferous and mixed forests while breeding; wooded, shrubby, or forest-edge habitats during migration.*
LENGTH *5in (13cm)*
WINGSPAN *8½in (21cm)*

Yellow Warbler

Ⓢ

Setophaga petechia

By May, the song of the Yellow Warbler can be heard across North America as the birds arrive for the summer. This warbler is treated as a single species with about 35 subspecies, mostly in its tropical range (West Indies and South America). It is known to build another nest on top of an old one when cowbird eggs appear in it, which can result in up to six different tiers. The Yellow Warbler does not walk, but rather hops from branch to branch.

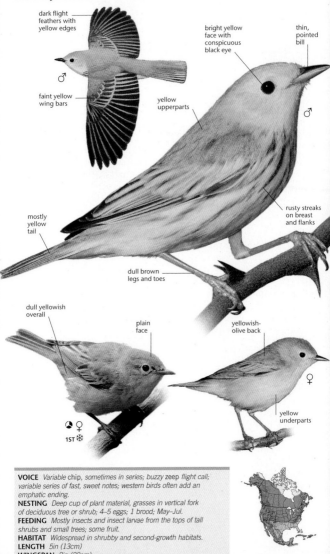

dark flight feathers with yellow edges

bright yellow face with conspicuous black eye

thin, pointed bill

♂

faint yellow wing bars

yellow upperparts

♂

mostly yellow tail

rusty streaks on breast and flanks

dull brown legs and toes

dull yellowish overall

plain face

yellowish-olive back

♀

yellow underparts

♀ 1ST

VOICE *Variable* chip, *sometimes in series; buzzy* zeep *flight call; variable series of fast, sweet notes; western birds often add an emphatic ending.*
NESTING *Deep cup of plant material, grasses in vertical fork of deciduous tree or shrub; 4–5 eggs; 1 brood; May–Jul.*
FEEDING *Mostly insects and insect larvae from the tops of tall shrubs and small trees; some fruit.*
HABITAT *Widespread in shrubby and second-growth habitats.*
LENGTH *5in (13cm)*
WINGSPAN *8in (20cm)*

Chestnut-sided Warbler Ⓢ

Setophaga pensylvanica

The Chestnut-sided Warbler depends on deciduous second-growth and forest edges for breeding. These birds vary in appearance, immature females looking quite unlike adult males in breeding. In all plumages, yellowish wing bars and whitish belly are the most distinguishing characteristics. Its pleasant song has long been transcribed as *pleased pleased pleased to MEET'cha.*

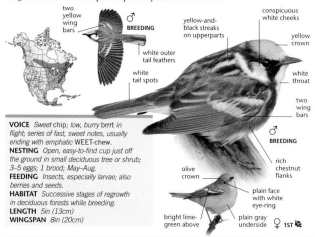

two yellow wing bars

♂ BREEDING

white outer tail feathers

white tail spots

yellow-and-black streaks on upperparts

conspicuous white cheeks

yellow crown

white throat

two wing bars

♂ BREEDING

rich chestnut flanks

olive crown

plain face with white eye-ring

bright lime-green above

plain gray underside ♀ 1ST

VOICE *Sweet chip; low, burry* brrrt *in flight; series of fast, sweet notes, usually ending with emphatic WEET-chew.*
NESTING *Open, easy-to-find cup just off the ground in small deciduous tree or shrub; 3–5 eggs; 1 brood; May–Aug.*
FEEDING *Insects, especially larvae; also berries and seeds.*
HABITAT *Successive stages of regrowth in deciduous forests while breeding.*
LENGTH *5in (13cm)*
WINGSPAN *8in (20cm)*

Blackpoll Warbler Ⓢ

Setophaga striata

The Blackpoll Warbler is known for undergoing a remarkable fall migration that takes it over the Atlantic Ocean from southern Canada and the northeastern US to northern Venezuela. Before departing, it almost doubles its body weight with fat to serve as fuel for the nonstop journey. In spring, most of these birds travel the shorter Caribbean route back north.

white tail spots

♂

two white wing bars

greenish upperparts with fine black streaks

♀ BREEDING

faint, fine streaking on underparts

black cap

white cheek

bold black streaks on gray back

streaked underparts

white undertail feathers

orange legs

♂ BREEDING

VOICE *Piercing chip; high, buzzy, sharp tzzzt in flight; crescendo of fast, extremely high-pitched ticks, ending with a decrescendo tsst tsst TSST TSST TSST tsst tsst.*
NESTING *Well-hidden cup placed low against conifer trunk; 3–5 eggs; 1–2 broods; May–Jul.*
FEEDING *Arthropods, such as beetles; worms; small fruit in fall and winter.*
HABITAT *Spruce-fir forests and coastal coniferous forests while breeding.*
LENGTH *5½in (14cm)*
WINGSPAN *9in (23cm)*

Black-throated Blue Warbler (S)

Setophaga caerulescens

Male and female Black-throated Blue Warblers look so dissimilar that they were originally considered different species. Many of the females have a blue wash to their wings and tail, and almost all have a subdued version of the male's white "kerchief." These warblers migrate northward in spring along the Appalachians, but a small number of birds fly northwestward to the Great Lakes.

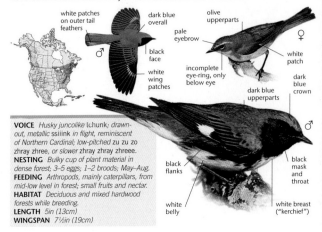

white patches on outer tail feathers

dark blue overall

black face

white wing patches

olive upperparts

pale eyebrow

♀

white patch

incomplete eye-ring, only below eye

dark blue upperparts

dark blue crown

♂

black mask and throat

black flanks

black breast ("kerchief")

white belly

white breast ("kerchief")

VOICE Husky juncolike tchunk; drawn-out, metallic ssiiink in flight, reminiscent of Northern Cardinal; low-pitched zu zu zo zhray zhree, or slower zhray zhray zhreee.
NESTING Bulky cup of plant material in dense forest; 3–5 eggs; 1–2 broods; May–Aug.
FEEDING Arthropods, mainly caterpillars, from mid-low level in forest; small fruits and nectar.
HABITAT Deciduous and mixed hardwood forests while breeding.
LENGTH 5in (13cm)
WINGSPAN 7½in (19cm)

Palm Warbler (S)

Setophaga palmarum

The Palm Warbler is one of North America's most abundant warblers. Its tail-pumping habit makes it easy to identify in any plumage. The western subspecies (*S. p. palmarum*), found in western and central Canada, is grayish-brown above and lacks the chestnut streaks of the eastern subspecies (*S. p. hypochrysea*), which has a yellower face and breeds in southeastern Canada and the northeastern US.

chestnut crown

dark upperparts

white-edged tail

◆ EASTERN

yellow eye-stripe

grayish-green "mustache"

dull gray upperparts

yellow undertail feathers

ring below eye

dark gray upperparts

chestnut streaks on breast

rich yellow underparts

yellow throat

S. p. hypochrysea
EASTERN; BREEDING

yellowish rump

dusky streaks on breast and belly

♂ ◆
S. p. palmarum
WESTERN; BREEDING

VOICE Husky chik or tsip; light ziint in flight; slow, loose, buzzy trill: zwi zwi zwi zwi zwi zwi zwi zwi.
NESTING Cup of grasses on or near ground, often in peat moss, at base of small coniferous tree or shrub; 4–5 eggs; 1 brood; May–Jul.
FEEDING Insects, sometimes caught in flight; seeds and berries.
HABITAT Spruce bogs within the northerly forest zone while breeding.
LENGTH 5½in (14cm)
WINGSPAN 8in (20cm)

Pine Warbler

S

Setophaga pinus

This appropriately named species is a common bird in its namesake habitat—eastern US pine forests—where its distinctive musical trilling song can often be heard. A hardy bird, the Pine Warbler stays within the US throughout the winter. The Pine Warbler is the only warbler that eats large quantities of seeds—primarily pine seeds. This seed-eating ability makes it one of the few warblers to visit bird feeders.

two white wing bars

round wings

♂

white sides to long tail

overall similar to male, but duller

♀

yellow eye-ring

olive upperparts

bright yellow throat

♂

brownish streaks on breast and flanks

VOICE *Soft* tsip; *high, thin, slightly rolling, descending* ziit *in flight; lazy, musical trill.*
NESTING *Cup of grass high up, far out on horizontal branch, concealed by pine needles; 3–5 eggs; 1–2 broods; Mar–Jul.*
FEEDING *Arthropods, especially caterpillars, from pine needles; also seeds and fruit in nonbreeding season.*
HABITAT *Pine and mixed forests; will nest in deciduous forests with small stands of pine.*
LENGTH *5in (13cm)*
WINGSPAN *9in (23cm)*

Yellow-rumped Warbler Ⓢ

Setophaga coronata

The abundant and widespread Yellow-rumped Warbler is not choosy about its wintering habitats. It was once considered to consist of two species; "Myrtle" (*S. c. coronata*) in the North, and "Audubon's" (*S. c. auduboni*) in the West. Because they interbreed freely in a narrow zone of contact in British Columbia and Alberta, the American Ornithological Society merged them. The two forms differ in plumage and voice, and their hybrid zone appears stable.

♂ MYRTLE · white wing bars

♀ *S. c. auduboni* AUDUBON'S · yellowish throat · grayish overall

♂ *S. c. coronata* MYRTLE · dark cheeks · black streaks on gray back · white throat · black streaks across breast · bright yellow rump

♀ *S. c. coronata* MYRTLE · whitish eyebrow · whitish throat · yellow flanks · same pattern as male's, but duller

♂ *S. c. auduboni* AUDUBON'S · white corners on outer tail feathers · white lower and upper eye crescents · solid black breast · large white wing patch · unmarked undertail

VOICE coronata: *flat, husky* tchik; auduboni: *higher-pitched, rising* jip; *both: clear, upslurred* sviiit *in flight; loose, warbled trill with an inflected ending.*
NESTING *Bulky cup of plant matter in conifer; 4–5 eggs; 1 brood; Mar–Aug.*
FEEDING *Flies, beetles, wasps, and spiders while breeding; fruit and berries at other times of the year; often sallies to catch prey.*
HABITAT *Coniferous and mixed hardwood-coniferous forests.*
LENGTH 5in (13cm)
WINGSPAN 9in (23cm)

Yellow-throated Warbler (S)

Setophaga dominica

Yellow-throated Warblers are known for their habit of creeping along branches to glean prey, especially caterpillars, from foliage and bark. They are one of the earliest warblers to return from the southern wintering grounds to eastern US forests; in fact, some birds arrive in March. There are four subspecies; their range has recently extended northward. These warblers interbreed with Northern Parulas, creating "Sutton's Warblers."

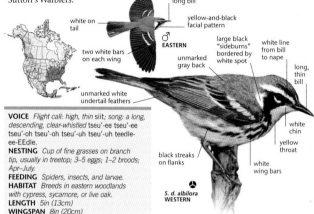

long bill

white on tail

yellow-and-black facial pattern

♂ **EASTERN**

two white bars on each wing

large black "sideburns" bordered by white spot

white line from bill to nape

unmarked gray back

long, thin bill

unmarked white undertail feathers

white chin

yellow throat

black streaks on flanks

white wing bars

S. d. albilora **WESTERN**

VOICE Flight call: high, thin siit; song: a long, descending, clear-whistled tseu'-ee tseu'-ee tseu'-oh tseu'-oh tseu'-uh tseu'-uh teedle-ee-EEdle.
NESTING Cup of fine grasses on branch tip, usually in treetop; 3–5 eggs; 1–2 broods; Apr–July.
FEEDING Spiders, insects, and larvae.
HABITAT Breeds in eastern woodlands with cypress, sycamore, or live oak.
LENGTH 5in (13cm)
WINGSPAN 8in (20cm)

Prairie Warbler (S)

Setophaga discolor

Despite its name, the Prairie Warbler does not live on the prairie. Its distinctive song is a quintessential sound of scrubby areas in its range. Although the population of this bird increased in the 19th century due to the widespread clearing of forests, the maturation of this habitat, along with human development, is having a negative impact on some populations.

pale yellowish wing bars

♂

white sides to tail

no rufous spots on back

paler markings on face

roundish wings

streaks on breast not as bold as male's

straight black bill

♀

yellow face with black markings

♂

rufous spots on back

black streaks on yellow underparts

white outer tail feathers

VOICE Thick tsik or tchip; high, thin sssip in flight; series of husky, buzzy notes that increase in pitch: zzu zzu zzu zzo zzo zzo zzee zzee.
NESTING Cup of plant material in fork of sapling or low trees; 3–5 eggs; 1 brood; May–Jul.
FEEDING Various insects, such as flies and crickets; also berries.
HABITAT Shrubby, open-canopied, second-growth habitats while breeding.
LENGTH 4¾in (12cm)
WINGSPAN 9in (23cm)

Black-throated Green Warbler (S)

Setophaga virens

This species is easy to distinguish because its bright yellow face is unique among birds inhabiting northeastern North America. It is a member of the *virens* "superspecies," a group of nonoverlapping species that are similar in plumage and vocalizations—the Black-throated Green, Golden-cheeked, Townsend's, and Hermit Warblers. Sadly, this species is vulnerable to habitat loss in parts of its wintering range.

greenish cap

two white wing bars

olive-green back

yellow face

♂

black bib and chin

heavily streaked underparts

yellowish flanks

white outer tail feathers

same as male's, but duller

greenish flanks

♀

VOICE Flat tchip; rising siii in flight; fast zee zoe zee zee 700 zee; slower zu zee zu-zu zee.
NESTING Cup of twigs and grasses high on branch near trunk; 3–5 eggs; 1 brood; May–Jul.
FEEDING Insects and larvae, especially caterpillars; also small fruit, including poison-ivy berries, in nonbreeding season.
HABITAT Forests, especially mix of conifers and hardwood while breeding; variety of habitats during migration and winter.
LENGTH 5in (13cm)
WINGSPAN 8in (20cm)

Canada Warbler (T)

Cardellina canadensis

One of the last species of wood warblers to arrive in the US and Canada in the spring, and among the first to leave in the fall, the Canada Warbler is recognizable by the conspicuous black markings on its chest. This bird is declining, probably because of the maturation and draining of its preferred breeding habitat of old mixed hardwood forests with moist undergrowth.

♂

plain gray tail

white undertail feathers

paler crown

bicolored eye-ring

faint necklace

♀

yellow patch between eye and bill

dark crown

conspicuous yellow eye-ring

yellow throat

plain gray upperparts

♂

yellow belly

black "necklace" across breast

VOICE Thick tchip; clear plip in flight; jumble of sweet notes, beginning with or interspersed with tchip, followed by a pause.
NESTING Concealed cup of leaves, in moss or grass, on or near ground; 4–5 eggs; 1 brood; May–Jun.
FEEDING Insects from midlevel foliage or in flight; also forages on ground.
HABITAT Moist forests with well-developed understory while breeding.
LENGTH 5in (13cm)
WINGSPAN 8in (20cm)

Wilson's Warbler

Cardellina pusilla

The tiny Wilson's Warbler is perhaps the most common spring migrant of all the wood warblers across many areas of the West. In the East, however, it is much scarcer in spring. Wilson's Warblers have a wide range of habitats, yet their numbers are declining, especially in the West, because their riverside breeding habitats are gradually being destroyed by development.

♂

long, narrow tail

olive or blackish crown

yellow eyebrow and chin

♀

black cap

large black eye

olive upperparts

yellow brightest on face

♂

VOICE *Rich* chimp *or* champ; *sharp, liquid* tsik *in flight; chattering trill, often increasing in speed:* che che che che chi-chi-chi-chit.
NESTING *Cup of leaves and grass placed on or near ground in mosses or grass; 4–6 eggs; 1 brood; Apr–Jun.*
FEEDING *Insects from foliage, leaf litter, or during flight; berries and honeydew.*
HABITAT *Wet shrubby thickets with no canopy while breeding, often near streams and lakes.*
LENGTH *4¾in (12cm)*
WINGSPAN *7in (17.5cm)*

New World Sparrows

New World sparrows are closer to Old World buntings than other sparrows but familiar names were given to quite different birds by early European settlers and have stayed with us. New World sparrows are rounded but long-tailed, and have small, conical or triangular bills adapted to feed on grass seeds. While some birds are distinctive, many are small, "streaky-brown" species that are hard to identify. Range, habitat, behavior, and voice are all often used together for identification.

TYPICAL SPARROW
A White-crowned Sparrow shows the typical stout beak of New World sparrows.

Cardinals and Relatives

Birds in the family Cardinalidae are visually stunning and noisy. Some tanagers, grosbeaks, and buntings are grouped with the Northern Cardinal in this family. Tanagers are slender-bodied, cone-billed birds that feed on insects and fruits. The striking cardinals have pointed crests and short, stout bills. Grosbeaks are heavily built and have deeply triangular bills. The buntings in this family are similar to the grosbeaks, but with more delicate, triangular bills.

MALE COLORS
Male Scarlet Tanagers are among North America's most colorful birds.

Eastern Towhee

S

Pipilo erythrophthalmus

The Eastern Towhee is famous for its vocalizations and has one of the best-known mnemonics for its song: "drink your tea." Like all towhees, the Eastern Towhee feeds noisily by jumping backward with both feet at once to move leaves and reveal the insects and seeds hidden underneath.

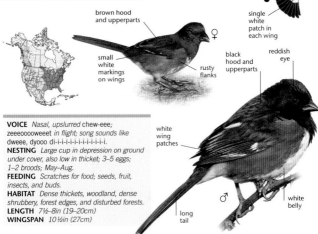

white corners to tail

single white patch in each wing

brown hood and upperparts ♀

small white markings on wings

rusty flanks

black hood and upperparts

reddish eye

white wing patches

white belly

♂

long tail

VOICE Nasal, upslurred chew-eee; zeeeooooweeet in flight; song sounds like dwee, dyooo di-i-i-i-i-i-i-i-i-i-i-i-i.
NESTING Large cup in depression on ground under cover, also low in thicket; 3–5 eggs; 1–2 broods; May–Aug.
FEEDING Scratches for food; seeds, fruit, insects, and buds.
HABITAT Dense thickets, woodland, dense shrubbery, forest edges, and disturbed forests.
LENGTH 7½–8in (19–20cm)
WINGSPAN 10½in (27cm)

Bachman's Sparrow

D

Peucaea aestivalis

This rather shy, skulking sparrow is predominantly associated with the pine woods of the southeastern US; it is often identified by its melodious song. This species was first described in 1834 by John James Audubon in honor of his friend John Bachman. Bachman's Sparrow populations have been declining for some time, primarily as a result of habitat loss.

brown, lightly streaked upperparts

yellowish-tan breast

rufous eyestripe

EASTERN

long, dark, round tail

P. a. illinoensis **WESTERN**

streaked crown

gray eyebrow

brownish-gray cheek

bold rufous-and-black streaks on back

long grayish bill

tan-buffy breast

VOICE Call a thin tseep; song a melodious, high whistle followed by a musical trill.
NESTING Grass cup, sometimes domed, placed on ground, often in thicket; 2–5 eggs; 1–3 broods; May–Sep.
FEEDING Forages for insects, including weevils and beetles; also eats seeds.
HABITAT Prefers open, grassy old-growth, younger pine woods with dense undergrowth, and orchards.
LENGTH 6in (15cm)
WINGSPAN 7¼in (18.5cm)

long tail

P. a. aestivalis **EASTERN**

pale gray belly

American Tree Sparrow

S

Spizelloides arborea

The first heavy snowfalls of winter often bring large flocks of American Tree Sparrows to bird feeders. Sometimes they are mistaken for the smaller Chipping Sparrow, but the American Tree Sparrow is larger and has a central breast spot and a bicolored bill. A highly social and vocal species, noisy winter flocks numbering in the hundreds frequent northern US roadsides, weedy fields, and bird feeders during winter months.

BREEDING

striped back

NONBREEDING

cleft tail

rufous crown

gray head and nape

black-and-yellow bill

rusty stripe behind eye

rust patch on shoulder

black-and-rust streaking on back

dark central spot

long, squarish tail

BREEDING

VOICE *Call a bell-like* teedle-ee; *flight call a thin, slightly descending* tsiiiu; *song* seee seee di-di-di di-di-di dyew dyew.
NESTING *Nest cup on ground concealed within thicket; 4–6 eggs; 1 brood; Jun–Jul.*
FEEDING *Seeds, berries, and variety of insects.*
HABITAT *Scrubby thickets of birch and willows while breeding; open brushy habitats for nonbreeders.*
LENGTH *6¼in (16cm)*
WINGSPAN *9½in (24cm)*

Chipping Sparrow S

Spizella passerina

The Chipping Sparrow is a common, trusting bird, which breeds in backyards across most of North America. While they are easily identifiable in the summer, "Chippers" molt into a drab, nonbreeding plumage during fall, at which point they are easily confused with the Clay-colored and Brewer's Sparrows they flock with. Most reports of this species across the North in winter are actually of the larger American Tree Sparrow.

pale underparts

rusty cast to crown

pinkish bill

bright rufous crown

white eyebrow

black eye-line

blackish bill

heavily streaked, especially on breast

gray underparts

cleft tail

BREEDING

VOICE *Sharp* tsip; *sharp, thin* tsiiit *in flight; insectlike trill of* chip *notes, variable in duration.*
NESTING *Nest cup usually placed well off the ground in tree or shrub; 3–5 eggs; 1–2 broods; Apr–Aug.*
FEEDING *Seeds of grasses and annuals, some fruit; insects and other invertebrates while breeding.*
HABITAT *Open forest, woodlands, grassy parklike areas, shorelines, and backyards.*
LENGTH *5½in (14cm)*
WINGSPAN *8½in (21cm)*

Clay-colored Sparrow

S

Spizella pallida

The little Clay-colored Sparrow is best known for its mechanical, buzzy song. It spends much of its foraging time away from the breeding habitat; consequently, males' territories are quite small, allowing for dense breeding populations. During the nonbreeding season, they form large flocks in open country, associating with other *Spizella* sparrows, especially Chipping and Brewer's.

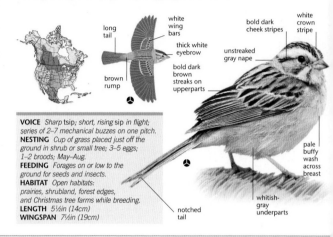

long tail

white wing bars

thick white eyebrow

brown rump

bold dark brown streaks on upperparts

bold dark cheek stripes

unstreaked gray nape

white crown stripe

pale buffy wash across breast

whitish-gray underparts

notched tail

VOICE *Sharp* tsip; *short, rising* sip *in flight; series of 2–7 mechanical buzzes on one pitch.*
NESTING *Cup of grass placed just off the ground in shrub or small tree; 3–5 eggs; 1–2 broods; May–Aug.*
FEEDING *Forages on or low to the ground for seeds and insects.*
HABITAT *Open habitats: prairies, shrubland, forest edges, and Christmas tree farms while breeding.*
LENGTH 5½in (14cm)
WINGSPAN 7½in (19cm)

Field Sparrow

S

Spizella pusilla

The distinctive trill of the Field Sparrow's song is a characteristic sound of scrubby areas in the eastern US. Its bright pink bill, plain "baby face," and white eye-ring make this sparrow one of the easiest to identify. It has a brighter plumage in the East, and drabber plumage in the interior part of its range.

rusty markings on head

long, notched tail

REDDISH FORM

white eye-ring

streaking on back

white wing bars

GRAYISH FORM

small pink bill

light rust cheek and crown

tan underparts

long tail

distinctive pink legs

REDDISH FORM

VOICE *Sharp* tsik; *strongly descending* tsiiiu *in flight; series of sweet, downslurred whistles accelerating to a rapid trill.*
NESTING *Grass cup placed on or just above ground in grass or bush; 3–5 eggs; 1–3 broods; Mar–Aug.*
FEEDING *Seeds; insects, insect larvae, and spiders in summer.*
HABITAT *Overgrown fields, woodland edges, and roadsides while breeding.*
LENGTH 5½in (14cm)
WINGSPAN 8in (20cm)

Vesper Sparrow

D C

Pooecetes gramineus

The Vesper Sparrow is named for its sweet evening song. The Vesper Sparrow needs areas with bare ground to breed, so it is one of the few species that can successfully nest in areas of intense agriculture. Despite that, its numbers are declining to the point of being endangered in some regions.

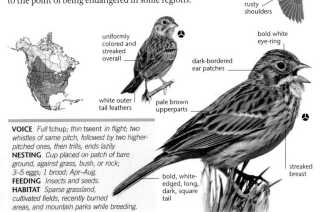

rusty shoulders

uniformly colored and streaked overall

bold white eye-ring

dark-bordered ear patches

white outer tail feathers

pale brown upperparts

streaked breast

bold, white-edged, long, dark, square tail

VOICE *Full tchup; thin tseent in flight; two whistles of same pitch, followed by two higher-pitched ones, then trills, ends lazily.*
NESTING *Cup placed on patch of bare ground, against grass, bush, or rock; 3–5 eggs; 1 brood; Apr–Aug.*
FEEDING *Insects and seeds.*
HABITAT *Sparse grassland, cultivated fields, recently burned areas, and mountain parks while breeding.*
LENGTH *6¼in (16cm)*
WINGSPAN *10in (25cm)*

Savannah Sparrow

S D

Passerculus sandwichensis

The Savannah Sparrow shows tremendous variation—21 subspecies—across its vast range, but it is always brown with dark streaks above and white with dark streaks below. The pale "Ipswich Sparrow" (*P. s. princeps*) breeds on Sable Island, Nova Scotia, and winters along the East Coast.

brown overall

pale sandy overall

pale yellow eyebrows

small bill

reddish streaks on underparts

P. s. princeps
IPSWICH SPARROW

white belly

WESTERN

VOICE *Sharp, full stip; downslurred tseew in flight; song: sit sit sit sit suh-EEEEE say.*
NESTING *Concealed grass cup in depression on ground under cover; 2–6 eggs; 1–2 broods; Jun–Aug.*
FEEDING *Insects; seeds in summer; berries and fruit in winter; small snails, crustaceans.*
HABITAT *Meadows, grasslands, pastures, bushy tundra, and cultivated land when breeding.*
LENGTH *5½–6in (14–15cm)*
WINGSPAN *6¾in (17cm)*

whitish tail edgings

Grasshopper Sparrow

D

Ammodramus savannarum

The Grasshopper Sparrow is small, with a large head, spiky tail, and plain breast. It is one of the few North American sparrows that has two completely different songs. Its common name derives from its song, which resembles the sounds grasshoppers make. It varies geographically, with about 12 subspecies.

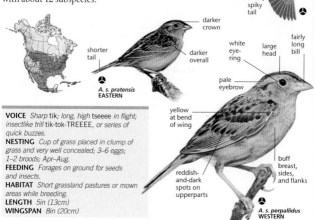

buff overall

short, spiky tail

shorter tail

darker crown

darker overall

A. s. pratensis
EASTERN

white eye-ring

large head

fairly long bill

pale eyebrow

yellow at bend of wing

reddish-and-dark spots on upperparts

buff breast, sides, and flanks

A. s. perpallidus
WESTERN

VOICE *Sharp tik; long, high tseeee in flight; insectlike trill tik-tok-TREEEE, or series of quick buzzes.*
NESTING *Cup of grass placed in clump of grass and very well concealed; 3–6 eggs; 1–2 broods; Apr–Aug.*
FEEDING *Forages on ground for seeds and insects.*
HABITAT *Short grassland pastures or mown areas while breeding.*
LENGTH *5in (13cm)*
WINGSPAN *8in (20cm)*

Henslow's Sparrow

E

Centronyx henslowii

The combination of a large, flat greenish head and purplish back are unique to the Henslow's Sparrow. While it has suffered greatly from the drainage, cultivation, and urbanization of much of its preferred breeding grounds, the Henslow's Sparrow has also recently started to use reclaimed strip mines in northwest Missouri and Iowa for breeding.

dark reddish overall

round, spiky tail

flat greenish head with black stripes

heavy bill

whitish scaling on purplish back

rufous-edged wing feathers

black streaks on buffy breast

VOICE *Sharp tsik; long, high, shrill tseeeeee in flight; hiccuping sputter with second note higher tsih-LIK!*
NESTING *Cup of loosely woven grass placed on or near ground; 2–5 eggs; 1–2 broods; May–Aug.*
FEEDING *Seeds; forages for insects and insect larvae, and spiders in summer.*
HABITAT *Tallgrass prairie and wet grasslands while breeding.*
LENGTH *4¾–5in (12–13cm)*
WINGSPAN *6½in (16cm)*

Saltmarsh Sparrow

Ⓓ

Ammospiza caudacuta

For a short time, this species was grouped with Nelson's Sparrow as a single species, called the Sharp-tailed Sparrow. The Saltmarsh Sparrow has a much smaller range; its restriction to the East Coast provides the simplest means of distinguishing the two sparrows. The Saltmarsh Sparrow also has more clearly defined facial markings, darker streaks on its breast, and a slightly longer bill.

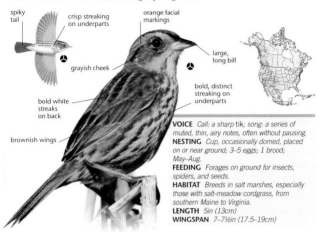

spiky tail

crisp streaking on underparts

orange facial markings

large, long bill

grayish cheek

bold, distinct streaking on underparts

bold white streaks on back

brownish wings

VOICE Call: a sharp tik; song: a series of muted, thin, airy notes, often without pausing.
NESTING Cup, occasionally domed, placed on or near ground; 3–5 eggs; 1 brood; May–Aug.
FEEDING Forages on ground for insects, spiders, and seeds.
HABITAT Breeds in salt marshes, especially those with salt-meadow cordgrass, from southern Maine to Virginia.
LENGTH 5in (13cm)
WINGSPAN 7–7½in (17.5–19cm)

Seaside Sparrow

Ⓣ

Ammospiza maritima

The Seaside Sparrow's song is a characteristic summer sound of East Coast salt marshes. Seaside Sparrow subspecies vary geographically. East Coast birds are the dullest. Gulf Coast birds are more boldly marked. Sadly, marsh drainage in eastern Florida caused the extinction of the endemic Dusky Seaside Sparrow in 1987. The crisply marked Cape Sable Seaside Sparrow of southwest Florida is now endangered.

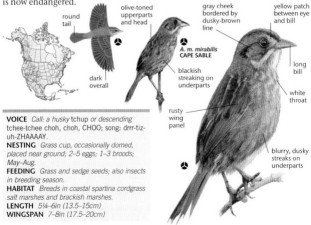

round tail

olive-toned upperparts and head

gray cheek bordered by dusky-brown line

yellow patch between eye and bill

A. m. mirabilis
CAPE SABLE

dark overall

blackish streaking on underparts

long bill

white throat

rusty wing panel

blurry, dusky streaks on underparts

VOICE Call: a husky tchup or descending tchee-tchee choh, choh, CHOO; song: drrr-tiz-uh-ZHAAAAY.
NESTING Grass cup, occasionally domed, placed near ground; 2–5 eggs; 1–3 broods; May–Aug.
FEEDING Grass and sedge seeds; also insects in breeding season.
HABITAT Breeds in coastal spartina cordgrass salt marshes and brackish marshes.
LENGTH 5¼–6in (13.5–15cm)
WINGSPAN 7–8in (17.5–20cm)

Fox Sparrow

S

Passerella iliaca

Fox Sparrows are larger and more robust than other related sparrows. They forage in backyards during migration, especially under shrubs and in fence-rows, where they claw through decomposing leaves, kicking them aside in search of spiders, insects, and other invertebrates. Fox Sparrows' appearance varies over their large range, from thick-billed birds in the Sierras to dark populations in the Northwest, and distinctive red Fox Sparrows in taiga forest from Newfoundland to Alaska. Their musical song is distinctive and they sing while in migration.

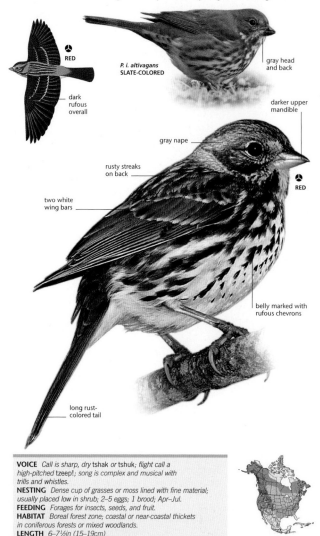

RED

dark rufous overall

P. i. altivagans
SLATE-COLORED

gray head and back

darker upper mandible

gray nape

rusty streaks on back

RED

two white wing bars

belly marked with rufous chevrons

long rust-colored tail

VOICE *Call is sharp, dry* tshak *or* tshuk; *flight call a high-pitched* tzeep!; *song is complex and musical with trills and whistles.*
NESTING *Dense cup of grasses or moss lined with fine material; usually placed low in shrub; 2–5 eggs; 1 brood; Apr–Jul.*
FEEDING *Forages for insects, seeds, and fruit.*
HABITAT *Boreal forest zone; coastal or near-coastal thickets in coniferous forests or mixed woodlands.*
LENGTH 6–7½in (15–19cm)
WINGSPAN 10½–11½in (27–29cm)

Song Sparrow

Ⓢ

Melospiza melodia

The familiar song of this species can be heard in backyards across the continent, including in winter, although it varies both individually and geographically. The Song Sparrow may be the North American champion of geographic variation: about 30 subspecies have been described; most have streaky plumage and are widespread in a range of habitats. Males sing in spring and summer on an exposed perch around eye level.

grayish head with dark chestnut-brown crown

heavily streaked brownish-gray upperparts

WEST COAST

streaked underparts

dark "mustache" bordering whitish throat

heavily streaked underparts

WEST COAST

long, dark, rounded tail

whitish lower belly

paler neck

more rusty overall

M. m. saltonis **SOUTHWEST**

grayish head with brown markings

central breast spot

M. m. melodia **EASTERN**

VOICE *Dry tchip; clear siiiti in flight; jumble of variable whistles and trills,* deeep deeep deep-deep chrrrr tiiiiiiiiiiii tyeeur.
NESTING *Bulky cup on or near ground, in brush or marsh vegetation; 3–5 eggs; 1–3 broods; Mar–Aug.*
FEEDING *Mainly insects in summer; mainly seeds, but also fruit, in winter.*
HABITAT *Variety of open habitats, including fields and pastures, the edges of forests and wetlands, and suburbs.*
LENGTH *5–7½in (13–19cm)*
WINGSPAN *8½–12in (21–31cm)*

Lincoln's Sparrow

S

Melospiza lincolnii

In the breeding season, the Lincoln's Sparrow seeks out predominantly moist willow scrub at the tundra–taiga timberline. It may occasionally visit backyard feeders in winter, but it generally prefers to stay within fairly dense cover. Its rich, musical song is unmistakable and varies remarkably little from region to region.

rounded tail

broad gray eyebrow

crested or peaked rufous crown

small, thin bill

bold eye-ring

dark brown streak under cheek

streaks on throat

pencil-thin streaking on buffy breast

rufous-edged wings

VOICE *Variable, loud tchip; rolling ziiiit in flight; rich, musical trills: ju-ju-ju dodododo didididid whrrrrr.*
NESTING *Grass cup hidden in depression in ground under overhanging sedges or grasses; 3–5 eggs; 1 brood; Jun–Aug.*
FEEDING *Seeds in winter; in summer, insects, such as beetles, mosquitoes, and moths.*
HABITAT *Muskeg, wet thickets while breeding; scrubby habitats during migration and winter.*
LENGTH *5¼–6in (13.5–15cm)*
WINGSPAN *7½–8½in (19–22cm)*

Swamp Sparrow

S

Melospiza georgiana

The Swamp Sparrow is a common breeder in wet habitats, especially tall reed marshes. It is skittish and often seen darting rapidly into cover. Although often confused with the Song and Lincoln's Sparrows, the Swamp Sparrow has very faint, blurry streaking on its gray breast, and sports conspicuous rusty-edged wing feathers.

rufous crown

gray-and-rufous face

rufous flanks

BREEDING

tan upperparts with dark streaks

dark, rounded tail

gray breast with fine streaking

BREEDING

rusty margins to wing feathers

unstreaked gray nape

tawny flanks

NONBREEDING

VOICE *Slightly nasal, forceful chimp; high, buzzy ziiiiii in flight; slow, monotonous, loose trill of chirps.*
NESTING *Bulky cup of dry plants placed above water in marsh vegetation; 3–5 eggs; 1–2 broods; May–Jul.*
FEEDING *Mostly insects while breeding, especially grasshoppers; seeds in winter.*
HABITAT *Marshes, cedar bogs, damp meadows, and wet hayfields.*
LENGTH *5–6in (12.5–15cm)*
WINGSPAN *7–7½in (18–19cm)*

White-throated Sparrow

Zonotrichia albicollis

White-throated Sparrows sing all year round; their whistled, rhythmic song can be remembered with the mnemonic *Oh sweet Canada Canada Canada*. This species has two different color forms: one with a white stripe above its eye, and one with a tan stripe. In the nonbreeding season, large flocks roam the leaf litter of woodlands in search of food.

two white wing bars

tan stripe
browner face

TAN-STRIPED

bold white stripe
bright rufous back and tail

yellow patch
white throat

gray underparts

WHITE-STRIPED

VOICE Loud, sharp jink; lisping tsssssst! in flight; clear whistle comprising 1–2 higher notes, then three triplets.
NESTING Cup placed on or near ground in dense shrubbery; 2–6 eggs; 1 brood; May–Aug.
FEEDING Seeds, fruit, insects, buds, and various grasses.
HABITAT Forests while breeding; wooded thickets and hedges.
LENGTH 6½–7½in (16–17.5cm)
WINGSPAN 9–10in (23–26cm)

fairly long tail

Harris's Sparrow

Zonotrichia querula

An unmistakable black-faced, pink-billed bird, the Harris's Sparrow is the only breeding bird endemic to Canada. It can be seen in the US during migration or in winter on the Great Plains and is occasionally found among large flocks of White-throated and White-crowned Sparrows. It is a large sparrow, approaching the Northern Cardinal in size.

indistinct facial markings

NONBREEDING

pinkish bill
two wing bars

NONBREEDING

black crown
gray cheeks
black cheek patch
gray rump and undertail feathers

pinkish or yellow bill

black chin and throat

BREEDING

VOICE Sharp weeek; melancholy series of 2–4 whistles on the same pitch.
NESTING Bulky cup placed on ground among vegetation or near ground in brush; 3–5 eggs; 1 brood; Jun–Aug.
FEEDING Seeds, insects, buds, and even young conifer needles in summer.
HABITAT Scrub-tundra along taiga–tundra timberline while breeding; winters in prairies.
LENGTH 6¾–7½in (17–19cm)
WINGSPAN 10½–11in (27–28cm)

White-crowned Sparrow

S

Zonotrichia leucophrys

The White-crowned Sparrow's black-and-white head, pale bill, and gray breast make it a striking bird. This sparrow's four subspecies all have slightly different field marks. White-crowned Sparrows scurry through overgrown fields, visit feeders, and like towhees, hop backward to turn over leaves. Young males learn the sweet whistling adult song during their first few months of life. Since they usually breed near where they were raised, song dialects frequently develop.

brown crown

gray rump and uppertail

longish tail

two wing bars

gray breast

white crown with two black stripes

yellowish bill

black line

gray cheek

two wing bars

white streaking on brown upperparts

unmarked grayish underparts

Z. l. oriantha
INTERIOR MOUNTAIN WEST

VOICE *Call: a sharp* tink; *flight call a thin* seep;
song: a buzzy whistle followed by buzzes, trills,
and whistles.
NESTING *Bulky cup of grass placed on or near the*
ground in bushes; 4–6 eggs; 1–3 broods; Mar–Aug.
FEEDING *Seeds, insects, fruit, buds, and grass.*
HABITAT *Boreal forest and tundra limit; nests in dense brush*
near open grasslands; in winter, open woods and gardens.
LENGTH *6½–7in (16–18cm)*
WINGSPAN *9½–10in (24–26cm)*

Dark-eyed Junco

Junco hyemalis

The Dark-eyed Junco's appearance at bird feeders during snowstorms has earned it the colloquial name of "snowbird." Sixteen subspecies have been described. "Slate-colored" populations occur in central Alaska, Canada, and the northeastern US, "Pink-sided" birds breed in Idaho, Montana, and Wyoming, and "Oregon" birds breed in the Pacific West, from coastal Alaska to British Columbia and the mountainous western US in the Sierras south to Mexico.

white outer tail feathers

♂ SLATE-COLORED

dark area between eye and bill

bluish-gray hood

dull brownish back

pinkish flanks

♀ PINK-SIDED

blackish hood

rust back

reddish flanks

♂ OREGON

dark gray head

gray body with brown wash to back

white belly

♂ SLATE-COLORED

VOICE *Loud, smacking* tick *and soft* dyew; *rapid twittering, and buzzy* zzeet *in flight; simple, liquid, one-pitch trill.*
NESTING *Cup placed on ground hidden under vegetation or next to rocks; 3–5 eggs; 1–2 broods; May–Aug.*
FEEDING *Insects and seeds; also berries; forages on ground at base of trees and shrubs or under feeders.*
HABITAT *Coniferous and mixed forests while breeding; open woodlands, fields, parks, and backyards in winter.*
LENGTH *6–6¾in (15–17cm)*
WINGSPAN *8–10in (20–26cm)*

Summer Tanager   Ⓢ

Piranga rubra

The stunning male Summer Tanager is the only entirely red bird in North America. Molting immature males are also striking, with bright yellow-and-red plumage; females are yellow. Summer Tanagers catch bees and wasps in flight, kill their prey by beating it against a branch, then rub it on a branch to remove the stinger before eating it.

tail appears short in flight

♂ BREEDING

lacks grayish cheek patches

red wash overall

♀ *P. r. rubra* EASTERN

thick, long yellowish bill

dark eye

bright red upperparts

brownish legs and toes

♂ BREEDING

VOICE Call: an explosive pit-ti-tuck; muffled, airy vreee in flight; whistling song like American Robin.
NESTING Loosely built grass cup high in tree; 3–4 eggs; 1 brood; May–Aug.
FEEDING Specializes in bees and wasps; also fruit, especially mulberries.
HABITAT P. r. rubra subspecies breeds in Eastern deciduous and mixed woodlands; P. r. cooperi in Western cottonwood-willow riversides.
LENGTH 8in (20cm)
WINGSPAN 12in (31cm)

Scarlet Tanager   Ⓢ

Piranga olivacea

Although the male breeding Scarlet Tanager is one of the brightest and most easily identified North American birds, its secretive nature and preference for the canopies of well-shaded oak woodlands make it difficult to spot. Males can vary in appearance—some are orange, not scarlet, and others have a faint reddish wing bar.

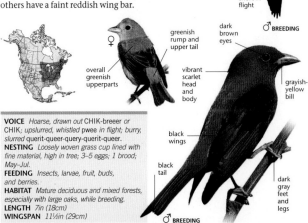

black wings

tail appears short in flight

red body

♂ BREEDING

♀

greenish rump and upper tail

overall greenish upperparts

dark brown eyes

vibrant scarlet head and body

grayish-yellow bill

black wings

black tail

dark gray feet and legs

♂ BREEDING

VOICE Hoarse, drawn out CHIK-breeer or CHIK; upslurred, whistled pwee in flight; burry, slurred querit-queer-query-querit-queer.
NESTING Loosely woven grass cup lined with fine material, high in tree; 3–5 eggs; 1 brood; May–Jul.
FEEDING Insects, larvae, fruit, buds, and berries.
HABITAT Mature deciduous and mixed forests, especially with large oaks, while breeding.
LENGTH 7in (18cm)
WINGSPAN 11½in (29cm)

Northern Cardinal

S

Cardinalis cardinalis

The male Northern Cardinal, or "redbird," is a familiar sight across southeastern Canada and the eastern US. Females are less showy, but have a prominent, reddish crest and red accents on their tan-colored outer tail and wing feathers. The male aggressively repels intruders and will occasionally attack his own reflection in windows and various shiny surfaces. Northern Cardinals neither migrate nor molt to a duller plumage, making identification easy.

warm red overall ♂

reddish crest

buff-olive upperparts

dark patch not as extensive as male's

red on outer tail feathers

grayish-brown underparts

♀

darker bill

smaller, duller crest

brownish wings

prominent crest

thick orange-red bill

bright red back and wings

black patch on face, extends onto throat

♂

long red tail

brownish toes and legs

VOICE *Sharp, metallic* tik, *also bubbly chatters; loud, variable, sweet, slurred whistle:* tsee-ew-tsee-ew-whoit-whoit-whoit-whoit-whoit.
NESTING *Loose, flimsy cup of grass, bark, and leaves in deciduous thicket; 2–4 eggs; 1–3 broods; Apr–Sep.*
FEEDING *Seeds and insects, such as beetles and caterpillars; also buds and fruit.*
HABITAT *Thickets of relatively moist habitats, such as deciduous woodland, scrub, desert washes, and backyards.*
LENGTH *8½ in (22cm)*
WINGSPAN *12in (30cm)*

Rose-breasted Grosbeak ⓢ

Pheucticus ludovicianus

For many birders in the East, the appearance of a flock of dazzling male Rose-breasted Grosbeaks in early May signals the peak of spring songbird migration. Females and immature males have more somber plumage. In the fall, immature male Rose-breasted Grosbeaks often have orange breasts and are commonly mistaken for female Black-headed Grosbeaks where both species occur in the Midwest. The latter, however, have pink wing linings that are usually visible on perched birds, pink bills, and streaking across the center of the breast.

white rump

white wing bars

white marks on head

large pinkish bill

short tail with white corners

thick streaks on underparts

♀

♂ BREEDING

brown patches on back

streaked underparts

black head and back

bold white wing patches

rose-red breast

white belly

♂ NONBREEDING

♂ BREEDING

VOICE *High, sharp, explosive* sink *or* eeuk, *like squeak of sneakers on floor tiles; airy* vree *in flight; liquid, flutelike warble, slow and relaxed.*
NESTING *Loose, open cup or platform, usually in deciduous saplings, mid- to high level; 2–5 eggs; 1–2 broods; May–Jul.*
FEEDING *Arthropods, fruit, seeds, and buds.*
HABITAT *Deciduous and mixed woods, parks, and orchards while breeding.*
LENGTH *8in (20cm)*
WINGSPAN *12½in (32cm)*

Blue Grosbeak

Ⓓ

Passerina caerulea

The Blue Grosbeak is truly indigo in color; the species'
huge bill inspired the name "grosbeak." Blue Grosbeaks,
previously seen only in the South, have expanded their
range northward in recent years. Nevertheless, they are
not abundant and seeing one is fairly rare. Grosbeaks can
be distinguished from similar Indigo Buntings by their large
bill, black face, and reddish shoulders.

rufous
wing bars

blue
upperparts

♂

uniform dark
indigo head

black patch
between
eye and bill

♂

tawny
wing bars

huge
bill

pale tan
overall

♀

black
streaks on
shoulder
feathers

rufous
shoulder

VOICE *Loud, sharp, metallic tchink call;
rambling, husky song.*
NESTING *Compact cup placed low in deciduous
tangle; 3–5 eggs; 1–2 broods; Apr–Jul.*
FEEDING *Seeds in winter; insects, including
beetles, caterpillars, and grasshoppers, in
summer; also fruit.*
HABITAT *Breeds in dense undergrowth of
disturbed habitats: old fields, hedges, and
desert scrub across the southern US.*
LENGTH *6¾in (17cm)*
WINGSPAN *11in (28cm)*

Indigo Bunting

Ⓢ

Passerina cyanea

The brilliantly colored Indigo Bunting is actually a vibrant,
almost cyan-blue, turning to indigo on the male's head
before finally becoming a rich violet on the face. Indigo
Buntings are specialists of disturbed habitats, originally
depending on tree-falls within forests and the grassland-
forest edge. Human activity, however, has radically
increased suitable breeding habitats.

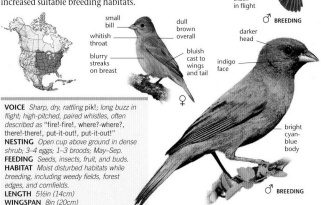

blue
overall;
often
appears
black
in flight

♂ BREEDING

small
bill

whitish
throat

blurry
streaks
on breast

dull
brown
overall

bluish
cast to
wings
and tail

♀

darker
head

indigo
face

bright
cyan-
blue
body

♂ BREEDING

VOICE *Sharp, dry, rattling pik!; long buzz in
flight; high-pitched, paired whistles, often
described as "fire!-fire!, where?-where?,
there!-there!, put-it-out!, put-it-out!"*
NESTING *Open cup above ground in dense
shrub; 3–4 eggs; 1–3 broods; May–Sep.*
FEEDING *Seeds, insects, fruit, and buds.*
HABITAT *Moist disturbed habitats while
breeding, including weedy fields, forest
edges, and cornfields.*
LENGTH *5½in (14cm)*
WINGSPAN *8in (20cm)*

Painted Bunting

D

Passerina ciris

With its violet head, red underparts, and lime-green back, the male Painted Bunting is a colorful sight. The females are also distinctive as one of the region's few green songbirds. There are two populations: western birds molt after leaving the breeding grounds, while eastern birds molt before their winter departure. In Louisiana, "nonpareil," (French for "unparalleled") is fittingly used to describe this beautiful bunting.

blue head

♂ **BREEDING**

lime-green above ♀

yellowish underparts

violet-blue hood

glowing chartreuse back

red-and-green wings

♂

red rump

red underparts

VOICE Call: a soft, ringing, upward-slurred pwip!; song: a sweet, rambling, clear warble.
NESTING Deep cup in dense tangle or shrub, just above ground; 3–4 eggs; 1–3 broods; May–August.
FEEDING Eats seeds, fruit, and insects.
HABITAT Breeds in dense thickets, tangles, and disturbed areas.
LENGTH 5½in (14cm)
WINGSPAN 8½in (22cm)

Dickcissel

S

Spiza americana

The Dickcissel is a tallgrass prairie specialist and seldom breeds outside this core range. Immature birds, without yellow-and-rusty plumage, are very similar to female House Sparrows—vagrant and wintering Dickcissels in North America are often mistaken for sparrows. It winters in Venezuela, where it is a notorious pest to seed crops.

streaked back

♂ **BREEDING**

long, yellow-tinged eye-line

bold braces on back

♀

large, pointed bill

yellow eyebrow

gray nape

rufous shoulder

black "V" on yellow breast

finely streaked underparts

VOICE Flat chik; low, electric buzz frrrrrrrt in flight; insectlike stutters followed by longer chirps or trill dick-dick-dick-SISS-SISS-suhl.
NESTING Bulky cup near ground in dense vegetation; 3–6 eggs; 1–2 broods; May–Aug.
FEEDING Insects, spiders, and seeds from ground.
HABITAT Tallgrass prairie, grassland, hayfields, unmown roadsides, and untilled cropfields while breeding.
LENGTH 6½in (16cm)
WINGSPAN 9½in (24cm)

♂ **BREEDING**

Blackbirds and Orioles

Members of this diverse family of birds are common and widespread, occurring from coast to coast in nearly every habitat in North America.

Blackbirds are largely covered in dark feathers, and their long, pointed bills and tails add to their streamlined appearance. They are among the most numerous birds on the continent after the breeding season.

Meadowlarks are birds of the open country. They can be recognized by a characteristic bright yellow chest with a black V-shaped bib and a sweet singing voice.

Brightly colored orioles build intricate hanging nests that are an impressive combination of engineering and weaving. Most species boast a melodious song and tolerance for humans.

Cowbirds are parasitic birds that lay eggs in the nests of close to 300 different species in the Americas. All three species found in North America are readily identified by their thick bill and dark, iridescent plumage.

NECTAR-LOVER
A Baltimore Oriole inserts its bill into the base of a flower, to get at the nectar.

Yellow-breasted Chat

Icteria virens

This unique species puzzled ornithologists for a long time: even recent DNA studies give conflicting results about its relationship with the wood warblers. Now placed between the tanagers and icterids, such as the Bobolink, it is the only species in the family Icteriidae. Sometimes this chat is difficult to spot, skulking in dense vegetation; at other times, it sings atop small trees in full view. One behavioral quirk is to fly upward suddenly, then glide slowly down while singing.

rounded wings

♂

yellow underwing feathers

duller olive upperparts

buff patch between eye and bill

black patch between eye and bill

white "spectacles"

olive upperparts

thick blackish bill

long, rounded tail

bright yellow breast

♂

black legs and feet

VOICE *Calls include low, soft* tuk *and nasal, downslurred* tiyew; *song: a repeated, decelerating series of monosyllabic grunts, clucks, and whistles.*
NESTING *Concealed, bulky structure of dead plants, in thicket near eye level; 3–5 eggs; 1–2 broods; May–Aug.*
FEEDING *Insects; also fruit and berries.*
HABITAT *Breeds in dense shrubby areas, including forest edges.*
LENGTH *7½in (19cm)*
WINGSPAN *9½in (24cm)*

Bobolink

Dolichonyx oryzivorus

The Bobolink is a common summer resident of open fallow fields through much of the northern US and southern Canada. In spring, the males perform a conspicuous circling or "helicoptering" display while singing, to establish territory and attract females. Bobolink populations have declined on both the breeding grounds and in wintering areas because of habitat loss and haying practices during nesting.

black wings

♂ **BREEDING**

buff-colored hindneck

blackish-brown crown

pinkish bill

gold-buff overall

♀ **BREEDING**

white shoulder feathers

black face and crown

white rump

black underparts

♂ **BREEDING**

black tail with pointed feathers

VOICE Link; long, complex babbling series of musical notes varying in length and pitch.
NESTING Woven cup of grass close to or on the ground, well hidden in tall grass; 3–7 eggs; 1 brood; May–Jul.
FEEDING Mostly insects, spiders, grubs in breeding season; cereal grains and grass seeds.
HABITAT Open fields with mixture of tall grasses and other herbaceous vegetation with breeding; especially old hayfields.
LENGTH 6–8in (15–20cm)
WINGSPAN 10–12in (25–30cm)

Red-winged Blackbird

Agelaius phoeniceus

One of the most abundant native bird species in North America, the Red-winged Blackbird is conspicuous in wetland habitats, even in suburbia. The sight and sound of males singing from the tops of cattails is a sure sign that spring is near. This adaptable species migrates and roosts in huge flocks. There are numerous subspecies, one of the most distinctive being the "Bicolored" Blackbird (*A. p. gubernator*).

red-and-yellow "flags"

♂

black outer wings

black eye

pointed bill

all-black back and tail

bright red shoulder patches with yellow edge

♂

light brown eyebrow

♀

off-white underparts with dark streaks

VOICE Various brusk chek, chit, or chet; males: kronk-a-rhee with a characteristic nasal rolling and metallic "undulating" ending.
NESTING Cup of grasses and mud in reeds or cattails; 3–4 eggs; 1–2 broods; Mar–Jun.
FEEDING Seeds and grains; largely insects when breeding; feeders.
HABITAT Wetlands, especially freshwater marshes; wet meadows with tallgrass, and open woodlands with reedy vegetation.
LENGTH 7–10in (18–25cm)
WINGSPAN 11–14in (28–35cm)

Eastern Meadowlark

Sturnella magna

A bird of eastern grassy fields, the colorful Eastern Meadowlark is known for its plaintive-sounding song. During courtship, males sing enthusiastically from the highest available perch. Eastern Meadowlarks overlap with Western Meadowlarks in the Great Plains, where the two species are best distinguished by their different calls and songs. Throughout its range, Eastern Meadowlark numbers have declined due to habitat destruction from mowing and regrowth of abandoned farmland to forest. Management is leading to a slow comeback in some locations.

black-and-white striped crown

rounded wings

buffy wash on face

buffy mottling in black breastband

black stripe behind eye

long, pointed bill

whitish face

yellow throat

brown upperparts streaked with buff and black

yellow breast with black "V"

short tail with white outer tail feathers

yellow belly

BREEDING

long toes

VOICE Sharp dzzeer; clear, descending, 3–8 note whistles, tseeeooou tseeeeou.
NESTING Loosely woven, usually domed, cup of grasses and other plants, located on the ground in tall grass fields; 3–8 eggs; 1 brood; Mar–May.
FEEDING Insects from ground; seeds and grain in winter.
HABITAT Native tallgrass prairie openings, pastures, and overgrown roadsides while breeding.
LENGTH 7–10in (18–25cm)
WINGSPAN 13–15in (33–38cm)

Western Meadowlark

Sturnella neglecta

The Western Meadowlark is one of the most abundant and widespread grassland birds in North America. It inhabits open country in the western Great Plains, the Great Basin, and the Central Valley of California. It is frequently encountered along roadsides, singing its melodious song from atop a fencepost or utility pole. Although the range of the Western Meadowlark overlaps widely with that of its eastern counterpart, hybrids between the two species are very rare and usually sterile.

duller pattern than breeding bird

short wings

white outer tail feathers

yellow throat

yellow patch between bill and eye

blackish-brown stripe behind eye

NONBREEDING

long, pointed bill

chunky body

black "V" on yellow chest

black spots and streaks on sides and flanks

yellow underparts

BREEDING

short, wide tail

long toes

VOICE *Series of complex, bubbling whistled notes descending in pitch.*
NESTING *Domed grass cup, well hidden in tall grasses; 3–7 eggs; 1 brood; Mar–Aug.*
FEEDING *Insects, including beetles, grubs, and grasshoppers; also grains and grass seeds.*
HABITAT *Open grassy plains while breeding; also agricultural fields with overgrown edges and hayfields.*
LENGTH *7–10in (18–26cm)*
WINGSPAN *13–15in (33–38cm)*

Rusty Blackbird

D

Euphagus carolinus

The Rusty Blackbird breeds in remote, inaccessible, swampy areas, and is much less of a pest to agricultural operations than some of the other members of its family. The plumage on the male Rusty Blackbird changes to a dull reddish-brown during the fall. This species is most easily observed during fall migration, as it moves south in long, wide flocks.

short narrow bill

long tail

♂
BREEDING

green sheen on head

gray-brown eyebrow

pale whitish or yellow eye

pale gray to rusty-brown underparts

♀

black overall with blue-green to greenish sheen

♂
BREEDING

VOICE Chuk *during migration flights; males: musical* too-ta-lee.
NESTING *Small bowl of branches and sticks, lined with wet plants and dry grass, usually near water; 3–5 eggs; 1 brood; May–Jul.*
FEEDING *Seasonally available insects, spiders, grains, seeds of trees, and fleshy fruit or berries.*
HABITAT *Moist to wet forests up to the northern timberline while breeding.*
LENGTH *8–10in (20–25cm)*
WINGSPAN *12–15in (30–38cm)*

Brewer's Blackbird

S

Euphagus cyanocephalus

The Brewer's Blackbird seems to prefer areas disturbed by humans to natural ones throughout much of its range. Interestingly, when the Brewer's Blackbird range overlaps with that of the Common Grackle, it wins out in rural areas, but loses out in urban areas. This species can be found feasting on waste grains left behind after the harvest.

stout bill

♂

long, dark tail

brown eyes

gray-brown overall

♀

purplish sheen on head

whitish-yellow eyes

black body with greenish-blue sheen

♂

VOICE Buzzy tshrrep *song ascending in tone.*
NESTING *Bulky cup of dry grass, stem, and twig framework lined with soft grasses and animal hair; 3–6 eggs; 1–2 broods; Apr–Jul.*
FEEDING *Insects from the ground during breeding season; snails; seeds, grain, and occasional fruit in fall and winter.*
HABITAT *Open, disturbed areas and human development, including parks, gardens, cleared forests, and fallow fields.*
LENGTH *10–12in (25–30cm)*
WINGSPAN *13–16in (33–41cm)*

black legs and feet

Common Grackle

Quiscalus quiscula

The Common Grackle is so well suited to urban and suburban habitats that it successfully excludes other species from them and even kills and eats House Sparrows. During migration and winter, Common Grackles form immense flocks, sometimes comprising more than a million individuals. This tendency, combined with its preference for cultivated areas, has made this species an agricultural pest in some regions.

dark wings

pale yellow eye

iridescent bluish-purple head

iridescent brownish-bronze back

long, thick bill

♂ **BRONZED FORM**

long, V-shaped tail

dull purplish-bronze overall

pale eye

♀

VOICE Low, harsh *chek*; loud series of odd squeaks and whistles.
NESTING Small bowl in trees, with a frame of sticks filled with mud and grasses; 4–6 eggs; 1–2 broods; Apr–Jul.
FEEDING Beetles, flies, spiders, and worms; small vertebrates; seeds and grain, especially in nonbreeding season.
HABITAT Open woodlands, suburban woodlots, city parks, gardens, and hedges.
LENGTH 11–13½in (28–34cm)
WINGSPAN 15–18in (38–46cm)

Boat-tailed Grackle

Quiscalus major

The Boat-tailed Grackle is so similar to the Great-tailed Grackle that the two birds were once thought to be the same species. This grackle resides in coastal marshes and neighboring uplands, but readily scavenges in nearby human settlements. Unlike the glossy blue-black males, females are brown. In spring, females form large nesting colonies that attract many males; only the most dominant males succeed in mating.

long, black bill

long, spread out, wedge-shaped tail

tawny-cinnamon eyebrow

round head

brown or yellow eyes

dark brown upperparts

glossy blue-black overall

♂

much smaller overall

♀

black wings

black legs and feet

VOICE Long, loud, three-part, high-pitched *chreeet chreeet*, low growl, then *sheet sheet*.
NESTING Rough grass and mud cup, woven into marsh vegetation; 2–5 eggs; 1–2 broods; Mar–Jun.
FEEDING Varied diet includes insects, crayfish, clams, seeds, fruit, fish, frogs, lizards, nestlings, and trash.
HABITAT Resides in coastal marshes; also urban habitats.
LENGTH 13–18in (33–46cm)
WINGSPAN 16–24in (41–61cm)

very long tail, often spread out

Shiny Cowbird

S

Molothrus bonariensis

Native to South America, the glossy purplish Shiny Cowbird has recently expanded into Florida and farther north, perhaps aided by introductions on various islands, including Barbados. This brood parasite lays its eggs in the nests of more than 200 different birds, 80 of which raise the young as their own. Shiny Cowbird nestlings grow quickly, leaving the host's nest within two weeks. Their impact on native birds is as yet unknown.

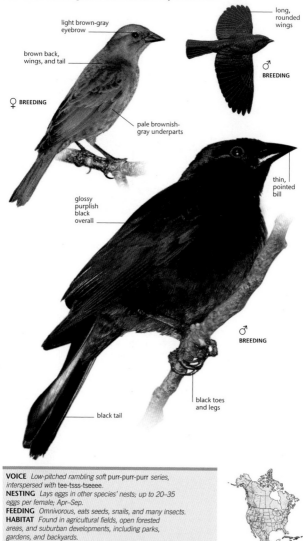

long, rounded wings

♂ BREEDING

light brown-gray eyebrow

brown back, wings, and tail

♀ BREEDING

pale brownish-gray underparts

thin, pointed bill

glossy purplish black overall

♂ BREEDING

black toes and legs

black tail

VOICE *Low-pitched rambling soft* purr-purr-purr *series, interspersed with* tee-tsss-tseeee.
NESTING *Lays eggs in other species' nests; up to 20–35 eggs per female; Apr–Sep.*
FEEDING *Omnivorous, eats seeds, snails, and many insects.*
HABITAT *Found in agricultural fields, open forested areas, and suburban developments, including parks, gardens, and backyards.*
LENGTH *7in (18cm)*
WINGSPAN *10–12in (25–30cm)*

Brown-headed Cowbird

Molothrus ater

North America's most common brood parasite, the Brown-headed
Cowbird was once a bird of the Great Plains, following bison to prey
on insects kicked up by their hooves. Now it is found continent-
wide. It is a serious threat to many smaller North American songbirds,
laying its eggs in the nests of more than 220 different species, and
having its young raised to fledging by more than 140 species.

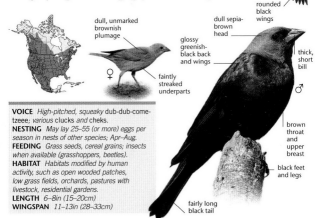

rounded
black
wings

dull, unmarked
brownish
plumage

dull sepia-
brown
head

glossy
greenish-
black back
and wings

thick,
short
bill

faintly
streaked
underparts

♀

♂

brown
throat
and
upper
breast

black feet
and legs

fairly long
black tail

VOICE *High-pitched, squeaky dub-dub-come-
tzeee; various clucks and cheks.*
NESTING *May lay 25–55 (or more) eggs per
season in nests of other species; Apr–Aug.*
FEEDING *Grass seeds, cereal grains; insects
when available (grasshoppers, beetles).*
HABITAT *Habitats modified by human
activity, such as open wooded patches,
low grass fields, orchards, pastures with
livestock, residential gardens.*
LENGTH *6–8in (15–20cm)*
WINGSPAN *11–13in (28–33cm)*

Orchard Oriole

Icterus spurius

The Orchard Oriole resembles a large warbler in size, color,
and the way it flits among leaves while foraging for insects.
Unlike other orioles, it bobs its tail, and spends less time on
the breeding grounds, often arriving there as late as mid-May
and leaving as early as late July. It tolerates humans and can
be found breeding in suburban parks and gardens.

black
back

♂

olive
upperparts

slightly
curved
blue-gray
black-
tipped bill

rich
chestnut
shoulders

two
white
wing
bars

yellowish
underparts

♀

chestnut
rump

♂

dark
chestnut
belly

white-
edged
flight
feathers

black
tail

VOICE *Fast, not very melodious, series of high
warbling notes ending in slurred shheere.*
NESTING *Woven nest of grass in fork between
branches; 4–5 eggs; 1 brood; Apr–Jul.*
FEEDING *Mainly insects while breeding;
also seeds, fruit, and occasionally nectar.*
HABITAT *Open forest and woodland edges
with evergreen and deciduous trees while
breeding; along river bottoms and near
agricultural land.*
LENGTH *7–8in (18–20cm)*
WINGSPAN *9in (23cm)*

Baltimore Oriole

(S)

Icterus galbula

The Baltimore Oriole's brilliant colors are familiar to many in eastern North America because this bird is so tolerant of humans. This species originally favored the American elm for nesting, but the Dutch elm disease decimated these trees. The oriole has since adapted to using sycamores, cottonwoods, and other tall trees as nesting sites. Its ability to use suburban yards and parks has helped expand its range to incorporate areas densely occupied by humans.

orange-yellow head

white-edged black wings

♂ 1ST

black-and-orange tail

orange-yellow shoulder patch

yellow-olive rump

olive upperparts

two wing bars

pale orange underparts

♀

straight blue-gray bill

black head

black back

♂

black upper breast

orange rump

orange underparts

black tail with orange outer tail feathers

VOICE *Loud, clear, melodious song comprising several short notes in series, often of varying lengths.*
NESTING *Round-bottomed basket usually woven from grass, hung toward the end of branches; 4–5 eggs; 1 brood; May–Jul.*
FEEDING *Hops or flits among leaves and branches, picking insects and spiders; caterpillars; also fruit and nectar.*
HABITAT *Forest edges and tall, open mixed hardwoods, close to rivers; forested parks, urban areas with tall trees.*
LENGTH *8–10in (20–26cm)*
WINGSPAN *10–12in (26–30cm)*

Finches

Finches in the family Fringillidae comprise a family of seed-eating birds, of which 16 species can be found in North America. They vary in size and shape—from the small, fragile-looking redpolls to the robust, chunky Evening Grosbeak. Finch colors range from whitish with some pink (redpolls) to gold (American Goldfinch), bright red (crossbills), and yellow, white, and black (Evening Grosbeak). They all have conical bills with razor-sharp edges, used to cut open hard seed hulls. The bills of conifer-loving crossbills are crossed at the tip, a unique arrangement that permits them to pry open tough-hulled pine cones. Crossbills wander widely to find abundant cone crops to allow breeding. Most finches are social and form flocks after nesting. All finches are vocal, calling constantly while flying, and singing in the spring. Their open cup-shaped nests of grasses and lichens hidden in trees or shrubs are hard to find.

GARDEN GLOW
Even pink flower buds cannot compete with the brilliant yellow of a male American Goldfinch.

Pine Grosbeak

(S)

Pinicola enucleator

The largest of the North American finches, Pine Grosbeaks are distinguishable by the male's pinkish-red color and thick, stubby bill. Four subspecies are found in North America. Due to extensive individual plumage color variation, the age and sex of these birds is challenging to determine. Pine Grosbeaks favor boreal forests across Canada and Alaska and some mountain ranges in the western US. In winter, northern birds occasionally move south into the northern US. They are often observed hanging from branches, gorging on ripe fruit, and they readily visit feeders.

two white wing bars

♂

greenish head

pale patch under eye

greenish rump

♀

gray belly

stubby, roundish blackish bill

pinkish-red head

short neck

♂

pinkish-red underparts (but regionally variable)

pinkish rump

long blackish tail

VOICE Contact calls of eastern birds tee-tew, or tee-tee-tew; western forms give more complex tweedle; warbling song.
NESTING Well-hidden, open cup nest in spruce or larch trees; 2–5 eggs, 1 brood; Jun–Jul.
FEEDING Spruce buds, maple seeds, and mountain ash berries throughout the year; feeding stations in winter; insects in summer.
HABITAT Open, northerly coniferous forests usually near fresh water.
LENGTH 8–10in (20–25cm)
WINGSPAN 13in (33cm)

House Finch

S

Haemorhous mexicanus

Historically, the House Finch was a western bird, and was first reported in the East on Long Island, New York City, in 1941. These birds are said to have originated from released birds that had been caught for the illegal bird trade. The population of the eastern birds started expanding in the 1960s; by the late 1990s, the eastern and western populations had linked up. The male House Finch is distinguished from the Purple and Cassin's Finches by its brown-streaked underparts and more strawberry-colored wash, while the females have plainer faces and generally blurrier streaking.

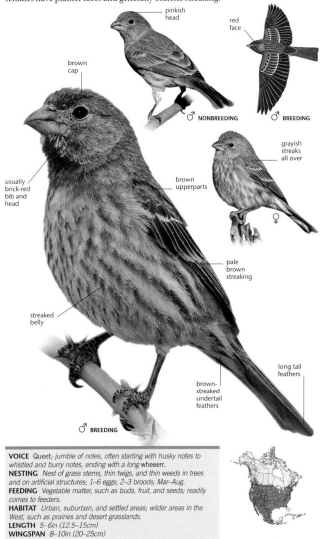

pinkish head

red face

brown cap

♂ **NONBREEDING**

♂ **BREEDING**

grayish streaks all over

brown upperparts

usually brick-red bib and head

♀

pale brown streaking

streaked belly

long tail feathers

brown-streaked undertail feathers

♂ **BREEDING**

VOICE *Queet*; jumble of notes, often starting with husky notes to whistled and burry notes, ending with a long *wheeerr*.
NESTING Nest of grass stems, thin twigs, and thin weeds in trees and on artificial structures; 1–6 eggs; 2–3 broods; Mar–Aug.
FEEDING Vegetable matter, such as buds, fruit, and seeds; readily comes to feeders.
HABITAT Urban, suburban, and settled areas; wilder areas in the West, such as prairies and desert grasslands.
LENGTH 5–6in (12.5–15cm)
WINGSPAN 8–10in (20–25cm)

Purple Finch

Haemorhous purpureus

The Purple Finch is more often seen than heard, even on its breeding grounds in open and mixed coniferous forest. The western subspecies (*californicus*) is slightly darker and duller than the eastern form (*purpureus*). The raspberry-red male Purple Finches are easily distinguished from male House Finches, which have a strawberry-red face and brown-striped underparts; the brown-streaked females are harder to identify.

pinkish-red body

♂

rounded brownish wings

raspberry-red crown

♂

pink-and-brown streaked upperparts

whitish belly with rosy patches

brown stripe between eye and bill

pink rump and upper tail

lightly streaked overall

darker, streaked wings

brownish conical bill

pale brown overall

♀

VOICE *Single, rough* pikh *in flight; rich series of notes, up and down in pitch.*
NESTING *Cup of sticks and grasses on a conifer branch; 4 eggs; 2 broods; May–Jul.*
FEEDING *Buds, seeds, flowers of deciduous trees; insects and caterpillars in summer; also seeds and berries; feeding stations, especially in winter.*
HABITAT *Northern mixed conifer and hardwood forests while breeding.*
LENGTH *4¾–6in (12–15cm)*
WINGSPAN *8½–10in (22–26cm)*

Red Crossbill

Loxia curvirostra

Crossbills push the tips of their slightly open, cross-tipped bills between the scales of a conifer cone to pry it apart and lift out the seeds with their tongues. They occur in many forms, varying in size and bill shape. They have slightly different flight calls and rarely interbreed. It is nearly impossible to identify the different forms of the Red Crossbill other than by voice or DNA.

red body

♂

black wings

crown usually brick-red

crossed mandibles

♂

black stripe over eye

♀

dark wings

greenish breast

dark brown wings

red rump

VOICE *Jit* repeated 2–5 times; complex, continuous warbling of notes, whistles, and buzzes.
NESTING *Cup nest on lateral conifer branch; 3–5 eggs; 2 broods; can breed year-round.*
FEEDING *Pine seeds; also insects and larvae, particularly aphids; other seeds.*
HABITAT *Coniferous or mixed-coniferous and deciduous forests; mountain forests in the Rockies.*
LENGTH *5–6¾in (13–17cm)*
WINGSPAN *10–10½in (25–27cm)*

White-winged Crossbill (S)

Loxia leucoptera

Few other creatures of the northern forest go about their business with such determined energy as the White-winged Crossbill, and no others accent a winter woodland with hot pink and magenta. Flocks of these birds gather in spruce trees, calling with a chorus of metallic, yanking notes, then erupt into the air.

red body

variable dark patch on cheek

two conspicuous white wing bars

brownish-green head

dark brown wings

greenish streaked underparts

♂

crossed mandibles

♀

blackish wings

pinkish-red underparts

notched tail

VOICE Sharp, chattering plik, or deeper tyoop, repeated in series of 3–7 notes; song: melodious trilling.
NESTING Open cup nest, usually high on end of a spruce branch; 3–5 eggs; 2 broods; Jul, Jan–Feb.
FEEDING Seeds from small-coned conifers: spruces, firs, larches; insects when available.
HABITAT Nomadic; coniferous forests, especially with spruce and tamarack.
LENGTH 5½–6in (14–15cm)
WINGSPAN 10–10½in (26–27cm)

Common Redpoll (S)

Acanthis flammea

Every other year, spruce, birch, and other trees in the northern forest zone fail to produce a good crop of seeds, forcing the Common Redpoll to look for food farther south than usual. It is tame around people and easily attracted to winter feeders. The degree of whiteness in its plumage varies greatly among individuals, due to sex and age.

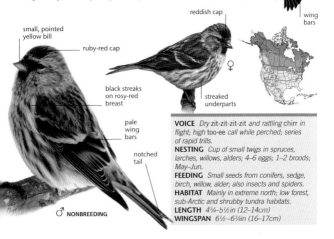

red cap

♂

wing bars

reddish cap

small, pointed yellow bill

ruby-red cap

♀

black streaks on rosy-red breast

streaked underparts

pale wing bars

notched tail

♂ NONBREEDING

VOICE Dry zit-zit-zit-zit and rattling chirr in flight; high too-ee call while perched; series of rapid trills.
NESTING Cup of small twigs in spruces, larches, willows, alders; 4–6 eggs; 1–2 broods; May–Jun.
FEEDING Small seeds from conifers, sedge, birch, willow, alder; also insects and spiders.
HABITAT Mainly in extreme north; low forest, sub-Arctic and shrubby tundra habitats.
LENGTH 4¾–5½in (12–14cm)
WINGSPAN 6½–6¾in (16–17cm)

Hoary Redpoll Ⓢ

Acanthis hornemanni

This bird of the high Arctic has two recognized subspecies—*A. h. exilipes* and *A. h. hornemanni*. Hoary Redpolls are close relatives of the Common Redpoll and often breed in the same areas. Like Common Redpolls, their chattering flocks buzz rapidly over trees and fields. Recent DNA studies may see the Hoary Redpoll lumped in with the Common Redpoll in the near future.

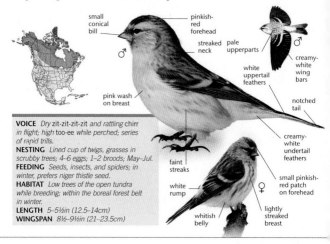

small conical bill

pinkish-red forehead

streaked neck

pale upperparts

creamy-white wing bars

white uppertail feathers

notched tail

pink wash on breast

creamy-white undertail feathers

faint streaks

small pinkish-red patch on forehead

white rump

♀

whitish belly

lightly streaked breast

VOICE *Dry* zit-zit-zit-zit *and rattling* chirr *in flight; high* too-ee *while perched; series of rapid trills.*
NESTING *Lined cup of twigs, grasses in scrubby trees; 4–6 eggs; 1–2 broods; May–Jul.*
FEEDING *Seeds, insects, and spiders; in winter, prefers niger thistle seed.*
HABITAT *Low trees of the open tundra while breeding; within the boreal forest belt in winter.*
LENGTH *5–5½in (12.5–14cm)*
WINGSPAN *8½–9½in (21–23.5cm)*

Pine Siskin Ⓢ

Spinus pinus

This energetic, fearless little bird of the conifer belt runs in gangs, zipping over the trees with incessant twittering. An expert at disguise, the Pine Siskin can resemble a cluster of pine needles or cones. Often abundant wherever there are pines, spruces, and other conifers, they may still make a mass exodus from a region if the food supply is not to their liking.

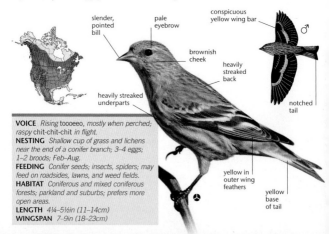

slender, pointed bill

pale eyebrow

conspicuous yellow wing bar

♂

brownish cheek

heavily streaked back

heavily streaked underparts

notched tail

yellow in outer wing feathers

yellow base of tail

VOICE *Rising* tooooeo, *mostly when perched; raspy* chit-chit-chit *in flight.*
NESTING *Shallow cup of grass and lichens near the end of a conifer branch; 3–4 eggs; 1–2 broods; Feb–Aug.*
FEEDING *Conifer seeds; insects, spiders; may feed on roadsides, lawns, and weed fields.*
HABITAT *Coniferous and mixed coniferous forests; parkland and suburbs; prefers more open areas.*
LENGTH *4¼–5½in (11–14cm)*
WINGSPAN *7–9in (18–23cm)*

American Goldfinch

Spinus tristis

The male American Goldfinch in sunny yellow breeding plumage is a cheerful and common summer sight. Even when unseen, its presence is quickly given away by its tinkling, bell-like calls in flight. American Goldfinches are one of summer's latest birds to breed and build nests. They relish weed seeds, particularly thistle, and will readily visit niger-seed feeders.

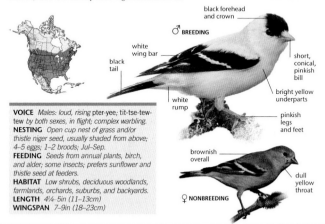

bright yellow back

♂ BREEDING

black forehead and crown

♂ BREEDING

white wing bar

black tail

white rump

short, conical, pinkish bill

bright yellow underparts

pinkish legs and feet

brownish overall

dull yellow throat

♀ NONBREEDING

VOICE Males: loud, rising pter-yee; tit-tse-tew-tew by both sexes, in flight; complex warbling.
NESTING Open cup nest of grass and/or thistle niger seed, usually shaded from above; 4–5 eggs; 1–2 broods; Jul–Sep.
FEEDING Seeds from annual plants, birch, and alder; some insects; prefers sunflower and thistle seed at feeders.
HABITAT Low shrubs, deciduous woodlands, farmlands, orchards, suburbs, and backyards.
LENGTH 4½–5in (11–13cm)
WINGSPAN 7–9in (18–23cm)

Evening Grosbeak

Coccothraustes vespertinus

The husky Evening Grosbeak feeds in noisy flocks at bird feeders in the winter. It has extended its range eastward in the past 200 years and now nests as far as Newfoundland, partly due to the planting of ornamental box elder, whose seeds ensure a ready food supply in winter. Recently though, its eastern range is rescinding northward, possibly due to spruce budworm control measures.

black wingtips

♂

large white wing patches

conspicuous yellow eyebrow

very dark gray head and shoulders

♂

large white wing patch

yellow rump

short, square tail

huge yellowish-white bill

black outer wing feathers

mustard-yellow underparts

large grayish bill

♀

grayish wing patch

VOICE Descending feeew; also buzzy notes and beeping chatter.
NESTING Loose, grass-lined twig cup on conifer branch; 3–4 eggs; 1–2 broods; May–Jul.
FEEDING Seeds of pines and other conifers, maples, and box elders; also insects and their larvae, particularly spruce budworm.
HABITAT Mixed conifer and spruce forests while breeding; coniferous or deciduous woodlands, often near suburbs, in winter.
LENGTH 6½–7in (16–18cm)
WINGSPAN 12–14in (30–36cm)

Old World Sparrows

These small, short-legged, short-billed, principally seed-eating birds were introduced to North America from Europe and Asia, and their name has carried over to many unrelated New World species. They are related to African and Asian weavers, although they lack the weavers' nest-building capabilities.

House and Tree Sparrows are small and finchlike, but always unstreaked below. Male and female House Sparrows differ in appearance, while Tree Sparrows of both sexes are more like the male House Sparrow. House Sparrows are familiar urban and suburban birds, always associated with buildings, parks, or farmsteads. House Sparrows have a variety of simple, cheeping calls, and a structured, nonmusical song. They nest in cavities, although they may create loose, domed structures out in the open.

DECLINING POPULATIONS
Due to changing land-use patterns and possible competition from the House Finch, which has expanded its range eastward, House Sparrow numbers are on the decline.

House Sparrow

Passer domesticus

The familiar "sparrow" of towns, cities, suburbs, and farms, House Sparrows actually belong to a Eurasian family called Passeridae. From their first modest introduction in Brooklyn, New York, in 1850, these hardy and aggressive birds have since spread throughout the North American continent. In just 150 years, the House Sparrow has evolved similar geographic variations to those of native species: it is pale in the arid Southwest, and darker in wetter regions.

yellowish bill

buff eye-stripe

♀

pale rump

white wing bar

drab brown underparts

gray crown

brown nape

white wing bar

black-and-brown streaks on upperparts

black throat

gray breast

♂ ☼

VOICE Variety of calls, including a cheery chirp, a dull jurv, and a rough jigga; song consists of chirp notes repeated endlessly.
NESTING Untidy mass of dried vegetable material in either natural or artificial cavities; 3–5 eggs; 2–3 broods; Apr–Aug.
FEEDING Mostly seeds; sometimes gleans insects and fruit.
HABITAT Downtown sections of cities and near human habitations, including agricultural areas.
LENGTH 6in (15.5cm)
WINGSPAN 9½in (24cm)

Index

Acknowledgments

Dorling Kindersley would like to thank the following people: for editorial help Frankie Piscitelli, for design support Sharon Spencer, and for proofreading Jamie Ambrose, John Cox and Andrew Mackay for the flight illustrations. The publisher would also like to thank the following contributors: François Vuilleumier, Joseph DiCostanzo, David M. Bird, Nicholas L. Block, Peter Capainolo, Matthew Commons, Malcolm Coulter, Shawneen Finnegan, Neil Fletcher, Ted Floyd, Jeff Groth, Paul Hess, Brian Hiller, Rob Hume, Thomas Brodie Johnson, Kevin T. Karlson, Stephen Kress, William Moskoff, Bill Pranty, Michael L.P. Retter, Noah Strycker, Paul Sweet, Rodger Titman, Elissa Wolfson, and Paul Lehman (Map editor).

Dorling Kindersley would also like to thank Nandini Gupta, Nishtha Kapil, Antara Moitra, Priyanjali Narain, Janashree Singha, and Arani Sinha for editorial assistance; Avinash Kumar, Rohit Bhardwaj, and Vishal Bhatia for design assistance; Jaypal Chauhan and Bimlesh Tiwary for DTP assistance; Mohd. Zishan for help with flight illustrations; and Sakshi Saluja for picture research assistance.

For the revised edition, Dorling Kindersley would like to thank Aashline R. Avarachan, Ekta Chadha, Madhurima Chatterjee, Ankita Gupta, Priyanjali Narain, and Nandini Tripathy for editorial assistance; Shanker Prasad for CTS assistance; and Rakesh Kumar, Priyanka Sharma Saddi, and Saloni Singh for jackets assistance.

The publisher would like to thank the following for their kind permission to reproduce their photographs:

(Key: a-above; b-below/bottom; c-center; f-far; l-left; r-right; t-top)

1 Brian E. Small: (c). 3 Garth McElroy: (clb). Markus Varesvuo: (cb,crb). 6-7 Doug Backlund: (ca). 6 Markus Varesvuo: (b). 7 Alamy Stock Photo: Juniors Bildachiv (c). 11 Getty Images: Brad Sharp (c). Alamy Stock Photo: Bruce Coleman Inc. (tc); Nancy Camel (ca). Alamy Stock Photo: Derrick Alderman (cla); Gay Bumgarner (cr). FLPA: S & D & K Maslowski (cl). 12 naturepl.com: Barry Mansell (b). 13 Bob Steele: (cl). Dudley Edmondson: (crb). 14 Bill Schmoker: (cb). Bob Steele: (cb). 15 Brian E. Small: (cla). Neil Fletcher: (cb). 16 Bill Schmoker: (cra). Garth McElroy: (cb). Dorling Kindersley: Roger Tidman (crb, br). 17 Bill Schmoker: (br). Brian E. Small: (ca, cra). Neil Fletcher: (cb). 18 Dorling Kindersley: Roger Tidman (crb). E. J. Peiker: (cra, br). 19 Brian E. Small: (crb, bl). Dorling Kindersley: Mike Lane (cra). Neil Fletcher: (cr). 20 E. J. Peiker: (cb). 21 Bob Steele: (c). Dorling Kindersley: Chris Gomersall Photography (b). 22 Brian E. Small: (cr, br). Dorling Kindersley: Mark Hamblin (cra). Peter S Weber: (cra). 23. E. J. Peiker: (cra, cr). Dorling Kindersley: David Tipling Photo Library (clb). E. J. Peiker: (br). 24 Markus Varesvuo: (cra, cr). E. J. Peiker: (crb, br). 25 Brian E. Small: (crb, bl). E. J. Peiker: (cra, cr). 26 Brian E. Small: (br). E. J. Peiker: (cr). Dorling Kindersley: Mark Hamblin (cra); Mike Lane (cr). 28 Markus Varesvuo: (cra, cr, br). Dorling Kindersley: Roger Tidman (crb). 29 Brian E. Small: (cra). Garth McElroy: (br). Peter S Weber: (cr). Robert Royse: (crb). 30 Garth McElroy: (cr, crb). Kevin T. Karlson: (cra). 31 Brian E. Small: (cb). Garth McElroy: (c). 32 Dorling Kindersley: Roger Tidman (cra); Steve Young (cb). 33 Bob Steele: (cr). Brian E. Small: (crb). E. J. Peiker: (br). Markus Varesvuo: (cra). 34 Dorling Kindersley: David Tipling Photo Library (cr). Markus Varesvuo: (cra); Steve Young (crb, br). 35 Dorling Kindersley: Mike Lane (c); Roger Tidman (c). 36 Markus Varesvuo: (b). 37 Brian E. Small: (cla, cb). 38 Dorling Kindersley: George McCarthy (cra). Markus Varesvuo: (b) 39 Bob Steele: (ca). Dudley Edmondson: (c). Kevin T. Karlson: (clb). 40 Brian E. Small: (cb). Robert Royse: (cla). 41 Jari Peltomäki: (ca). Robert Royse: (c). 42 Dorling Kindersley: Chris Gomersall Photography (cl); Mike Lane (cra, cb). 43 Brian F. Small: (cr). Doug Backlund: (cla). 44 Brian E. Small: (cb). 45 Jari Peltomäki: (b). 46 Garth McElroy: (bl). Dorling Kindersley: Mark Hamblin (cla);

Roger Tidman (cra). Markus Varesvuo: (crb). 47 Markus Varesvuo: (b). 48 Alan Murphy: (cb). Bob Steele: (cl). 49 Dorling Kindersley: David Tipling Photo Library (c). Markus Varesvuo: (b). 50 Bob Moul: (cl). Dorling Kindersley: Mike Lane (cb). 51 NHPA / Photoshot: Kevin Schafer (b). 52 Arto Juvonen: (crb, clb). Bill Schmoker: (cra). Bob Steele: (cla). 53 Dorling Kindersley: Chris Gomersall Photography (cla, cr). FLPA: David Hosking (br). Vireo: Robert L. Pitman (cl). 54 Bill Schmoker: (crb, cb). Mike Danzenbaker: (cra). 55 Bill Schmoker: (c). Mike Danzenbaker: (crb). Ardea: Peter Steyn (cra). Dorling Kindersley: Steve Young (cb). 56 Alamy Stock Photo: imageBROKER (cl). iStockphoto.com: Trevorplatt (b) 57 Brian E. Small: (cla, cb). 58 Ian Montgomery / Birdway. com.au: (cra). Judd Patterson: (cl, br) 59 Dorling Kindersley: Roger Tidman (cb); Mike Lane (cla). 60 Bob Steele: (b). Dreamstime.com: Ciaoarturo (cra). 61 Garth McElroy: (cla). Joe Fuhrman: (cb). 62 Dorling Kindersley: Mark Hamblin (cb); Steve Young (cla). 63 Dudley Edmondson: (cla). Bob Steele: (cr). Brian E. Small: (cb). 64 Judd Patterson: (bc). 65 Brian E. Small: (cl; br). Dudley Edmondson: (cra; cla). 66 Bill Schmoker: (cr). Melvin Grey: (cb, br). 67 Garth McElroy: (cra). E. J. Peiker: (cb). Peter S Weber: (cr). 68 Bob Steele: (ca). E. J. Peiker: (crb). Garth McElroy: (br). Dorling Kindersley: George McCarthy (cl). 69 Brian E. Small: (br). Garth McElroy: (ca). Judd Patterson: (cra). 70 Brian E. Small: (cla; bl). Dudley Edmondson: (cb). Melvin Grey: (cl). 71 WorldWildlifeImages.com / Andy & Gill Swash: (cla). Garth McElroy: (cb). Peter S Weber: (cr). 72 Garth McElroy: (cra). Dorling Kindersley: George McCarthy (cl). 73 Brian E. Small: (cla, cr). E. J. Peiker: (cra). Dorling Kindersley: Roger Tidman (br). 74 Bob Steele: (cb). Brian E. Small: (cla). 75 Jari Peltomäki: (b). Brian E. Small: (cr). 76 Brian E. Small: (cr). 77 Brian E. Small: (cla, cb). 78 Dorling Kindersley: Chris Gomersall Photography (ca, cr). Lee Zieger: (b). Melvin Grey: (cb). 79 Alan Murphy: (cla, c). Brian E. Small: (bl). Dudley Edmondson: (cb). 80 Bob Steele: (ca). Brian E. Small: (cr). Dudley Edmondson: (cb, br). 81 Bob Steele: (ca). Brian E. Small: (bl). Markus Varesvuo: (cb, bl). 82 Bob Steele: (cb). E. J. Peiker: (cr). Judd Patterson: (br). Kevin T. Karlson: (cb). 83 Bill Schmoker: (clb). Doug Backlund: (c). 84 Arto Juvonen: (cra). Bob Steele: (b). Brian E. Small: (cla). Jari Peltomäki: (crb, bl). Tomi Muukkonen: (cla). 85 Bob Steele: (cb). 86 Brian E. Small: (cla). 87 Alan Murphy: (cb). Brian E. Small: (cra). 88 Bob Steele: (cla). Garth McElroy: (cb). 89 Bob Steele: (cra, cr). Brian E. Small: (cb). Melvin Grey: (br). 90 FLPA: Jim Brandenburg / Minden Pictures: (cb). Corbis: Neil Bowman / Frank Lane Picture Library (cr). 91 Bob Steele: (cla). Melvin Grey: (cb). 92 Brian E. Small: (cr, fbr). Bob Steele: (br). 93 Wayne Nicholas: (r, clb). 94 NHPA / Photoshot: Bill Coster (b). 95 Bob Steele: (c). Dudley Edmondson: (cb). 96 Bob Steele: (cl). E. J. Peiker: (cla). 97 Garth McElroy: (cb). Kevin T. Karlson: (cra). 98 Bob Steele: (cb). Garth McElroy: (cr). Melvin Grey: (cla). 99 Brian E. Small: (cr). E. J. Peiker: (cb). 100 Dudley Edmondson: (cr). Melvin Grey: (cb). 101 E. J. Peiker: (cb). Garth McElroy: (br). Dorling Kindersley: Gordon Langsbury (c). 102 Garth McElroy: (cb). Dreamstime.com: Rusty Dodson (cra) 103 Brian E. Small: (cb). Garth McElroy: (cl). Dorling Kindersley: Gordon Langsbury (ca) 104 Bob Steele: (ca). Brian E. Small: (cr). Garth McElroy: (bc). Robert Royse: (cb). 105 Brian E. Small: (cb). Garth McElroy: (cr). Robert Royse: (br). 106 Bob Steele: (cr). Dorling Kindersley: Gordon Langsbury (ca). Joe Fuhrman: (br). 107 Brian E. Small: (ca, cr). Kevin T. Karlson: (cb, br). 108 Melvin Grey: (ca). Robert Royse: (cra). Dorling Kindersley: George McCarthy (bl); Roger Tidman (clb). 109 Glenn Bartley / BIA / Minden Pictures: (cla); Bob Steele: (cb). 110 Garth McElroy: (cra). Melvin Grey: (cr). Dorling Kindersley: Mike Lane (cb). 111 Bob Steele: (cra). Dorling Kindersley: David Tipling Photo Library (cr); Mike Lane (br). Markus Varesvuo: (b). 112 Brian E. Small: (br). Bob Steele: (cb). Dudley Edmondson: (cr). Garth McElroy: (cb). 113 Garth McElroy: (ca).). Kevin T. Karlson: (cb). Robert Royse: (cra). Tom Ennis: (br). 114 Bob Steele: (cra). Brian E. Small: (cb). Dorling Kindersley: Mike Lane (cr); Roger Tidman (br). 115 Brian E. Small: (ca, cr). Garth McElroy: (br). Kevin T. Karlson: (cb, crb). 116 Bob Steele: (cra). E. J. Peiker: (cr). Garth McElroy: (br). 117 Bob Steele: (br, cb). Garth McElroy: (cr). 118 Bob Steele: (cr). Dorling Kindersley: Roger Tidman (cra, cb, br). 119 Bob Steele: (c). Dorling Kindersley: Roger Tidman (crb). 120 Dorling Kindersley: George McCarthy (cra); Mike Lane (crb); Steve Young (br). Markus Varesvuo: (cr). 121 Dorling Kindersley: Chris Gomersall Photography (cb, br); Roger Tidman (ca). Hanne & Jens Eriksen: (cr). 122 Bob Steele: (cr). Dorling Kindersley: Chris Gomersall Photography (br); Kevin T. Karlson: (cb). Mike Danzenbaker: (ca). 123 Dorling Kindersley: Mike Lane (cb); Roger Tidman (c). 124 Dorling Kindersley: Chris Gomersall Photography (cla); Kim Taylor (cr); Mike Lane (cb). 125 Dudley Edmondson: (b). 126 Bob Steele: Brian E. Small: (cb). E. J. Peiker: (cra). Tomi Muukkonen: (c). 127 Bob Steele: (cb). Dorling Kindersley: Chris Gomersall Photography (cb); Mike Lane (cb). Garth McElroy: (cr). 128 Brian E. Small: (crb, b). Dorling Kindersley: David Tipling Photo Library (cr); Steve Young (cra). 129 Bob Steele: (c). 130 Bob Steele: (c). Brian E. Small: (cb). Dudley Edmondson: (cla). 131 Bob Steele: (cl). Dorling Kindersley: Chris Gomersall Photography (clb); David Tipling Photo Library (cra). 132 Garth McElroy: (cla, br). 133 Dorling Kindersley: David Tipling Photo Library (ca). Garth McElroy: (br). Robert Royse: (crb). 134 Dorling Kindersley: David Tipling Photo Library (c, cb). 135 Garth McElroy: (cr, cb). 136 Bob Steele: (cla). Hanne & Jens Friksen: (br). Robert Royse: (crb). Dorling Kindersley: Roger Tidman (cra). 137 Arthur Morris/Birds As Art: (br). Bob Steele: (ca). Brian E. Small: (cr). Dorling Kindersley: Chris Gomersall Photography (crb). 138 Dorling Kindersley: George McCarthy (br). Dorling Kindersley: Mike Lane (cra); Steve Young (cr). Tomi Muukkonen: (crb). 139 Brian E. Small: (ca, crb, br). E. J. Peiker: (c). 140 Brian E. Small: (cb). E. J. Peiker: (c). 141 Brian E. Small: (b). 142 Brian E. Small: (cb). Dorling Kindersley: Chris Gomersall Photography (cra); David Tipling Photo Library (cr). 143 Brian E. Small: (b). Dorling Kindersley: Roger Tidman (cra). Tom Grey: (br). 144 Bob Steele: (br). Garth McElroy: (cr). 145 Alan Murphy: (b). 146 Brian E. Small: (bc, clb). Robert Royse: (cra). 147 Brian E. Small: (cb). Mike Danzenbaker: (ca). 148 Jari Peltomäki: (b). 149 Brian E. Small: (b). E. J. Peiker: (ca). Dorling Kindersley: Mark Hamblin (cr). 150 Bob Steele: (cla, crb). 151 Brian E. Small: (cb, cb, crb). E. J. Peiker: (l). 152 Brian E. Small: (cra, cb). 153 Brian E. Small: (cra). 154 Bob Steele: (br). Brian E. Small: (cr). Dudley Edmondson: (br). 155 Bob Steele: (cla, br). 156 Garth McElroy: (cb). Dorling Kindersley: Mark Hamblin (br). Markus Varesvuo: (cr). 157 Brian E. Small: (r). 158 Bob Steele: (br). Peter S Weber: (c). 159 Bob Steele: (ca). Mike Danzenbaker: (cb). 160 DK Images: Roger Tidman (t). Alan Murphy: (b). 161 Alamy Stock Photo: Rick & Nora Bowers (r). 162 Bob Steele: (cra, cb). Garth McElroy: (ca). Robert Royse: (br). 163 Alan Murphy: (b). 164 Alan Murphy: (cb). Brian E. Small: (cla, crb). 165 Alan Murphy: (b). 166 Bob Steele: (br). Brian E. Small: (r, cr, cb). Peter S. Weber: (ca, cb). 167 Brian E. Small: (r, crb, br). Peter S Weber: (br). 168 Bob Steele: (c, cr). Brian E. Small: (bc, br). 169 Garth McElroy: (bc, br). Robert Royse: (ca, cra). 170 Bob Steele: (ca, cr). Brian E. Small: (br). 171 Brian E. Small: (cb, r). 172 Photoshot: Picture Alliance (b). 173 Bob Moul: (cr). Bob Steele: (br). E. J. Peiker: (cb). Kevin T. Karlson: (cr). 174 Dorling Kindersley: Chris Gomersall Photography (cl). Doug Backlund: (br). Tom Grey: (cla). 175 Dudley Edmondson: (b). 176 Brian E. Small: (b). 177 Brian E. Small: (cr, br) 178 Bob Steele: (cr, ca). Brian E. Small: (br). 179 Brian E. Small: (cra, br). 180 Garth McElroy: (cl). Robert Royse: (br). 181 Bob Steele: (br). Brian E. Small: (cra). Garth McElroy: (c). 182 Brian E. Small: (cr). Garth McElroy: (ca). Judd Patterson: (cb). 183 Bob Steele: (b). Brian E. Small: (ca, cb,) 184 NHPA/Photoshot: NHPA / Lee Dalton (b). Brian E. Small: (ca). 185 Bill Schmoker: (ca). Bob Steele: (cra, cb). Markus Varesvuo: (br). 186 Brian E. Small: (bc). E. J. Peiker: (cl). 187 Bob Steele: (br). Brian E. Small: (ca, crb). 188 Brian E. Small: (br). Garth McElroy: (cl). Robert Royse: (cl). 190 Brian E. Small: (cb). Garth McElroy: (ca). 191 Dudley Edmondson: (cb). E. J. Peiker: (ca). 192 Bob Steele: (cr). Robert Royse: (bc). Tom Grey: (ca). 193 Dorling Kindersley: Chris Gomersall Photography (cla); Mike Lane (cb). 194 Alan Murphy: (t). Bob Steele: (b). 195 Bob Steele: (cr, cb, br). Brian E. Small: (ca). 196 Bob Steele: (cl, ca). Garth McElroy: (cb). 197 Bob Steele: (ca). Brian E. Small: (cb). Garth McElroy: (cr). 198 Bob Steele: (ca). Garth McElroy: (cb). 199 Bob Steele: (cr). Brian E. Small: (clb). 200 Bob Steele: (cr). Robert Royse: (crb). 201 Alan Murphy: (crb). Garth McElroy: (cl). 202 Garth McElroy: (cra, crb). 203 E. J. Peiker: (b). Garth McElroy: (t, c). 204 Brian E. Small: (cb, cl). 205 Brian E. Small: (cr). Garth McElroy: (cb). 206 Garth McElroy. 207 Bob Steele: (cb). Robert Royse: (ca). 208 Brian E. Small: (br). Dorling Kindersley: Steve Young (cr). 209 Bob Steele: (cr, cb). Brian E. Small: (br). 210 Bob Steele: (bl). Brian E. Small: (cb). Garth McElroy: (cr). 211 Bob Steele: (crb). Brian E. Small: (cla). 212 Brian E. Small: (cr). Robert Royse: (cr). Garth McElroy: (br). 213 Dorling Kindersley: Mark Hamblin (ca); Roger Tidman (cb). 214 Brian E. Small: (cr, bc). Garth McElroy: (cb, cl). 215 Brian E. Small: (cr, bc). Garth McElroy: (ca). 216 Brian E. Small: (cb, br). Garth McElroy: (cra). 217 Brian E. Small: (ca, br). Garth McElroy: (cra). 218 Bob Steele: (cl, crb). Garth McElroy: (ca). 219 Bob Steele: (bc). Brian E. Small: (ca, cr). Dorling Kindersley: Chris Gomersall Photography (cb). Neil Fletcher: (br). 221 Brian E. Small: (cl). Garth McElroy: (cla, bc). 222 E. J. Peiker: (cr). Garth McElroy: (cla). Tom Grey: (clb). 223 naturepl.com: Markus Varesvuo (ca). 224 Jari Peltomäki: (cla). Markus Varesvuo: (cla). 225 Dorling Kindersley: Roger Tidman (cl); Steve Young (cb). 226 Alan Murphy: (b). 227 Brian E. Small: (br). Garth McElroy: (cr). 228 Brian E. Small: (cra, br). 229 Brian E. Small: (cra, c, bc, br). 230 Brian E. Small: (cla, cb, br). Garth McElroy: (c). 231 Bob Steele: (br). Brian E. Small: (cra, tc). E. J. Peiker: (bc). 232 Bob Steele: (ca, cb). Robert Royse: (br). 233 Brian E. Small: (cra, cb, br). Robert Royse: (ca). 234 Bob Moul: (ca). Bob Steele: (cb). Brian E. Small: (br). Garth McElroy: (ca). 235 Bob Steele: (br). Brian E. Small: (cla, cb). 236 Brian E. Small: (cla, fcla, cb, br). 237 Brian E. Small: (cla). Garth McElroy: (cb). 238 Brian E. Small: (cb). Garth McElroy: (cra, cl). 239 Brian E. Small: (cla, cr, br). Garth McElroy: (cb). 240 Alan Murphy: (cb). Robert Royse: (clb). Brian E. Small: (cr). 241 Garth McElroy: (cra, cb, br). Bob Steele: (ca). 242 Brian E. Small: (cr, crb). Mike Danzenbaker: (cra). Robert Royse: (br). 243 Brian E. Small: (c, crb). 244 Bob Steele: (cla, clb). Brian E. Small: (c). E. J. Peiker: (cb). 245 Bob Steele: (br). Brian E. Small: (ca). Garth McElroy: (br). Kevin T. Karlson: (cb). 246 Brian E. Small: (cl, cb). Garth McElroy: (cla). 247 Brian E. Small: (ca, crb). 248 Brian E. Small: (ca). Alan Murphy: (br). 249 Bob Steele: (crb). Brian E. Small: (ca, br). Garth McElroy: (cb). 250 Brian E. Small: (cla). Garth McElroy: (crb). 251 Brian E. Small: (cl). Dudley Edmondson: (cb). Garth McElroy: (cra). 252 Alan Murphy: (cb). Garth McElroy: (cra). Robert Royse: (br). 253 Brian E. Small: (ca, br). Garth McElroy: (cr). Kevin T. Karlson: (cb). 254 Brian E. Small: (cr, br). Garth McElroy: (ca). 255 Brian E. Small: (cla, cb, br). 256 Bob Steele: (ca). Dudley Edmondson: (cb). 257 Bob Steele: (clb). Brian E. Small: (c). Garth McElroy: (crb). 258 Brian E. Small: (cb). Garth McElroy: (br). 259 Bob Steele: (cb). Brian E. Small: (cra, br). Garth McElroy: (cla). 260 Brian E. Small: (crb, ca). 261 Brian E. Small: (cra, cl). Garth McElroy: (cb). 262 Brian E. Small: (ca, cra). Robert Royse: (br). 263 Brian E. Small: (cra, cl, crb). 264 Brian E. Small: (cra, cl). Garth McElroy: (cb). 265 Brian E. Small: (ca, cra, cb, br). 266 Brian E. Small: (cr, cra, cb, br). 267 Alan Murphy: (b). 268 Brian E. Small: (crb, ca). 269 Bob Steele: (br). Brian E. Small: (cra, cb). Garth McElroy: (ca). 270 Brian E. Small: (cb, ca). E. J. Peiker: (cla). 271 Tom Grey: (cla). Garth McElroy: (ca). Mike Danzenbaker: (cb). 272 Bob Steele: (br, cb). Garth McElroy: (ca). Mike Danzenbaker: (cb). 273 Bob Steele: Brian E. Small: (ca, cl, br). 274 Brian E. Small: (cla, crb). 275 Brian E. Small: (ca, cb, br). E. J. Peiker: (cra). 276 Brian E. Small: (cla, cl, crb). 277 Bob Steele: (b). 278 Bob Steele: (br). Garth McElroy: (b). 279 Bob Steele: (ca, cb). E. J. Peiker: (cr). 280 Brian E. Small: (b). Garth McElroy: (ca, cr, crb). 281 Brian E. Small: (bl). Garth McElroy: (ca, cra). Dorling Kindersley: Tim Loseby (cb). 282 Brian E. Small: (bc). Markus Varesvuo: (ca, cra). 283 Bob Steele: (cr, br). Garth McElroy: (cb). 284 Neil Fletcher: (cb). 285 Dorling Kindersley: Chris Gomersall Photography (ca).

All other images © Dorling Kindersley
For further information see: www.dkimages.com